D0049863

BYT

Swimming in the Congo

WITHDRAWN

Swimming in the Congo

Margaret Meyers

ECTOR COUNTY LIBRARY
321 W. 5th St.
Odessa, Texas 79761

MILKWEED
EDITIONS

The characters and events in this book are fictitious. Any similarity to real persons, living or dead, is coincidental and not intended by the author.

© 1995, Text by Margaret Meyers
All rights reserved. Except for brief quotations in critical articles or reviews, no part of this book may be reproduced in any manner without prior written permission from the publisher: Milkweed Editions, 430 First Avenue North, Suite 400, Minneapolis, MN 55401
Distributed by Publishers Group West

Published 1995 by Milkweed Editions
Printed in the United States of America
Book design by Will Powers. The text of this book is set in Charlotte.
95 96 97 98 99   5 4 3 2 1
First Edition

Milkweed Editions is a not-for-profit publisher. We gratefully acknowledge support from the Dayton Hudson Foundation for Dayton's and Target Stores; Ecolab Foundation; General Mills Foundation; Honeywell Foundation; Jerome Foundation; John S. and James L. Knight Foundation; The McKnight Foundation; Andrew W. Mellon Foundation; Minnesota State Arts Board through an appropriation by the Minnesota State Legislature; Musser Fund; Challenge and Literature Programs of the National Endowment for the Arts; I. A. O'Shaughnessy Foundation; Piper Family Fund of the Minneapolis Foundation; Piper Jaffray Companies, Inc.; John and Beverly Rollwagen Fund of the Minneapolis Foundation; The St. Paul Companies, Inc.; Star Tribune/Cowles Media Foundation; Surdna Foundation; James R. Thorpe Foundation; Unity Avenue Foundation; Wallace-Reader's Digest Literary Publishers Marketing Development Program, funded through a grant to the Council of Literary Magazines and Presses; and generous individuals.

Library of Congress Cataloging-in-Publication Data

Meyers, Margaret.
    Swimming in the Congo / Margaret Meyers. — 1st ed.
        p.   cm.
    Based on the author's thesis (M.F.A., University of Virginia, 1995).
    ISBN 1-57131-006-1 (alk. paper)
    1. Zaire—Social life and customs—Fiction.   2. Children of missionairies—Zaire—Fiction.   3. Missionaries—Zaire—Fiction.
I. Title.
PS3563.E944S95   1995
813'.54—dc20   95–17162
                                                                          CIP

This book is printed on acid-free paper.

F
MEY
LC# 9517162

963516

#13.95

97-9-96

For my sisters, Janet and Marilyn, with love

My warm thanks to Melissa Mahood Lambrecht, who encouraged me to write these stories and critiqued my earliest drafts with insight and humor. My thanks also to Douglas Thorpe, for his unflagging enthusiasm for this project and his invaluable lessons in "clean writing." And a very special *merci mingi* to Anne Borchardt, Ellen Douglas, and John Casey.

My parents, Ronald Bruce and Alice Linnea Meyers, graciously helped with fact checking and served as my own personal Lingala dictionary. They also gave me a childhood with no television but with plenty of books, for which I am eternally grateful.

And finally, my affectionate thanks to Estelle, truly the Best!

Swimming in the Congo

AUTHOR'S NOTE

Although geographical and historical accuracy is important to me, I have taken liberties with both in "Simbas in Little America." I have relocated Léopoldville's "Little America" to suit my story purposes, and I have merged the U.S. State Department's response to the 1964 crisis with its response to the Independence crisis four years earlier. Léopoldville was never seriously threatened in 1964, so only a few State Department families left. In 1960, however, they all left, as did the vast majority of expatriates. The Red Cross evacuated many missionary families, including mine—with the exception of my father, who stayed behind.

Swimming in the Congo

Prologue

THE BELGIAN DOCTOR drops me off and drives away before I can thank him. I shake out my skirt, raising a cloud of fine red dry-season dust, and shrug on my backpack. The sign is gone, but I know where I am. The avenue looks shabby, dead branches dangling untrimmed from the royal palms. A khaki lizard scoots across the gravel road and disappears into the hedge of poinsettia blooming beside the Catholic elementary school.

"Those Catholics!" Mrs. Frykman fumes. "They've got a nerve, building their school on the very edge of Boanda Mission property!"

I walk slowly up the avenue. Twenty years ago Alain's house was standard-issue Belgian colonial, red brick with wide arches and high cool ceilings and a deep veranda. It has been replaced by a small boxy house of concrete blocks topped with aluminum roofing. An uneven stump is all that remains of the Nandi flame tree in the front yard. Once the Protestant church was the finest in the Equateur province, but now it desperately needs a coat of paint. The bells are missing from the bell tower. Behind the pulpit there used to be a twelve-foot cross of ebony inlaid with ivory, made by

Wamba, a local artist and convert. I wonder if it's still there, but I pass the church without stopping.

"Awfully fancy cross for a Protestant church," Mr. Frykman *grumbles. "But I suppose we ought to be thankful it's not a cruci-fix, since Wamba got his education from the Belgian Fathers at Bamania."*

Overgrown crimson bougainvillea threatens to crush the roof of Miss Renquist's house, but the Carlson and Frykman homes are unchanged. The mission cemetery, filled with pioneer missionaries dead of malaria, yellow fever, dysentery, and snakebite, still awaits the Resurrection. From a distance I see no recent graves, and I know the mostly Swedish names on the ill-kept stones: Nygren and Andersson, Sandstrom and Blomberg. The oldest stones have English names on them, from the time before the British Baptist Mission sold Boanda to the Evangelical Swedish-American Mission.

The path to the agriculture school has been widened into a road, the jungle cut back. I catch a glimpse of low whitewashed buildings and small square fields full of struggling crops. I can't make out what is growing in those fields, but I know it isn't soybeans. Soybeans are the one crop I can recognize without fail at any stage of development.

"Soybeans are an amazing source of protein, absolutely amazing!" says my father. *"They're the future of sub-Saharan Africa. I predict by 1970 every Congolese family will grow more soybeans than corn and manioc put together."*

The circle of bricks around the base of the Madagascar plum tree is still here, arranged in a herringbone pattern. Plums are not in season, but I remember their mouth-twisting tartness and thin scarlet skin. Yellow curtains have replaced my mother's green-striped ones in the living-room window. A lazy white column of smoke floats up from the cookhouse chimney, and I smell roasting breadfruit, Nile perch, and *pilipili* peppers. An invisible transistor blares

Kanda Bongo Man jazz. A loud, off-key voice sings along in Lingala.

"I know he wants to practice his English, but if Makua sings 'I Heard the Bells on Christmas Day' one more time, I'll go berserk!" My mother covers her ears with her hands. "Go out to the cookhouse, Grace, and teach him 'What A Friend We Have in Jesus.'"

At the umbrella tree I turn off the royal-palm avenue and pick my way carefully down the jungled bluff. Sunlight pierces the green ceiling above me, dancing a frenetic golden dance on the overgrown path. Every tree, baby papaya to aging mahogany, is hung from top to bottom with kudzu vine. The air smells moldy, and the underbrush vibrates with a harsh cicada buzz. Mindful of snakes, I give wide berth to the pale green stand of bamboo. I listen for monkey chatter but hear nothing. Maybe it's too early in the afternoon for monkeys, maybe they've been hunted out. The path grows muddy as I descend, orange clay caking and weighting my sandals. Black and aqua butterflies soar and drop above a stagnant puddle. *Papilio bromius?* My father would know.

"What a field day for lepidopterists the Congo is! I've gone through all my books, and this one with the emerald speckles isn't in any of them. Come take a look, Grace. You'll probably never see one of these again!"

The trees give way to a wide sandy bank flecked red with iron ore. I ease my backpack from my shoulders, kick off my sandals, and walk to the water's edge. The river flows broad and strong-willed, undeterred by the occasional slender green strip of island. It reflects the hot blue sky of dry season like a monstrous cobalt chameleon. White-gold dimples of sunshine scatter the surface of the water.

Once upon a time every day was like this, appropriate for heroic journeys and monumental quests. In my mind I was

Henry Stanley's Girl Friday and accompanied the great journalist-explorer on his first trip down the Congo River, his loyal companion in spite of an age difference of more than a century. I recognized the devoutly Christian soul beneath his cruelties, his grandiose boastings, and in return he trusted me. Together we paddled north, surviving the Falls by fervent prayer as well as endless portages through the jungle. Together we curved west with the Great Bend, past Isangi and Basoko, Bumba and Lisala, past the Upoto hills, past Mankanza and Lulonga, our travel-weary eyes finally resting upon the gentle green bluffs of Boanda. "The perfect site for a mission!" Henry Stanley cried, leaping to his feet. He waved his long-barreled rifle with glee, water dripping from his shaggy hair. "This is exactly where the river and the equator meet! Thanks be to God for this sign of His blessing." He ordered me to hand over his water-stained journal so he could make one of his flowery entries. He wrote standing up, confidently balanced in the drifting pirogue, while I shaded my eyes with a sunburned hand and squinted at the jungle-crusted bluffs where my very own home was to be.

"If you're daydreaming again, Grace, I could use some help with this marmalade." My mother briskly hands me a knife and a bowl filled with tangerines, oranges, and lemons. "Section this fruit, will you? And make sure to get all the seeds out."

My view downriver is obstructed by something dark and bulky. It rears out of the water, throwing a short equatorial shadow that doesn't quite reach the bank. One of the great forty-person war pirogues that Henry Stanley so admired? The carcass of the legendary Congo dragon, unseen since the sixteenth century? I hike my skirt to my knees and wade downstream. I have forgotten the force of the current; even this close to shore, tiny whirlpools suck like leeches at my ankles. I reach my goal and find not ancient but recent river history. An abandoned barge is beached in the shallows, worn out by countless trips up and down the seventeen hundred kilometers of navigable river. Faint rainbow colors slick the surrounding water, and I assume the barge once carried oil. Although the steel body is orange with rust, small flecks of black paint here and there reveal the original color. I peer over the side. Trapped on the barge's flat bottom are several clumps of water hyacinths floating in a bit of brackish water.

"A noxious weed, the water hyacinth," says my father. "The curse of the Congo River, and not even indigenous! Just another of Europe's thoughtless gifts to Africa."

Straight flowering stalks rise up from the porous green leaves and shaggy gray roots. The petals are transparent lavender, at their base a tiny candlelike flame of yellow. Nothing is more delicate, more luminous. One stroke of a fingertip, and they dissolve in a watery streak of color.

I climb inside the decaying barge and gather all the trapped hyacinths by their dripping roots. Climbing out is an awkward business with my hands full, but I manage it. I stand again in the sun-warmed water, my arms overflowing, my mind undecided. I'd like to keep them, take them with me, but they are so many, so heavy, so fragile.

Besides, I am here only for the day. Tomorrow morning I catch a bush plane to Brazzaville, then a commercial flight to Angola. My luggage, self-limited to one backpack, plus my camera gear, is locked away in the hotel manager's office back in Coquilhatville. (No, it's called Mbandaka now, I remind myself. It has been for twenty-two years. The statue of Henry Stanley's Captain Coquilhat is long gone, replaced by a monument to the Mouvement Populaire de la Révolution, and just as well.)

Suppose I save one tiny hyacinth—this one, with three undersized leaves and a few scraggly roots. Will it be content in the still world of a jar? Can it survive roaming the continent in a half liter of tap water?

My unmanageable bouquet soaks me to the skin, a living armload of my own memories. Memories rooted in water. Memories undomesticated, ungrounded . . .

Does the solid earth they could flourish in exist anymore? Not for me. I am just one more of Europe's thoughtless gifts to Africa. And yet I claim my right to survive, my floating space on the river.

I set the wanderlusting hyacinths in the water one by one.

"Try not to clog the main channel," I tell them. "You're here on sufferance."

They are swept away, spinning but upright, heading west with the current. Brazzaville waits seven hundred kilometers downriver. I'll get there before my hyacinths do, but in time they will make it.

Ndokis and the Equator

ACCORDING TO MY FATHER, the equator ran somewhere between our whitewashed brick house and the
Boanda Mission Agricultural Institute.

"Just think about it, Grace," he said in his earnest
professional-educator voice. "There it is, zero degrees latitude, cutting right through that hundred meters of jungle
behind our own back yard! And consider the implications:
because the equator's really in there somewhere, we travel
casually from one hemisphere to the other several times a
day. Amazing, don't you think?"

"Amazing," I echoed enthusiastically.

That hundred meters of jungle—a green tangle of trees,
vines, and undergrowth—was bisected by a narrow, often
muddy path. The year I was six, I haunted that path, inhaling the smell of plant decay and small dead animals, wondering what the equator was really like and where it might
be found.

My father told me I had misunderstood him. "The equator
isn't anything you can see, Grace. At least not in the ordinary
way." His bright eyes gentled, and his voice went dreamy, almost reverent. "The equator has a *scientific* reality."

Undeterred, I stalked the equator like a Congolese hunter in my flowered shorts, thongs, and T-shirt. It was there in that jungle; my father had said so. If I was stealthy enough, cunning enough, one day I would catch the equator unawares. And when I did, I expected something both fabulous and terrible: a thin burning trail of orange dragon fire, perhaps, or a splendid red and purple rainbow weaving fiercely through the jungle. All I needed was perseverance, and eventually I would surprise it at the right magical moment. My best hope was early in the morning, I thought, before the mist was gone. However gorgeous and imposing, the equator was doubtless shy, or possibly even unfriendly, preferring to be seen when the mission was quiet and few people were about.

I got distracted from my equatorial quest when my mother hired a new cook to replace Matthieu, who had moved back to his village after the death of his father.

"Poor Matthieu wasn't very dependable, but he had a lot to bear," my mother told Mrs. Elmer Frykman over mid-morning coffee break. "His family suffered an unbelievable number of deaths last year."

"Unbelievable is right!" Mrs. Frykman snorted, fanning her fleshy neck with our latest *Reader's Digest*. "Something like twenty, according to my cook, who says you gave Matthieu paid leave every time! Now honestly, June, don't you think the Lord expects us to show some Biblical Discernment about truth and fiction—particularly when it comes to the Congolese?"

My mother's quick, nervous frown made me wonder what Mrs. Frykman meant, but I didn't find out, because my mother sent me to the cookhouse to wait for the new cook.

"He should be arriving any minute, Grace," she said. "And when he does, come get me—after you've introduced yourself, of course."

Our new cook turned out to be a tall, skeletal man named Makua, which I thought very funny, as *makua* meant "bones" in Lingala. He was a Banza from the far northwest corner of the Congo, right across the border from the Central African Republic. The other mission cooks laughed at Makua because he came from "the sticks," had unusually black skin, and couldn't speak a word of French. ("How can anyone be such a *sauvage* in 1963, even a Banza?" they wanted to know.) I hoped Makua would stay. He promised to teach me how to whistle between my teeth, the way he did when he pumped water from the cistern. He even allowed me take over the dry-season job of checking the water level in the cistern, though he insisted on removing the round concrete lid himself.

"*Bana basi na mindele bajali makasi te,*" he explained, heaving the lid aside. "Little white girls aren't strong like Congolese girls. You might hurt yourself. Then when you grow to be a woman you won't be able to have any children, and your husband and his family will curse you."

"*Wapi!*" I said, defending my future relations. "Nonsense! Americans don't do that."

"*Wapi!* They just curse quietly, that's all." Makua brushed his hands against his shorts, leaving long streaks of concrete dust on the black fabric. "*Yango wana.* There you are. Be careful not to fall in."

I dropped down flat on my stomach and hung my head deep inside the mouth of the cistern. As I peered at the slimy concrete wall, I tried to guess how far the water level had dropped since yesterday. Duty done, I shouted into the watery cavern and listened to my voice bounce around like a lost ball, waterlogged, hollow, but eerily familiar. A stale-smelling black scum floated on the surface of the water, and sometimes I thought I heard frogs croaking and splashing about, although I never saw them. My mother said there was no telling what disgusting creatures lived in there, and it was a good thing the cistern lid was so heavy and tight fitting.

"That water is a strange color lately," Makua remarked as he dragged the lid over the gaping hole. "Greenish black. Even river water looks better. I can tell you why, if you like. I think it might be good for you to know."

"To know what?"

"That you have a *ndoki* living inside your cistern."

Makua's Lingala from "the sticks" was sometimes different from Boanda Lingala, but I knew I hadn't misunderstood.

"A *ndoki*? Really? *Nakamwi!*"

"I heard about it the first day I worked for your mother. The Frykmans' cook told me."

A *ndoki* of my own all this time, and I hadn't known! The missionary adults talked about evil spirits, of course, but only the New Testament kind that Jesus was forever having to throw out of people. They never mentioned Congolese evil spirits at all. Yet everyone else understood how important *ndokis* were, that the world was filled with them and a person could run into one at any moment. Some *ndokis* were less exciting than others, I knew, but all deserved great respect. Seeing a *ndoki* gave a person special rights to brag about it and be listened to patiently. I had never imagined being able to tell my friends stories about my own personal cistern *ndoki*.

"Have you seen it?" I asked Makua.

"Many times. Your *ndoki* isn't a terribly evil one though. It's too *goigoi*, lazy. It changes the color of the water, but otherwise it just sleeps a lot."

"Oh," I said, trying not to sound disappointed. "What does it look like?"

"A ball of blue-white light. It's *moke moke*, very small. It lives just under the concrete ceiling, way over in the corner, so you can't see it easily, not even with your head hanging down inside. Sometimes when it feels playful it splashes around in the water. That's why you hear strange noises down there from time to time."

The frogs! Now I knew better.

"Ah, has it ever attacked you?" I asked Makua timidly.

"No, not this one." Makua sat down on the porch step, stretching his long skinny legs in front of him and tilting his head back. The day was already warm, and little rivers of sweat ran from the high dome of Makua's forehead to his hairline, losing themselves in the close-trimmed curls. "But not long ago I was chased by a *ndoki* through the big market in Coquilhatville."

Coquilhatville, capital of the Congo's Equateur province, was just seven kilometers from Boanda. I never missed a chance to visit the market there. You could buy everything from python steaks and phony Congo dragon fossils to Archie comics and Bazooka bubble gum.

"In the daytime?" I asked. "With the place so full of people?"

"Oh no! It was late at night. I was crossing the empty market square, heading for my friend Mobaya's house, when suddenly I saw a terribly large person skulking in the shadows. I guessed it was a man, but I couldn't see very well since there was no moon and I had no *mwinda*, lantern. I began to walk as fast as I could, and the shadowy person followed so silently that I knew he must be a *ndoki*. My heart grew cold within me, cold as death, and I decided not to go to Mobaya's house after all. Bringing a *ndoki* along as an un-invited guest would be a dreadful thing to do to a friend. So I ran *kilikili* all over that market, dodging behind stalls and dashing first one way and then another as I tried to escape him. I grew weary and breathless, panting like an old *basenji* dog on a hot day, but I couldn't get rid of that *ndoki*. He just kept following me, loping along without making a sound. Finally I could run no further. My eyes were blinded by sweat, and my legs wouldn't hold me up anymore. They were just like *potopoto*."

"*Potopoto?*"

"You know. That muddy clay we build houses with."

I nodded. Then I sat down beside him on the step, hugging my knees to my chest as he continued.

"I hid behind one of the fish stalls and watched the *ndoki* come toward me. Even in the darkness I could see that he was at least two meters tall. He was barefoot and wore only a loincloth, like some of the old-fashioned fathers in my village. And he carried a huge handmade spear as thick as my arm!"

Makua held out his own muscled arm, flexing his hand so I could see the sturdy corded lines where the blood ran beneath the skin.

"That spear wasn't just thick and heavy. It was also the longest spear I had ever seen. It was *molai mpenza*, longer even than my grandfather's spear, and my grandfather was a famous and strong hunter in his time. I knew that *ndoki* could pin me to the wall of the fish stall, and I could do nothing to save myself. I would just have to hang there until I died and my body was found by the fish women the next morning.

"As he drew near me, I forced myself to look directly into his face and meet his eyes. Somehow it seemed right that I know the eyes of this being who wished to kill me. So I looked, and what I saw made my tongue wither up like a leaf in dry season. The *ndoki* had no eyes—only two deep pits in his face, like empty cisterns. And even as I looked into those bottomless holes, the *ndoki* raised his arm and drew his spear back for a powerful throw. I knew I would never see my wife and children again. I knew I would never see my village again. I was going to die instead. Die a bad death in that stinking stall littered with fish scales and bones and catfish whiskers.

"And then, just across the road, someone opened the door of Frank Sinatra's Wild Bush Baby Bar. Electric light poured out, coloring the night red and green, blue and yellow. I heard South African jazz blaring from the bar owner's transistor and felt the heat of many people laughing and dancing in a small room."

Makua made a wondering sound in his throat as he slowly shook his head, his arms dangling over his knees.

"All the noise and colored lights must have given him *ntembe,* fear, because suddenly the *ndoki* wasn't there anymore. He didn't run away. He just faded like a bad smell into the darkness of the fish stalls."

I sighed, the painful knot in my throat slowly easing. I knew how my father must have felt when he came home from church and loosened his tie. For a long wordless moment, Makua and I stared across the back yard, seeing dark, spear-laden shadows in the trees. My mother's voice calling me in for breakfast broke the spell, and I jumped up, relieved.

After breakfast I set off to broadcast the news of my *ndoki.*

"That's not so great. I've seen one with my very own eyes," Davina Carlson informed me. Her nose had a snooty tilt, and her sun-bleached cowlick sprang wildly upward in spite of Mrs. Carlson's daily efforts to flatten it with Dippity-Do. "There's a *ndoki* at the burned-down house by the Catholic church. I saw it one night on our way home from prayer meeting. It was a little flickering light that made crying noises like a baby. And I know that's what it was, because the Belgian lady who lived there before Independence had a tiny boy who ate a whole bottle of quinine pills and died."

Davina clutched her neck, stuck her tongue out, and rolled her eyes back into her head. "It was instant."

Ronnie Nordstrom had a *ndoki* story too. So did his sister Pauline, although hers was from the Bible. ("Gospel text last Sunday, remember? The one where the Greek lady begs Jesus to throw the evil spirit out of her little girl.") It turned out that everyone I talked to had seen *ndokis* before. Alphonse, the Frykmans' cook, had a brother, Dawili, whose mother-in-law died of sleeping sickness and turned into a *ndoki*. Alphonse told us Dawili saw her with his own eyes one foggy morning two weeks after her death. Dawili was sitting down by the river mending a fishing net when suddenly she appeared before him, river water dripping from her naked limbs. Worms and bugs crawled across her wet, wrinkled skin, and Dawili saw that maggots had eaten out her eyes and nostrils. While he huddled behind an abandoned pirogue, gagging at her death-smell, she cursed him in a deep, thundering voice. Then she disappeared into the river, and Dawili went home and drank so much palm wine that he was sick for three days. Dawili hadn't always done well by his mother-in-law, Alphonse said, but he wasn't nearly cruel or wicked enough to deserve such punishment.

Even Mama Malia, my baby sister Faith's nanny, had seen a *ndoki* just last month while she was working in her manioc garden. This *ndoki* was disguised as an animal, she said.

"A pig?" I asked, thinking of Jesus and the evil-spirit-filled pigs, the ones He sent stampeding over a cliff into the sea.

"A wild dog," Mama Malia said. "But now I have a special wooden amulet, and I haven't seen a *ndoki* since."

I wondered where she got the amulet, but I didn't like to ask, and Mama Malia didn't offer to tell me.

I began to avoid the back porch, where my own personal *ndoki* lived unseen just inches beneath the concrete. Why had I been so foolishly pleased when Makua told me about it? Surely that *ndoki* hated its dark stagnant life and held me somehow responsible. Surely it spent all its underwater days planning terrible things to do to me if it had the chance. And one day it would, I was certain. One day Makua would take the lid off that ugly cistern mouth and forget to put it back. The *ndoki* would sneak out to look for me, and when it found me, it would kill me. Everyone knew *ndokis* did that, because people often died after seeing one. They might not die right away, they might linger for months or even years, but eventually the *ndoki* destroyed them. Some Congolese planted special broad-leaved vines around their houses to keep evil spirits away. I wondered if I could plant one next to our house without my parents noticing—and then I wondered if I could really stop an evil spirit with one little vine. Shouldn't something be done about the Coquilhatville market too? And what about the riverfront, Mama Malia's garden, the burned shell of the Belgians' house?

When I mentioned this to Davina, she put on her mother's most superior voice and told me I could end up planting vines until Our Lord's Second Coming. "And then it would all be for nothing, because Jesus will send all the evil spirits to Hell anyway," she said, adding, "But you know what I want to do, Grace? I want to explore that Belgian house. Come with me—unless you're scared."

I didn't want any more contact with the mysterious and the terrible, but Davina was younger than me by nearly a year; I couldn't allow her to think I was scared. So before Davina could believe her suspicions were justified, I gave in. Late on a Sunday afternoon, when it seemed reasonable to hope the average *ndoki* was drowsy and good-tempered, Davina and I headed for the burned-down Belgian house.

"You would never think this was fun if you had a *ndoki* in your cistern," I muttered as we walked along the palm-lined gravel road. "We could go swimming instead, you know. Play keep-away, maybe, or build a water-hyacinth fort. Or even stay in my back yard and hunt for the equator."

"We can hunt the equator tomorrow."

I said nothing more, but my dread deepened as we passed the bougainvillea-shaded Frykman and Renquist houses, then Dr. Birgie's unpainted concrete duplex. Now there remained just one inhabited house between us and the Catholic church.

"Grace! Davina! I haven't seen you children for days." Alain lounged on a veranda chair, waving his drink at us and smiling his sweet lopsided smile. His dark hair was rumpled, and his wire-rimmed glasses had slipped down to the tip of his long nose. "Come drink a Coca-Cola and talk English with me. It is needing practice, my English."

Alain Fougère was one of my favorite people in the world, yet somehow I couldn't tell him we were hunting for a *ndoki*. "We're hunting the equator," I said and watched Alain's smile grow even sweeter, more lopsided.

"How charming!" he said. "I wish you luck."

Davina and I exchanged glances of gleeful horror. We weren't allowed to use the word "luck," because the missionary adults said it meant God wasn't in charge of the world. Luck was unchristian, they told us, even primitive.

"Thank you," we chorused.

"But certainly." Alain took another sip of his licorice-scented drink. "Perhaps you will return when your hunt is finished. I have a new case of Coca-Cola. Also Côte D'or milk chocolates, the ones you are mad for, the ones filled with hazelnut praline."

Alain was always stuffing us with rare luxuries: imported soft drinks, chocolates, apples, Petit Beurre biscuits straight from France. Mrs. Frykman said it was obvious Alain came from money and took a lot for granted.

"It's easy to be generous when you can afford it," I'd heard her say. "And of course the children love him! For myself, though, I'd be ashamed to buy affection with chocolate bars."

Mrs. Frykman didn't know it, but we so adored Alain that we happily visited him the day before Madame Vaske's monthly shipment of European groceries was due at her Coquilhatville shop. On those days Alain had only quinine water to offer us. We swallowed it cheerfully, determined to keep our grimaces deep inside where they couldn't hurt his feelings.

The missionary adults often prayed for Alain at Wednesday-night prayer meeting, so we knew all about his terrible sins. From Mrs. Frykman's prayers, we knew Alain was a pacifist, avoiding French military service by teaching in Africa. From Mrs. Carlson's prayers, we learned Alain drank alcoholic beverages, and that it was wrong to smoke a pipe, even a pretty one made of African rosewood. Mr. Frykman's prayers told us Alain was a Catholic who didn't go to Mass anymore. It was no sin that Alain wouldn't go to Mass, according to Mr. Frykman, but that Alain was a Catholic in the first place was a scandalous slap in the faces of his Huguenot-martyr ancestors.

Alain also had several European lady friends in Coquilhatville. "Immoral to the core," Mrs. Frykman said. "Every last miniskirted one of them." The lady friend he saw most was Ghislaine, an elegant bony Frenchwoman who worked at the Air France office. Ghislaine had long red hair, short black skirts, and didn't shave her legs. She wore bright red polish on her toenails and drew thick black lines around her mournful eyes. We called her The Panda and made rude faces at her narrow back whenever we saw her in line for French bread at the Coquilhatville market. I wished we were there now, sniffing warm bread and jeering at

Ghislaine's back, rather than approaching the burned-
down house. At least it was some comfort to know that if we
survived this *ndoki*-hunt, we would return to Alain's.

The gravel was still hot on our naked feet, and I was almost
relieved to see our goal in sight. The crumbling walls of the
house were shaded by heavy-limbed mango trees, and
weeds blurred the fancy pattern of the orange brick walkway. Once the walls of the house had been that same sun-
faded orange. Now they were blackened by the fire that had
gutted the interior and made a giant torch of the thatched
roof, and they smelled of mold and wet moss. The front door
was gone, leaving a hole as alarming as the one beneath the
cistern lid at home. We stood just inside the rotting door
frame, staring through screenless, shutterless windows to
the river, glinting blue in the late afternoon sun. I could
hear village children laughing as they played behind the
Catholic elementary school. The concrete floor had cracked
into crazy spiderweb designs and was scattered with fallen
mangoes. It cooled my feet.

I had reached the middle of the room before I realized
Davina was still in the doorway, her eyes scanning the ruined walls and floor suspiciously. She hugged her crossed
arms, and her bright cowlick drooped on her forehead.

"Come on, Davina! This was your idea, remember?"

"I bet there are snakes in here," she quavered, following
slowly. "Green mambas. Gabon vipers. Spitting cobras."

I hoped not. Snakes frightened me almost as much as
ndokis. Having to worry about both in one place seemed
unfair.

"Let's get this over with. Show me where you saw that
ndoki," I ordered.

"I don't know, exactly," she replied. "I guess it was in the little dead baby's room. Anyway, not in here. This was the living room, I think."

I agreed, noticing a charred couch-like shape against one wall. I considered which room to try next. Just to the right of the couch was a mahogany door, tightly closed. The weighty dark wood intimidated me, as did the overhanging mango branches. I didn't want to explore such a gloomy place unless I absolutely had to.

"Let's see what's straight ahead," I said, heading for a sunny room facing the river.

Fragments of glass from a shattered cupboard littered the floor. The large table in the center of the room was covered with overripe mangoes. Only six years ago, the Belgian lady must have held dinner parties at this table. They would have been very grand, I knew. Alain went to European dinner parties all the time, and sometimes my mother and father were invited as well. Afterwards my mother sat on my bed in her pink-flowered Sunday dress and described the clothes, the conversation, the table, the food. I wondered if the Belgian lady had been entertaining on that terrible night. If she had, I knew the scene by heart, down to the smallest detail. She wore a low-cut black dress, pearls, and lemon-scented Guerlain eau de cologne. ("Or Shalimar, perhaps," Alain would say. "If the lady has a certain *volupté*.") Her hibiscus-red nail polish exactly matched her lipstick, and her dark hair had a fresh henna rinse. The table was set with real silverware, more forks and spoons per place setting than I was used to, white embroidered linens, and silver candlesticks. White jungle orchids with deep red hearts floated gently in a crystal bowl. The Belgian hostess ladled soup, something strange like turtle or oxtail, into shallow European soup plates. She passed around crusty French bread with lots of unsalted butter. For a while everyone ate quietly, chinking their spoons against the wide-brimmed porcelain plates. Then, gradually, everybody began to talk and laugh, the ladies waving their hands in the air and jangling their bracelets as they discussed the high price of imported cheese in Coquilhatville, plane fares to Brussels, and good Belgian boarding schools. The men shook their heads over the drop in rubber prices and the cost of shipping the cacao crop to Antwerp.

While Congolese servants in starched white jackets and white gloves cleared away the first course, the Belgian lady would have excused herself to check on the baby. I imagined her opening the door very softly, her black taffeta skirt rustling about her knees, sounding like a swarm of mosquitoes after a rain. She tripped over something lying in the middle of the floor. Was it a toy? She picked it up. It was a brown glass Nivaquine bottle, and it was empty. She clutched the bottle to her bosom and rushed to the little bed beneath the window. Her child lay facedown on the duvet, breathless and still . . .

"You know what, Grace? I think the *ndoki* lives in the other room, behind that door."

I followed Davina back to the living room, my head echoing with the Belgian lady's long-ago screams. I felt dizzy, and my knees, like Makua's, had turned to *potopoto*. A mango tree cast heavy shade, one dark leafy branch hanging so low it disappeared into the hidden room behind the roofless wall. The floor was a maze of mangoes with soft black-spotted skins. We picked our way carefully: one misstep and rotting fruit would ooze over our bare toes. The fire-blackened mahogany door was still there, still closed. The hinges, rusty from the long rains, looked like streaks of old blood.

Davina leaned against the door and pushed. Nothing happened. I decided I ought to help. Together we rammed the heavy wood with our skinny hips and shoulders, puffing and grunting, our hair falling into our eyes. I wondered if the *ndoki* was pushing against us on the other side.

"One more time," Davina panted.

In a sudden, desperate flash I knew I must open the door, must see the dreadful thing behind it. I wanted to run from this dead-smelling shell of a house, but where? My own home was no safer than this place! Hot frantic energy coursed through my veins, and I flung myself against the door like a stone from a slingshot. The ruined wood scraped slowly, painfully, across the concrete. Then, with a deafening crack, the door ripped completely out of the frame, hurtling us into the *ndoki*-filled room. Davina and I skidded across the floor and crashed against the far wall. Everything was a confused jumble of spoiled mangoes, dead branches, splintered wood, skinned knees. My right hand made horrible fleeting contact with something sleek and dry as snakeskin, and my fingers cramped up with panic. I shut my eyes, opened my mouth, and screamed.

"*Mon Dieu!* Grace! Davina! Where are you? Are you injured? *J'arrive. Ne bougez pas!*"

Usually Alain spoke in a soft lazy voice, words drifting from his mouth and curling gently around the smoky edges of his pipe. Now he sounded harsh and quick, his sandals slapping the floor as he hurried toward us, careless of the decaying mangoes. Shaking his head and muttering *"Bon sang,"* Alain stood us on our feet and examined our battered knees. I looked down too, noticing for the first time a sluggish river of rotten mango running down my left shin. It was the last straw. Tears and words spurted from me like a fountain. "We were looking for the *ndoki* that lives here, and we thought it would be in this room where the Belgian baby died."

"*Comment?*"

"Davina saw it!"

"Davina—" Alain turned to her.

"I did," she sniffed, rubbing her elbow. "Really. And once I heard it crying."

"I see. Let us leave this place. We will talk later," Alain said, hauling us limping and sobbing down the road to his house.

We sat on Alain's front veranda and watched the river change colors with the sunset. My legs were cleaned up, my knees sporting huge adhesive bandages that would stick to my hairs and be wonderfully painful and exciting to remove. I held a stubby glass filled with lemon ice cubes and Coca-Cola and nibbled the scalloped edges off my Petit Beurre, saving the center for last.

"Listen well, children," Alain said as he took the rosewood pipe and a box of matches from his trouser pocket. "There are no *ndokis* in that house or anywhere else. I have never seen a *ndoki,* and I do not expect to. I think perhaps you have been listening to silly Congolese stories, is that not so?"

I was stunned, afraid to believe. Afraid to disbelieve.

"Are you sure they're silly?" I asked cautiously.

Alain gave a sigh of patient aggravation and struck a match so hard that the match head snapped off, bounced down the steps, and landed in the flowering plumbago hedge.

"*Zut!*" He struck another match more gently and lit his pipe with care. "But of course I am sure!"

Even though he wasn't a missionary, wasn't even a Protestant, I knew Alain would never lie. All the same—

"And no *ndokis?* None at all?"

22

There was a short silence. Alain drew on his pipe, frowning into the smoky bowl like he'd seen something disgusting at the bottom—a tunneling termite maybe, or a patch of blue-green mold—and then he looked at us with fierce attention, his eyes bright in the settling gloom. When he spoke, his voice had the slow, sober authority of someone reading the Ten Commandments from the pulpit Bible, and I had a sudden crazy thought that perhaps Alain really was a missionary after all.

"It is important to listen to a Congolese with politeness, but now I will tell you children a true thing: whatever a Congolese says about *ndokis* is of no consequence, because *ndokis* are not real. Only the superstitious and uneducated believe in them. We Europeans do not."

We Europeans. There was a welcome lightness inside me, and a heady unfamiliar pride. Perhaps my grown-up future would include black dresses and pearls, turtle soup, and extra silverware at dinner parties . . .

Suddenly hungry, I ate two more biscuits and drained my glass of Coca-Cola. I leaned back on my elbows, puffed out my stomach, and burped comfortably, enjoying the sharp fizzle in my nose.

"That is enough of serious matters, I think," Alain said.

And then he told us all his latest Catholic-priest jokes, as well as a new installment of Tintin's adventures at the South Pole, while Davina and I watched the far-off islands dissolve in the darkness of the river.

The next morning I joined Makua on the back porch. He moved the cistern lid aside, and I dropped flat on my stomach to check the water level. It was a bit higher, due to an unexpected thunderstorm over the weekend, but otherwise the great grimy hole was just that, a stagnant underground necessity. A faint splash in the far corner no longer seemed mysterious (Didn't I know a frog when I heard one?) and all at once I had no heart for my shout-and-echo game. I stood up and brushed the dust from the front of my T-shirt. Ignoring Makua's protests (Wasn't he superstitious and uneducated?) I dragged the concrete lid over to the cistern mouth and shoved it into place all by myself.

"Little white girls are *kilikili*," Makua remarked, shaking his head. "And also bad tempered."

I sat down on the step and watched Makua whistle between his teeth as he emptied pails of cold water into a washtub, then checked the fuel supply in the washing machine motor. Today was Monday, laundry day, and I saw no reason for him to act so cheerful about pushing clothes through the wringer by hand and sweating in the dry-season heat. And it was going to be a horribly, miserably hot day, I could tell. The sun had already burned the dew from the grass, and the gardenia bush drooped, every leaf shriveled and dusty.

"It's a fine morning," my father announced, coming through the kitchen door with an armload of books and his moldy leather briefcase. "*Kitoko mpenza!*"

I said nothing, just stared across the back yard into the dark and vine-tangled trees.

"What's the trouble, Grace?" My father asked. "Why so glum?"

Instead of fierce dragon fire, instead of fabulous rainbows, a few leftover strands of morning mist floated between the jumbled branches. And the only bit of bright color I could see was the tiny orange beak of a pygmy kingfisher perching on a dead guava limb.

"There's no such thing as the equator," I said. "Not in that bit of jungle. Not anywhere."

"What in the world do you mean?" My father dropped his briefcase beside me on the step. "Of course there's an equator. It's a great circle around the Earth's surface at zero degrees latitude."

I folded my arms across my chest and looked at my father standing there in his teaching uniform of black wing tips, baggy black trousers, and white short-sleeved shirt, a sharpened yellow pencil tucked behind his left ear.

"No," I said flatly, sticking out my chin. "I have never seen the equator, and I do not expect to. The equator is not real, and only the—the superstitious and uneducated believe in it."

"Jumping Jehoshaphat!"

A redness crawled up my father's neck, his cheekbones, even his puckered forehead, until his whole face looked like an oversized Congolese *pilipili* pepper. I'd seen him turn that color just once before, when Mrs. Frykman said the mission shouldn't finance soybean farming because Jesus never mentioned soybeans in the Bible.

"Now you listen to me, Grace Linnea Berggren!" my father said in his sternest teaching voice. "The equator is critical to science! It is the absolutely vital reference line from which we figure all the other parallels of latitude. It is the backbone of the north-south grid of our global framework!" He plucked the yellow pencil from his ear and began drawing invisible lines in the air. "Why, we wouldn't be able to locate ourselves, our position on the earth, if we didn't postulate the equator as a starting point! Of course the equator is real!"

I said okay, where did you find these parallel-things, and my father looked at his wristwatch and groaned.

"I don't have time for this!" he said. "All right, it's a matter of degrees. You see, we use degrees to talk about parallels, and the value of each degree has been set at approximately sixty-nine miles. But this value is divisible as well, so we also use even smaller units—minutes and seconds—which increase our precision . . ."

As he talked, my father's brown eyes took on such a bright feverish glow that I wondered if he had a touch of malaria. His voice deepened, every word filled with a solemn churchlike excitement.

"Now we haven't even mentioned the east-west lines of longitude yet, which are reckoned from Greenwich, England, and intersect the parallels with the wonderful end result that science can determine the exact location of each degree, each minute, and even each tiny second on the entire globe! And that means no matter where you are, you can always *know* where you are—with respect to the equator, I mean, and of course Greenwich . . . Grace!" My father waved his pencil in my face. "Are you even listening to me?"

Maybe I had a malarial fever myself, the kind that made me see things all sideways and strange, but my father suddenly seemed more fierce, more fervent, than I'd ever dreamed possible. An evangelist missionary like Mr. Frykman, all hot-pepper-red and arm-waving, instead of an agriculture-teacher missionary.

"An object lesson, that's what you need," he exclaimed. "Come along. Quickly now."

He grabbed my arm and hurried me down the steps to the cookhouse, where a stack of concrete blocks and two rakes leaned up against one wall. He snatched the top block and headed across the yard while I trotted after him. He didn't pause when he reached the jungle, just rammed his way through several yards of undergrowth and spiraling gray vine, wild plantain trees, and shaggy waist-high ferns until he arrived at a small open space between two teak trees. He stopped, plunked the block down, and turned to me.

"There's your equator, Grace," my father said.

I stared mutely at the block of concrete lying on a thin bed of greasy-brown lichens and exposed teak roots. The block was all blunt gray edges, all drab and rough-grained ugliness.

"I've really got to run now."

The late afternoon sun stained my T-shirt orange as I squeezed through the jungle with leafy treasure in my cupped hands and one of my baby sister's bottles tucked under my arm. I knelt beside the concrete block, set both my treasure and Faith's bottle on top of it, then picked up a twig and scraped a shallow hole in the sandy lichen-crusted soil. Into this hole I carefully placed the tiny plant I'd up-rooted (without permission) from Mrs. Frykman's front yard, packing the light soil gently against the roots, shoring up the narrow stem. When I was certain the plant would stay upright, I unscrewed the plastic cap from Faith's bottle and poured a fine stream of water onto the broad clustering leaves of the loveliest little *ndoki* vine in Boanda.

Simbas in Little America

W<small>E CROUCHED</small> in the tall razor grass by the side of the road, our arms and legs slashed by the pale green blades. We waited, gulping air that smelled of earth—hot, lazy, and red. At last we heard the hoarse French bellowing of the commandant, the clatter of weapons, the heavy tread of military boots. Closer they came, closer and louder; in a moment they would be alongside us. I licked my upper lip, tasting salt.

"Five . . . four . . . three . . . two . . . one . . ."

Davina and I erupted from the knife-sharp grass, shrieking our lungs dry as we brandished our spears at the enemy soldiers. They screamed and reeled, dropping their guns, their eyes rolling back into their heads so only the whites were visible. They curled their arms over their skulls and fell dead on the road, splash-landing in the mud puddles left by last night's rain.

Except for Alison. She had the mysterious good fortune to fall on a tiny piece of dry ground. The other soldiers got up quickly, dimpled baby fat daubed with mud, eager for another ambush, but not Alison. She lay there staring up into the branches of a palm, one dainty elbow shading her eyes from the glaring Congo sun.

"This is a stupid game," she announced, unmoving.

Davina and I took off our lion masks and exchanged scornful glances over her prone body.

Finally Alison got up, craned her neck around, and brushed a fretful hand across the back of her once-white shorts. She frowned at the streaks of red dirt glittering with mica, then rearranged the ruffled collar of her pale pink blouse. "I don't see why all of us soldiers have to be such scaredy-cats," Alison said. "And anyway, this mud is disgusting. Just disgusting."

I considered calling Alison an Embassy Wimp right to her face, then changed my mind. She couldn't help being an Embassy Wimp. Besides, her parents hadn't evacuated to New York or Washington, D.C., like all the other American Embassy people in Léopoldville. They were staying, although they acted like frightful sissies about it. Alison's father wore a fancy bulletproof vest and hired two bodyguards, Maurice and Cecil, to accompany him everywhere. Maurice and Cecil were red-faced blond men with almost-but-not-quite-British accents. ("Rhodesian mercenaries," Alison told us. "They're the best, my father says.")

As for Alison's mother, she hadn't left her big hilltop house for two weeks now. She wouldn't take a walk around the yard, or even sit on the veranda. She spent all her time on her living-room couch, sipping gold-colored stuff out of short fat glasses and sighing as she flipped through European fashion magazines. Sometimes she pressed her hands to her forehead and wailed, "Oh, for chrissake *when* will this *end!*" With such parents, it was no wonder Alison liked to die carefully in between mud puddles.

"Alison, you're a soldier in the Congolese National Army, and we're the Simbas. You're supposed to be scared."

I tried to sound calm, saintly, and much older than seven. Dignified, like Mrs. Carlson when she told off her cook for breaking dishes or forgetting the salt in the oatmeal.

"Everybody is afraid of the Simbas," I explained. "They're protected by powerful *kisi*. No bullet can touch them."

"What is *kisi?*" Alison asked, still rubbing at the dirt on her shorts.

Davina and I rolled our eyes like dying soldiers in the National Army. Embassy Wimps really didn't know anything. We had always suspected it, but we hadn't known for sure until the rebellion started and we were sent down to Léopoldville.

"*Kisi* is magic. You know, witch-doctor medicine," I said. "The Simbas have got it, and it makes them extra brave, like lions. That's why they wear lion masks."

She knelt down to retie the loosened pink shoelaces that exactly matched her blouse. I couldn't tell if she was doubtful or just plain bored.

"And that's why the rebels are called Simbas," Davina added, her cowlick bouncing impatiently. "Because the Swahili word for lion is '*simba.*'"

"I'm going to ask my Dad," Alison replied, standing up and brushing off her knees. "He'll know."

How could he possibly know anything, I wondered. Embassy people never bothered to learn any languages except French—everyone knew that! Even as I opened my mouth to say so, Alison rearranged her fancy gold barrettes and revealed a new and shocking Embassy touch: tiny pearl earrings in the centers of her earlobes.

"You pierced your ears!" Davina and I cried.

Alison tossed her head and looked pleased with herself.

"My mother did," she said.

If only we'd known in time to talk Alison and her mother out of doing such a terrible thing! Congolese ladies had pierced ears, of course. Some even had pierced noses with little earrings or twigs to block up the hole. But most of the Congolese ladies had a good excuse: they honestly didn't realize their bodies were supposed to be Temples of God, undefiled by unnatural holes. Alison's mother, though, had no excuse at all. Even if she cried a lot and wasn't a missionary, Alison's mother was still a white American lady.

Indifferent to our horrified stares, Alison announced that real American kids played Cowboys and Indians, and she was going home. She said we could come along if we liked.

Davina and I held a silent conversation of shrugs and raised eyebrows:

Do you want to go?

I don't care.

Well, do you?

Oh, I guess so if you do.

"Sure," we said, "But we'll have to take the little kids home first."

We collected our stick spears and guns and followed the road up the hill, leaving Papaya Ravine behind. Papaya Ravine was our name for this little valley filled with razor grass, mauve savanna orchids, and flimsy baby papaya trees. It was a bit of wilderness inside the Léopoldville city limits, sudden and lovely, which we had discovered our first week here. The ravine almost made up for not living within walking distance of the river.

As we climbed the hill, I studied the lion face on my construction paper mask. I was pleased with my black Crayola efforts, though Gbadenu, our temporary cook, had laughed at it. "What do you children want to practice being warriors for? If you think any Simba would come up here to Little America, you're *kilikili!*" Gbadenu's open-throated laugh shook his entire body. "They're plenty brave, but even a Simba wouldn't dare!"

The Congolese called this hill Little America. Usually Little America was populated by several dozen American Embassy people, but right now wasn't usual. Right now most of the houses were empty, because the Embassy people had gone back to real America several months ago. Mrs. Carlson said they'd all left prematurely because they were just exactly what you'd expect from the Johnson administration: a gaggle of gutless weak-kneed Democrats. And though I never saw them, I pictured these evacuees without any bones or cartilage under their ashy paper-thin skin. I imagined them limp muscled and shapeless, like wet sheets hung out to dry, waiting for a breeze to fill out their flatness. They were long gone, these gutless Democrats, when the Simbas headed south toward Boanda, forcing all of us downriver to live in the dank shuttered Embassy houses and reclaim their weed-ridden clover lawns.

"All of us" weren't very many by that time. Dr. Birgie had gone off to Dr. Schweitzer's hospital in Lambarene, Gabon, and Alain Fougère had flown to France. ("Eager for a bit of Paris nightlife, I suppose," Mrs. Frykman said to my mother. "But why our Dr. Birgie wants to work for that Godless liberal in Lambarene is beyond me when I know for a fact the man doesn't believe in the divinity of Christ!") And then the Frykmans and a half dozen others had headed south to Katanga province to help out at a new Protestant orphanage until Things Calmed Down, and that left only our family and Davina's at Boanda—until the day my father told us the Simbas were on the move and we had to go down to Léopoldville without him. "I'm *not* going to let that bunch of communist rebels trash my experimental soybean fields!" he'd announced. "*Or* my chicken farm! And since Nils is worried about his chemistry lab, he's staying too."

My mother had gone pale as a blossom on a baobab tree. She clutched my father's sunburned arm and began crying,

"Oh Robert, you can't be heroic! It's suicide! They're taking white hostages, and we all know what happened to those poor Belgian nuns!"

My father had stroked her hand very gently and said, "Now honey, somebody's got to take care of the Rhode Island Reds or the Simbas'll eat them, and anyway, this can't last long. The Simbas aren't powerful enough, even with Soviet AK-47s and witch-doctor *kisi*."

So my mother had blown her nose and briskly told him he'd better make sure he ate properly or she'd give him a piece of her mind when things were back to normal, and my father had said, "That's the spirit, Junie!"

Then he'd taken us to the Coquilhatville airport, where he and my mother hugged and kissed for such a long time that my little sister Faith and I hid in the ladies' toilet out of embarrassment. After we'd boarded the plane, my father had climbed up the fire escape to the flat terminal roof. He stood there waving and smiling, his hair blowing like a wind sock, until our Air Congo DC-4 took off, skimmed the tops of the flamboyant trees at the end of the runway, and banked sharply, heading south toward Léopoldville and Little America.

"Hey, Grace!" Davina said, waving her stick spear in my face. "I almost forgot. Our cook says the river in Stanleyville is running red with dead bodies. Congolese, Europeans, even Russians. And so many the crocs can't eat them all!"

"Really?" I momentarily forgot about my father back at Boanda defending his chickens and soybeans. "But Stanleyville has millions of crocs!"

"He heard it on Radio Brazzaville," she said. "Ask him."

"We could ask Maurice and Cecil," Alison said. "They listen to the radio a lot. They're bored with backgammon, my mother says, and my father has run out of James Bond novels to loan them."

Davina and I glanced sideways at each other:

What's backgammon?

Something Rhodesian, I guess.

And James Bond novels?

They're probably Rhodesian too.

We stopped at the Carlson house to leave off Davina's little brother and sister, then went next door to my house. Davina and Alison sat on the back porch and talked to Gbadenu while I brought Faith inside. My mother was hovering over the kitchen stove, perspiring as she gently dropped flabby circlets of doughnut dough into a cast-iron pot of hot oil. I watched the pale rings sink down to the bottom of the pot, then explode to the surface sizzling and puffing out rich golden brown.

"Can I have one?"

"No, dear. They'll have to cool before I can frost them. You can have one for dessert tonight instead. How will that be?"

She'd been talking in that bright cheerful voice for several months now. I hated it.

"Okay, I guess," I said.

I watched her turn the doughnuts over with a long slotted spoon. I could usually tell in advance if pestering her would do any good, and today I knew it wouldn't. Being hot always made her extra strict, and she was obviously hot. Her face shone bright red, her blouse clung to her skin, and the curls at the back of her neck had grown tight, dark, and soggy. She kept drying her hands on the front of her blue-checked apron and humming distracted snatches of "O Savior, Our Comfort in Times of Distress." No, it was hopeless to try to change her mind, and anyway, I loved doughnut frosting, especially the little droplets that hung around the edges just begging to be licked off. I was willing to wait.

"We're going up to Alison's house," I said, dropping my lion mask on the counter.

My mother set down the slotted spoon and sighed, her forehead creasing up in wavy lines. She massaged the lines with her sweaty fingers, and I wished she wouldn't. The way she rubbed and poked at it lately, I was afraid her skin might fall off.

"Oh dear," she said. "I don't know if you should. We don't want to impose."

I'd never known my mother to worry about imposing until we met Alison's mother. It had something to do with clothes, I thought, remembering how my mother's mouth had dropped open when she saw Alison's mother for the first time. It was the afternoon of our arrival in Little America, and my mother and Mrs. Carlson had been drinking Nescafé at the kitchen table. ("Taking a breather from settling in," Mrs. Carlson said.) Alison and her mother had come down from the hilltop wearing matching pink linen dresses with huge mother-of-pearl buttons down the front. Alison's mother wore pink high heels that narrowed to sharp points at the toe, and carried gloves and a leather handbag, both dazzling white. She and Alison brought a tin of American cookies, Nabisco Nilla Wafers, and stayed just long enough to drink a cup of coffee and offer some advice about household help.

After they'd gone, my mother and Mrs. Carlson discussed her outfit for a solid hour, wondering how she kept her leather handbag from getting moldy and where she stored linen clothing so the moths couldn't ruin it. Davina and I finished all the American cookies, and they never noticed.

"What's so interesting about her clothes?" Davina had grumbled. I'd told her not to complain, that fancy clothes were much better than United Nations resolutions, Russian machine guns, and whispers of Emergency Evacuation Plans, Should Things Get Any Worse.

"I won't impose," I said. "Honestly."

"All right." My mother picked up the spoon and began scooping doughnuts from the boiling fat and setting them on a drying rack. "But don't be a nuisance. I guess Alison's mother is having a hard time, and the news wasn't very good this morning."

The kitchen door banged hard against the brick wall as I dashed out, shouting "Race you!" to Alison and Davina. My mother stuck her head around the door and cried, "Grace Linnea Berggren, you come back here this instant and shut the door nicely!" but I pretended not to hear. We sprinted to the top of the hill and leaned against the wooden gate, panting.

Alison's house was the only Little America house enclosed by a concrete wall and a locked gate. Alison fiddled with the combination lock while Davina and I stared up at the broken glass glued to the top of the wall to discourage intruders. I picked out bits and pieces of Fanta and Coca-Cola bottles, Miracle Whip and Tang jars, and noted some strange ones that said "Gordons" and "Seagrams V.O."

Alison finally managed to open the gate. We skipped up the walk, disrupting the careful whorls in the freshly-swept gravel, leaped the veranda steps, and burst into the house. The living room seemed very dark and gloomy after the rain-washed brightness outside. My eyes adjusted so slowly that for several moments I didn't even notice Alison's mother. Then she stood up, and I realized she had been sitting cross-legged on the floor by the couch. Our missionary mothers would have pierced their noses before they sat on the floor wearing a dress. Suddenly wondering at the safety of taking anything for granted, I scrutinized Alison's mother's nose. From a distance I could see nothing unusual about it.

"Hello girls!" she burbled, setting one of those thick short glasses on the coffee table. Except for one or two shrunken ice cubes, the glass was empty. "What've you been up to? Must be up to something! It's yet another lovely day of blood and butchery in the Congo!"

She talked sloppily, each word collapsing into the next like a line of dominoes. In the corner the record player played a song about wanting to be somebody's little teddy bear. The singer's voice had the smoky-dark tang of a burning grapefruit tree. It seemed to me that he sang with his lips up close to a pretty lady's ear, so close his breath mussed her hair. I was sure my mother wouldn't like him.

Alison's mother's feet were bare, her toenails painted a flaming bird-of-paradise orange. She wore a white dress with four big black buttons and black piping around the neck and armholes. My mother would like that dress, I knew, even though it was wrinkled and streaked with dust. My mother would say it was "terribly, terribly elegant," a phrase usually accompanied by a long sigh as she studied a picture of Mrs. Kennedy in *Time* magazine or window-shopped at Madame Tournier's fabric store on Avenue Bolenge in Coquilhatville.

"Nothing much," Alison said. "Just a stupid game Grace and Davina made up about the Simbas."

"Oh dear," Alison's mother said, the corners of her mouth slouching downwards. "I don't like the sound of that at all. Why can't you play Cowboys and Indians?"

My chest was suddenly tight as an overblown balloon. "Because our game is fun! We've even made lion masks!"

"Oh my God!" said Alison's mother. "And twenty thousand dead in Stanleyville."

She sank back down on the couch and made a sharp hiccuping sound, her eyes wide with shock. Then she began to giggle in a silly helpless way, like my three-year-old sister when my mother tickled her stomach and pretended to bite her neck. Alison's mother didn't sound like an adult at all.

"Let's go outside," Alison said abruptly. "I'll get my jump rope. Come on."

She scurried down the hall so fast that Davina and I had to run to catch up with her. We hated to miss even the briefest glimpse of Alison's room, an Aladdin's Cave of expensive American toys. She had a quartet of Barbies with hair color ranging from blond to black, all the Cherry Ames and Nancy Drew mysteries, and her own pink plastic record player. We hoped Alison believed we were unimpressed.

"Let's jump rope on the Dawsons' veranda," Alison said. "There's lots of shade."

I would have preferred to spend the afternoon feigning boredom in Alison's room or searching our lawn for poison-tipped arrows. Just yesterday Gbadenu had told us that even Little America wasn't safe from Simba arrows, not when any ordinary Simba warrior could hit a target at ten kilometers—or maybe even twelve if he had extra-good *kisi*. What was worse, the tiniest skin-graze from one of those arrows made you foam at the mouth in less than sixty seconds. Within the hour you were dead, Gbadenu said, and the Simbas gouged your heart out and ate it raw. I thought we should organize a daily arrow hunt from now on. Small animals, even small children like Faith, might accidentally kill themselves chewing on them. If we were very, very careful to wash the poison off, maybe we could use the arrows for our own games.

"Well, do you want to jump rope or not?" Alison asked.

I wanted to borrow Alison's Nancy Drew books sometime, so I had to stay on her good side.

"Jump rope is fine," I said.

The Dawson house was invisible from the road, isolated from the other Embassy houses like a leper from his village.

It had a deep gloomy veranda shaded by overgrown orange bougainvillea and a mammoth breadfruit tree. Scarlet hibiscus bloomed in a big clay pot decorated with a pretty Congolese design of x's and o's, like a game of tic-tac-toe. I picked a single hibiscus and twirled it between my thumb and forefinger, touching my nose to the red velvet tip of the nodding stamen.

"You better be careful not to get that fuzzy yellow pollen stuff on your clothes," Alison said. "It won't come out in the wash."

I ignored her. Only Embassy Wimps were fussy about clothes.

"My mother doesn't like Mrs. Dawson," Alison remarked. "My mother says cheating at bridge is vulgar."

Davina and I communed silently:

Bridge? Did she say bridge?

Yes, she did.

What kind of bridge can you cheat at?

I don't know, but I'm not going to ask an Embassy Wimp.

"Mrs. Dawson was the first to leave," Alison went on. "She came to our house the day we heard about the white hostages and told my mother she wouldn't stay another day in this frightful country. I heard her. She said, 'Listen Elaine, I can stand being bored, but I can't stand being terrified. I've got a standby seat on the flight to Monrovia, and David and the whole State Department be damned!'"

Davina and I exchanged shocked glances at this bit of Embassy profanity, and Alison puffed out her chest importantly.

"Then she said, 'Tell David there's leftover spaghetti in the fridge,' and my mother started laughing. Mrs. Dawson looked really mad, but after a bit she laughed too. And then they both started crying, and they cried and cried until Mrs. Dawson's taxi came to take her to the airport."

I wrinkled my nose, wondering if we were stuck with weepy worried mothers for the rest of our lives.

"Mrs. Dawson was in such a hurry she didn't even pack up her things first. Come on, I'll show you!"

We followed Alison around the side of the house, squeezing through the mock orange bushes in order to reach the back window. We stood on tiptoe and pressed our foreheads against the glass. The venetian blinds were open, revealing an unmade bed in the center of the room and an overstuffed chair littered with clothing. A jumble of bottles and three months' dust veiled the soft red glow of the African rosewood dresser. I thought some of the jumble was interesting: a simple squared-off cologne bottle with a black cap, a white jar with black lettering, and a white powder box, all with large intersecting gold C's on top. I didn't think they were as pretty as Avon bottles, which decorated the dressers of most missionary ladies, but I suspected my mother would call them "terribly, terribly elegant."

"Why didn't she at least take her fancy bottles and things?" I asked.

"She told my mother she just wanted out of here with a whole skin. The bloodthirsty Congolese vandals could have anything they liked, she said, except her alligator handbag and pearl choker." Alison shrugged. "When Mr. Dawson came home and found she'd gone, he packed a bag and then left too. The next week my mother made our cook clean their fridge and throw out the spaghetti."

A flock of military planes thundered over Little America, flying low. We were silent, our faces turned to the sky, until they dwindled to mere fly-specks above the palms. They were headed north, I thought. Toward Boanda, my father, and his Rhode Island Reds.

"C-130s," I said.

"Globemasters," Davina said.

"A really nasty shade of green," Alison said. "I don't feel like playing jump rope after all, do you?"

"No."

We leaned against the sun-soaked wall, lazy and vaguely anxious, until the heat penetrated our shoulder blades unbearably, forcing us to move away.

"Vandals haven't done anything to the Dawson house yet," I remarked, leaning over to inhale the heavy sweetness of the mock orange blossoms.

"No, but Mrs. Dawson was sure they would. She said you couldn't expect much from people who were stuck in the Stone Age. She said that without us the Congolese wouldn't even have the wheel yet. And *then* she said all the wheel had done for them was improve the techno-something of their tribal warfare."

My mother liked to quote Proverbs 21:23, "He who guards his mouth and his tongue guards his soul from troubles." She would have thought Mrs. Dawson deserved a few troubles, and certainly the Bible made it clear enough. Mrs. Dawson, so weepy and gutless, might even deserve to have her house wrecked by vandals. I looked at the window and considered. Then I looked down at the orange bricks bordering the flower bed. They were arranged in an ornamental pattern that reminded me of little bones neatly lined up inside a fish. I knelt and scrabbled around in the dirt with my hands. Davina looked at me, then squatted down and did the same.

"What are you doing?" Alison asked, staring.

"These bricks are just the right size," I said.

I picked up the loosened brick and wiped off the dirt that clung to the underside. The brick was damp and wonderfully cool against my palm. I swung it in an experimental arc, relishing the dragging sensation deep in my shoulder.

The concentrated weight of the brick in my hand was balanced by a giddy, back-home-at-Boanda lightness of body and spirit.

"I'm going to be a vandal," I announced grandly.

Alison clapped a hand over her mouth, her Coca-Cola brown eyes widening as much as the blinding sun would allow.

"Wait a minute," she said. "I want a brick too."

When we uprooted a third brick from the flower border, we discovered a small snail sticking to one side of it. He had two endearingly stubby antennae, and his frail shell was delicately marbled in brown, peach, and white, like the endpapers in my father's old copy of *Pilgrim's Progress*. I picked him up carefully and deposited him in the brick-shaped hole. This done, we lined up in a tidy row facing the window and drew back our right arms.

I said, "Five . . . four . . . three . . . two . . . one!"

"Hooray for the Brick Age vandals!" Davina shrieked.

The air shattered into jagged pieces of broken sunlight as we hurled all three bricks into Mrs. Dawson's bedroom window. Glittering fragments of glass pelted down like the rainbow-colored torrents of a dry-season cloudburst. We dropped onto our haunches and rocked back and forth on our heels, screaming with laughter, dazzlement, and the mysteriously satisfying *kisi* of strong action. We pounded the garden dirt with joyful fists until we lost our balance and fell on our backs, flattening the unweeded clover as we rolled from side to side. The very earth shook under our powerful hands, it seemed, and then we realized another pack of military planes was passing overhead. This time there were twice as many, twice as deafening, and their bloated green bellies blocked the sun.

We sat up. The glass-strewn flower bed shivered into

focus, and our hilarity died. Falling shards had crushed the tender white petals of the mock orange blossoms and slit the glossy leaves. We scarcely dared lift our eyes to the naked window, where a few glass spears clung to the edge of the frame and the wooden slats of the venetian blinds trembled in an unfamiliar breeze.

"Let's go!" I cried. "Now!"

I whirled around and promptly stepped in a hole left by one of the bricks. Glancing down, I found it was the hole with the marbled snail. I had crushed his thin shell into dozens of tiny pieces no larger than coarse sand, and his soft sticky insides were leaking snail blood all over the bottom of my shoe. Shuddering, I sprinted around the side of the house and down the driveway toward the road, making for my temporary home with desperate speed. Davina and Alison, panting like the Congolese National Army in full retreat, followed hard on my mud-and-snail-encrusted heels.

Guilt crowded my veins and clogged my throat as I flung the screen door wide, then reared back, ready to flee again. Alison's father sat at the table talking, while my mother poured coffee into his cup and Davina's mother offered him the sugar bowl. His voice was abnormally loud, and he waved his hands about, energetically displacing the thick humid air.

". . . U. S. planes brought them, of course, so I'm betting the United Nations condemns both Belgium and the U.S. for unwarranted intervention. But God knows *I'm* grateful, and you can't tell me that President Kasavubu isn't as well!"

My mother beamed when she saw us, but I noticed her eyes were teary. "Oh, girls!" she cried, "Come right on in."

Davina, Alison, and I looked at each other for a moment, shrugged, and proceeded cautiously into the room. The screen door banged behind us, but for once my mother didn't seem to mind. She had taken off her apron, and her damp neck curls had dried pale and fluffy. She was wearing her favorite lipstick, Avon's Peony Pink, for the first time in several months.

"Best doughnuts I've ever had," Alison's father said.

"Have another," my mother invited. "And you girls help yourselves."

She pushed the plate across the blue-speckled tabletop. It was a pretty sight, the fancy American Formica and the white china platter piled high with perfectly fried doughnuts, but there was one glaring deficiency: the doughnuts had no frosting. My mother had sprinkled them with a mixture of cinnamon and sugar instead. Why hadn't she frosted them like she promised? Why didn't she do things *right* anymore?

"Great news, kids!" said Alison's father. "And hot, too! I heard only twenty minutes ago." He stirred his coffee, smiling so broadly that all his teeth showed, two of them brightly capped in gold. "Belgian paratroopers have landed in Stanleyville and liberated the city from the Simbas!" he announced. "Except for a bit of mopping up, it's over. The rebellion is finally over."

"Praise the Lord!" said Mrs. Carlson, removing her aqua cat's-eye glasses and wiping her eyes with an embroidered hankie.

"Hmmm, yes, well . . ." Alison's father cleared his throat and looked uncomfortable. "I just thought you two would want to know the latest right away, considering where your husbands are. And now I'd better go back home and check on Elaine. She's gone to bed. This whole thing has been very, ah, hard on her, you know. Very hard."

"We do appreciate your thoughtfulness." Excitement laced my mother's best company voice. "This is a day to remember!"

"It certainly is!" said Mrs. Carlson.

Alison's father scooted his chair back and stood up.

"Now don't miss the Voice of America broadcast," he

said. "They might have more details. And if I hear anything new, I'll send Maurice or Cecil down to tell you."

He seemed to notice Alison properly for the first time.

"Hey, Ally-girl! Come and give your old dad a hug!" he said, scooping her up in his arms and rubbing the top of her head with his chin. "What've you been up to? Must be up to something on such a lovely day!"

"Nothing much," Alison said, her voice light and chatty. "Except we noticed a couple of strange Congolese walking up the Dawson driveway. I thought maybe I should tell you."

I stared, at last impressed by this weak-kneed Embassy Wimp. Who cared if it was a lie? At least it was a bold brave one—and better than you'd expect from a girl whose mother went to bed in the middle of the afternoon.

"Sounds suspicious," Alison's father said, his eyebrows shooting together above his nose. "I'll have Cecil and Maurice check it out."

"Could they have been Simbas, do you think?" Alison asked.

Her father smiled a tolerant smile, and his eyebrows smoothed back into place. "Here? Not a chance!" he said. "Though you were right to mention the matter, Little Miss Sharp-Eyes. Thank you."

"You're welcome, Daddy."

Alison wiggled out of his arms, grabbed his wrist, and hauled him toward the door. She didn't look at Davina or me. Her father followed agreeably, then paused halfway out the door and directed an unexpectedly charming smile at my mother.

"Absolutely delicious doughnuts, Mrs. Berggren," he said, his gold caps glinting.

Cinnamon and sugar? Absolutely delicious? I decided Alison's father must be taking bad witch-doctor *kisi* that made him stupid as well as gutless, but my mother clearly didn't agree. She looked pleased, shy, not quite like my mother.

"Why, thank you!"

The door banged hard, but once again my mother said nothing about it. She just threw her arms around Mrs. Carlson and cried, "Oh, Irma, isn't it marvelous!" They clutched each other, full skirts mingling as they swayed from side to side with their hands spread flat on each other's backs. Mrs. Carlson's shoulders were shaking, and my mother began to sniff.

Davina and I looked at each other and rolled our eyes, even though I saw that her bottom lip was trembling.

Now *what's wrong with them?*

Beats me. I thought they'd finally act normal *now everything's okay.*

I'm sick of this. I want to go home. I want to see my Dad.

Watch it! You're brave and powerful, remember?

We turned away from the spectacle of our unreliable mothers sobbing and hugging. Davina took a deep breath and said, "You're crumbling that doughnut to bits. Give it here. I'll finish it."

I handed over the doughnut and peered out the kitchen window. Alison and her father were taking their time about going home. They were only halfway up the hill, and now she was stopping to fish something out of her shoe. She stood on one leg, her left hand clutching her father's bullet-proof vest for support. For a moment I thought he was silly to keep that vest on when the rebellion was over, but then I changed my mind, remembering what Gbadenu told me when we first came to Little America. "A Simba practices his warrior skills and sleeps with his weapons even in peace-time," he'd said. "That's how a Simba preserves his courage and *makasi*, strength, in times of fear and war."

Alison finished fiddling with her shoe, and the two of

them started walking slowly uphill again. I stared at Alison's skinny white arms and ruffled pink blouse, wondering if she had anything to preserve her courage, her *makasi*. I snatched my lion mask off the counter and charged out the door.

"Alison! Alison, wait! This is for you."

Old Stories, Old Songs

Mama Malia leaned back in her chair and surveyed the items assembled on the rough cookhouse table: the Revereware kettle, the Tupperware measuring cups, the tin sugar canister, the wide enamel basin half filled with fruit, the dozen sterilized one-pint Mason jars with two-piece metal lids.

"*Nakamwi!*" she exclaimed. "There's no room left for the three of us to work! White-people food takes too much space and far too many containers."

I just shrugged and pitted another thumbnail-sized Madagascar plum, but Makua threw down his paring knife.

"I didn't ask you to help," he told her in an offended voice.

Mama Malia patted his hand and laughed, all her chins rippling like river waves on a stormy day. "*Likambo te,*" she said. "No problem. I want to help. I have nothing else to do. Madame Berggren has taken Faith to the French doctor in Coquilhatville. When such a very good child is bad-tempered, she is usually sick. Another earache, I think."

"*Ejali boye,*" I agreed. "My mother says the rebellion was bad for her ears. All the airplane noise, maybe."

Makua told Mama Malia she could stay in his cookhouse and help with his jam, but only so long as she kept her mouth shut. Mama Malia grinned at him across the crowded worktable, and Makua picked up his knife and went back to pitting fruit.

"I know a very old story about Madagascar plums," he said. "Also about a little girl. The parents of this little girl gave her a basket and sent her far, far away from her village to a strange and dangerous jungle well known for beautiful Madagascar plum trees and hostile spirits. Since the little girl had plenty of *mayele*, intelligence, she could feel those hostile spirits surrounding her, pressing closer and closer with each plum she picked. The little girl wanted to drop her basket and run away, but she kept on picking. She knew how highly her distant parents valued those plums. And because she was deeply sad and afraid, because the sound of the wind in the trees made her fingers tremble, the little girl sang a song as she worked."

"Do you remember the song?" I asked.

Makua closed his eyes and began to sing, his hands reaching up to pluck invisible plums from the warm cookhouse air:

> "If only my mother
> If only my father
> Had taken care of me
> I should have been with them now
> And not here all alone
> Oh, I shall surely die!
> Oh, I shall surely die!"

Makua's voice was sorrowful and grieving, a gentle wail that made my bones go limp with a terrible sadness. When he finished, Mama Malia said "Eee,eee,eee," and wiped her eyes with the sleeve of her blouse.

"Do you want to know the rest of the story?" Makua asked.

I thought I already knew the ending, and it wasn't a happy one. I started to say a reluctant yes, but Mama Malia rescued me.

"One small mistake," she said, leaning forward and planting her heavy elbows on the table. "That fruit, it wasn't Madagascar plums."

"Do you think I don't know this story?" he asked. "Of course it was."

"No, it wasn't plums," she said firmly. "It was something else. Red finger bananas, I think. Or maybe those soft spiky rambutans."

As I listened, I popped one tiny red plum in my mouth, and the tartness of it withered my tongue.

"It doesn't matter," Makua said. "The story is the same."

"Everybody into the pickup! Junie, where *are* you?" My father's normally soft voice was a hearty bellow. "Ready or not, we're leaving for the airport in two minutes!"

I hugged Kitoko one last time, listening to her quick breathing, burying my nose in her silky spaniel ears. The wet scrape of her tongue on my neck made me shiver, and I squeezed her until she moaned. Kitoko was my Christmas present from Alain, who'd returned from France to find his golden cocker, Musetta, with a litter of eight tiny puppies. ("Musetta must have seduced Dr. Birgie's spaniel as soon as the *doctoresse* left for Lambarene," Alain said, and Mrs. Frykman got mysteriously annoyed and told my mother he just *would* have to put it that way.) I adored Kitoko, who was every bit as beautiful as her mother, but I'd had her only a few weeks. What if she didn't remember me when I came home for Easter vacation?

"Wonder which you'll get, Grace, a DC-3 or a DC-4? A DC-4 would be nice. It's bigger, and you'd have a smoother flight. Not that it's very far—six hundred kilometers at most—but a smooth flight would still be nice, don't you think?" My father always said idle chatter was for silly people with too much time on their hands, but today he sounded a bit silly himself. Almost as silly as he sounded last month when the rebellion was finally over and he picked us up at the Coquilhatville airport. That day he'd chattered nonstop while trying to hold my mother's hand and shift gears at the same time.

"Sure," I said. "A smooth flight would be nice."

I climbed onto the tailgate and watched him stow my metal trunk where it couldn't bounce out if we hit a bad pothole. I had chosen that trunk at the Coquilhatville market last week. It was bright green, with a picture of a toothy leopard painted on it. My friend Davina, who was a year too young for boarding school, had decorated the trunk lid with so many Air Congo stickers that there was hardly any space left for addresses. Now I worried they weren't written large enough. Addresses were important. They told you where you belonged and where you were going. The address of my boarding school, in the Ubangi district, looked strange and far away, so I studied my home address in the upper left corner instead.

> Grace Linnea Berggren
> c/o Robert and June Berggren
> Boanda Mission
> Coquilhatville
> Democratic Republic of the Congo

My father said the democratic part was wishful thinking that got even more wishful all the time, but I thought it sounded pretty.

My mother rushed out the front door, her Congolese raffia purse in one hand, a typewritten list in the other. Usually my mother wore her favorite Peony Pink lipstick when she went to the airport, but today she had forgotten. She was mumbling through tight pale lips, "Toothbrush, check. Toothpaste, check. Sunday sandals, check. White shoe polish, check. Church offering money, check."

"Hurry *up*, Junie!" my father said. "And where's Faith?"

"Mama Malia's bringing her," my mother replied. "Grace, I don't think you should ride in the back today. Your dress will stay cleaner in the cab."

I nodded. Mama Malia appeared in her special-occasion orange-flowered *liputa* and matching turban. Faith, pulling on her still-sore ear, rode on Mama Malia's hip wearing a fearful scowl. Makua hurried out the front door behind them, drying his hands on his white cook's apron. Mama Malia put Faith down and hugged me, and then Makua took both my hands in his long bony ones. *"Kenda malamu,* go well," he said solemnly. "I come from the Ubangi, you remember. It is a good place."

"A good place?" Mama Malia shrieked. "You're *kilikili!* It's filled with inferior people and uncivilized tribes."

Makua laughed and told Mama Malia he'd never met any inferior people until he met her, and she punched his arm with her fist.

"Tikela malamu," I said. "Stay well."

We all piled in, my mother making room for Faith on her lap, and then we were off, the blue Ford jouncing past the royal palms that lined the river road from Boanda all the way to the outskirts of Coquilhatville. The palms were shot through with the dusty sunlight of January and the dry season, and Mrs. Carlson's white bougainvillea had yellowed from lack of rain. I meant to watch the river out my window, but the Ford kicked up such a gritty cloud that my eyes burned and I couldn't see a thing.

I stuck out my tongue as we drove by the Ecole Belgique de Coquilhatville, where I'd spent first grade. It wasn't supposed to be a Catholic school, just Belgian, but I'd soon discovered all the teachers were nuns, every single one. I'd told my parents and they'd exchanged worried frowns, headed off to my father's office, and stayed there for a long time. When they finally came out they said I should tell them pronto if I ever had to pray to the Virgin Mary, because the Evangelical Swedish-American Mission ran a good boarding school upcountry. "The nuns don't do anything terribly Catholic," I'd said, and my parents looked so relieved that I didn't tell them how much I disliked the nuns for other reasons. If you gave the wrong answer in geography class, Soeur Albertine threw an eraser at you. If you couldn't take dictation fast enough, Soeur Céleste rapped your knuckles with a wooden pointer. If you splattered ink from your fountain pen, Soeur Godwine raised one black eyebrow and made remarks about clumsy unaccomplished American children. Soeur Godwine was my least favorite nun. She had lots of ugly pictures of Jesus with a big open heart dripping blood.

It was Soeur Godwine's fault that I was going off to boarding school now, because she was the one who gave us all those tuberculosis inoculations. She'd claimed the more we had the healthier we would be, so I'd had five in the first grade. With the last one, my left arm had turned into a messy pus-filled volcano that erupted for three months. My mother had said this was absolutely the last straw and no more Catholic education for the Berggren family, but I was proud of my infected arm because Davina was so impressed. Davina had imagined I would develop a red streak running from my arm to my heart. When it reached my heart I would drop dead, just like Ingabritt Almquist, an old Boanda missionary lady who hadn't believed penicillin was Christian. I'd pictured Soeur Godwine at my funeral, weeping guilty tears over the stupid, dead American girl.

At the Coquilhatville airport, my father gave my trunk to an Air Congo official in dark glasses and a green uniform, and my mother gave me a key.

"This is for the Yale lock, Grace," she said brightly. "Keep it safe in your pocket, or you'll be in real trouble when you want to unpack."

I put the key inside my red plastic "First Federal Bank of Des Moines" coin purse. That was the city in America where my parents kept their money. I liked having that address too.

My mother reached in her purse and pulled out a book. "I mail-ordered this from the English bookstore in Léopoldville," she said, putting the book in my hand. "It's a collection of fairy tales. I know how you like them. You can read it on the plane."

My father was peering out the tinted-glass window. "Wouldn't you know it—a DC-3!" he said disgustedly. "I bet those things were obsolete before the Second World War. Trust Air Congo to keep on flying them."

I thought DC-3s were cute. They rested on their low back wheel like a hopeful dog sitting on his haunches waiting for a treat. I said so, and my father laughed.

"They're reliable as well, which is something these days," he told me. "Anyway, maybe you'll get a DC-4 when you come home for Easter."

The Air Congo official in dark glasses came over to say the plane was now boarding.

"Good-bye, honey." My mother's voice was suddenly thin. Her chin wobbled and the dimple in her left cheek disappeared. "We'll write you every week, I promise."

We hugged and kissed, and I squealed because my father's whiskers scratched my face. My little sister wouldn't kiss me, but my mother said not to mind it. ("Faith will be her own sweet self when this rotten ear infection is over.") I walked out on the tarmac while my parents waved and smiled from inside the terminal. Faith mashed her lips and nose flat against the glass, making horrible pig faces that I pretended not to see. Two uniformed men wheeled a movable staircase up to the passenger door of the DC-3, and I walked carefully to the top, hoping I wouldn't trip on the heat-sticky rubber-coated steps. I waved from the doorway of the plane, feeling important like President Johnson on the cover of *Newsweek*.

The pilot, a Belgian man with stout legs and a big stomach, stood beside the curtained-off cockpit, drinking coffee and talking to the Congolese steward. Both men said, *"B'jour,* Mademoiselle," and the pilot asked if I was going upcountry to the Swedish-American Mission boarding school. I said yes, and he said *magnifique.* Then he told me about his two little boys at boarding school in Antwerp. He said I would love school just as much as they did. The steward looked at me with sad, kind eyes and said *"Pauvre petite,"* and the pilot kicked him in the shin.

"My boys like window seats when they fly," the pilot said. "Come with me."

He found me a window seat in the third row, but I didn't thank him like I should have, or take proper advantage of my tiny oval view of Coquilhatville's royal palms and brick cathedral. I was too busy staring at the beautiful Belgian lady beside me. The lady had a face just like Jeanne d'Arc in Soeur Céleste's pamphlet about famous women martyrs.

She had a thin straight nose and short black hair, and she wore a sleeveless black linen two-piece dress with square white buttons. Although her belly ballooned hugely in the front, she was much more elegant than the missionary ladies I was used to, more elegant even than Alain's French girlfriend or the American Embassy ladies in Léopoldville. She smiled at me, her teeth white, her dark eyes warm, her lips red as a jungle orchid's heart. My breath stuck in my throat. I forgot to wave out my window, and I never even noticed the take-off.

The Congolese steward brought me a glass of Coca-Cola and called me *"la petite."* That was nice but not the same as being called *"Madame"* in the anxiously polite voice he used when he spoke to the Belgian lady. He served us hard rolls, Gruyère, and my favorite biscuits, Petit Beurre. I wished I had asked for coffee instead of Coca-Cola, because he brought the Belgian lady several sugar lumps in pale blue packets that she got to unwrap and drop into her cup with a delicious little plop. I sipped my Coca-Cola carefully since I was wearing my second-best dress and we were hitting so many air pockets. Being jostled up and down made it hard to act as ladylike and mannerly as I wished in front of the beautiful Madame.

The Belgian lady didn't seem interested in talking, so I decided I might as well look out my window. At first I was blinded by the glare on the silver wing, but then my eyes adjusted and I wished I had looked out sooner. The Congo River lay far below, a broad curving band the color of strong milky coffee. A tiny dark reflection of the DC-3 skimmed across the water's surface like a plane-shaped speedboat. Islands large and small dotted the river, and the rough green velvet of solid jungle flanked it on both sides. Except for a few white sand bars, deep jungle green and river brown stretched to the distant blurry edge of the sky. I thought of the river and jungle as quarreling giants, each competing for the same territory, each struggling to be most important. "The strength of the river is something even tourists can appreciate," I'd heard my father say. "But many people don't have a clue about heavy jungle. Your average Westerner wouldn't survive four hours of it. I doubt even I could make it overnight."

I stared out the window, my hands cold and sweaty. There were millions of trees down there, a thousand different varieties, and all with one thing in common: they wanted to kill my father. Would he be dead before I got home for Easter vacation? I fixed on the river, blocking out the jungle as hard as I could. Out in the main channel, a steamboat battled the current, pushing six huge barges oh-so-slowly upriver and leaving behind a trail of churning brown water. The steamboat was flying the Otraco Shipping Company flag. It had probably just left Coquilhatville too.

"And where are you going all by yourself, little one?"

I was relieved the beautiful Belgian lady had decided to talk, further relieved that her French was less rapid than the Coquilhatville Catholic sisters. Her name was Madame Van de Steen, she said, and she was married to an administrator of a rubber plantation near Coquilhatville. It turned out we were both going to the same Protestant mission eighty kilometers north of Gemena, I to the boarding school and she to the mission hospital.

"I should have flown home to Bruges before it was too late," she said. "Now the Evangelical Swedish-American Mission Hospital is my only option. It's truly insane to have a baby in this country, but at least they have an American obstetrician."

I wondered why it was insane to have a baby in the Congo. My sister and I were born here, and so was my friend Davina. Almost every Congolese woman carried a baby on her back or her hip. Yet Madame Van de Steen's dark eyes were fearful, and there was something automatic about her smile, as if smiling was just a habit like nail-biting. Her narrow white hand trembled as she touched her swollen belly.

"Move." Her voice was a sudden urgent whisper. "Please move." She sat very still, waiting for the thing inside her to respond. A pulse beat quick and hard at the base of her throat. After a moment she took a deep breath and looked straight at me.

"So you're going to boarding school," she said. "I did too. A French convent school. I won't lie to you like other grown-ups. Boarding school is dreadful."

For weeks everyone had been telling me how I would love boarding school, how I would love it so much I wouldn't even want to go home. I was almost grateful to her. "It is?"

"Yes. Absolutely. I hated it," Madame Van de Steen said flatly. "I hated the nuns who taught there too. They were very strict, very unkind. Soeur Polycarp used to beat our hands with her ruler."

"That's what Soeur Céleste did at the Ecole Belgique," I said. "Except she used a mahogany pointer. It hurt."

"I would suppose so," Madame Van de Steen replied. She set her coffee cup down so hard that the saucer rattled. "She probably came to Africa just so she could hit children with mahogany pointers."

I thought all missionaries came to Africa because they were Called By God, even the Catholic ones. I was shocked but I couldn't help snickering, and Madame Van de Steen smiled. This time her smile didn't look like a habit.

"I remember I missed my parents terribly," she went on. "And my friends. And Bruges. And speaking Flemish. And my dog."

I was so eager to tell her about Kitoko that I nearly

choked on my Coca-Cola. "I have a dog!" I said. "A golden cocker spaniel."

"Oh yes? Cocker spaniels are lovely dogs," she said. "Especially the golden ones. How old is yours?"

"She's just a puppy," I said. "I got her for Christmas. Do you think she'll remember me when I come home for Easter? I'm afraid she won't. It's a long time, three months."

"She'll remember," Madame Van de Steen promised firmly. "Any dog's memory is at least as good as a human's. And cocker spaniels are unusually smart dogs, you know. What is her name?"

"Kitoko," I said proudly. "I named her myself."

"Kitoko?" She looked surprised, her smooth white forehead crinkling, her black eyebrows shooting upward almost like Soeur Godwine's. "Isn't that some kind of Lingala word?"

"Yes," I answered, amazed she didn't know. "It means 'beautiful.'"

"You gave your dog a Lingala name?"

"Yes," I said again.

"I don't allow my cook or my laundry boy to speak Lingala. They have to practice their French. I try to correct their disgusting African accents—that 'petit-nègre,' you know—but it's very difficult."

I wondered if she thought my French was "petit-nègre" too. It didn't seem likely, since Soeur Godwine said my French was American, deplorably American.

"Madame, would you like more coffee?"

The steward had returned. Madame Van de Steen nodded, and he refilled her cup. I finished my last Petit Beurre, idly watching as he poured milk into her coffee. Suddenly I felt myself lighten and plunge downward. I clutched the armrests with both hands and pressed my head back. It's only an air pocket, I thought. I waited for the plane to find the bottom, but it kept falling. What if this air pocket didn't have a bottom? What if this air pocket dropped us all the way to the ground? Would it be worse to crash into the river or the jungle? Not the jungle, please, I prayed. Not all those millions of trees. Besides, I knew how to swim—or did I? What would my arms and legs remember when tons of rushing brown water closed over my head? I swallowed a mouthful of air mixed with panic, wondering how much river I would have to swallow before I drowned. Behind me someone started praying loudly in French. Someone else began to sob. Then the falling stopped, and the plane lurched forward once more. I grabbed my teetering glass of Coca-Cola and let out my breath just as Madame Van de Steen shrieked horribly, like a tree hyrax in the dead of night.

I turned to see her frantically sponging milk from her black skirt with a large cloth napkin. She glared at the steward. He looked embarrassed and horrified, staring at the silver milk pitcher as if he had never seen it before. He began to stutter apologies, but she interrupted him, speaking clearly into a perfect silence. Speaking Lingala instead of French.

"You stupid monkey!" she said.

I heard the harsh sound of indrawn breaths all around us, and the air thickened up like a pudding made with too much cornstarch. Only the hum of the plane engines went on as before. My neck and chest turned stiff and cold while my head swelled to bursting with a feverish prickling heat. Didn't Madame Van de Steen know what she had said?

My eyes burned as I stared at the glass in my hand. I didn't dare look at the steward. I didn't even dare blink, in case it drew attention to me. What if he and all the other Congolese passengers thought Madame Van de Steen and I were together? Yet as the terrible moment stretched on, I knew I had to look. I had to see how her words had marked him. I raised my eyes from my glass, peering up from beneath my bangs.

The cords of his neck stood out in polished black columns above his starched Nehru collar. His heavy shoulders pushed against the fabric of his white uniform, and the Air Congo insignia pin on his chest gleamed silvery and knifelike in the midday brightness. Though his face had a blank empty look, I could see him soaking up the insult like dry ground in a hard rain. He bent his torso in a brief bow. "Yes, Madame," the steward said, then turned away, but not before I saw the rage and loathing in his eyes.

"That's all the Lingala I know," Madame Van de Steen said, rubbing anxiously at the milky spot just above her bulging waistline. "But it's useful. You have to keep these people in their place. A generation ago they were swinging in the trees."

"Yes, Madame."

I stared out my window, dismayed to see no river, just the glossy green of uninterrupted jungle. I should have thought to watch the river until it was out of sight. I had lived in view of it for as long as I could remember—except this fall, during the Simba Rebellion.

"They don't understand an insult, you know," said Madame Van de Steen haughtily as she adjusted her seat belt. That done, she smiled at me, beautifully kind and warm. "Now then, little one!"

I huddled close to the window and hoped my skirt wasn't touching hers under the center armrest. She said nothing more, her hand once again stroking her belly.

Just as I was wondering what to do with myself for the rest of the trip, I remembered my mother's fairy-tale book and started reading the first story. It was about a lovely girl so good and kind that diamonds and rubies dripped from her lips when she talked. She had an older sister who was mean and nasty. When the older girl talked, snakes, toads, and spiders fell out of her mouth, and everyone scattered in all directions. A handsome prince had just asked the younger sister to marry him when the pilot announced we would be landing shortly and must refasten our seat belts.

The landing field at Gemena was red gravel, much bumpier than Coquilhatville's black tarmac. The airport terminal was small, boxy, and yellow as a ripe banana skin. We had a tall green-glassed control tower back home, and smooth-barked royal palms instead of this shabby avenue of everyday palms. At least the mango trees looked normal. A fat American missionary with big teeth and a freckled, hairless scalp was waiting to collect me and drive me to the school. He put my trunk in the back of his Chevy pickup.

"This little beauty is fresh off a boat from the good old U.S. of A.," he said. "The springs still work, even!"

As we drove off, I saw Madame Van de Steen awkwardly heaving herself into a Land Rover driven by a Congolese chauffeur. She waved when she saw me, but I thought of her toad-and-snake words and didn't wave back. We left them behind in a huge swirling cloud of red dust.

"Well, this is it—the Evangelical Swedish-American Mission School! You'll love it here. All the kids do." The fat hairless man chuckled. "They complain when they have to go home for vacation!"

He pulled into a fenced compound and parked the truck on a gravel drive facing a whitewashed brick dormitory. The dormitory was long and low, with a deep veranda and red bougainvillea blossoming against one wall. Off to the right, a spindly acacia grove shaded a classroom building. In the distance I could see pale gray-green hills covered with savanna grass instead of jungle.

"But where's the river?" I asked. "The Ubangi River?"

Last night (was it only last night?) my father had pointed it out on the old Belgian Congo map tacked to his office wall. "It's that skinny black line right there," he had said. "That one branching straight north off the Congo River, do you see? It forms a natural border with French Congo." My father wasn't sure where the Ubangi River was in relation to my new school, but he thought it was within walking distance, adding, "It's smaller than you're used to—just a Congo tributary, really. But it's still deep enough for big steamboats, and I'm told it hasn't got nearly so many dratted water hyacinths."

"About ninety-five kilometers west," said the fat hairless man. "The passenger door sticks a bit, so I'll come around and let you out."

Ninety-five kilometers! I sat perfectly still on the black vinyl seat, ignoring the open door and the fat hairless man's impatience until he said, "Come along now, we haven't got all day!"

I slid off the seat and followed him very slowly across the crunchy gravel to the dormitory steps, where a thin busy lady met us and said we'd made good time. She told me she was Mrs. Lindstrom, my dorm mother, and then whisked me inside and gave me a tour, apologizing for the gloom and the musty smell.

"We had to close up this fall during the Simba Rebellion when everyone evacuated. Everything is such a mess—half the windows still boarded over, and army ants and termites everywhere—but we've got to open before you children miss any more school. Most families aren't back yet, so we have lots of extra space. You get to have a room all to yourself, Grace. Aren't you lucky?" she asked brightly.

I said yes, but I wasn't sure. At home I shared a bed with my little sister. I'd grown used to her mumbles and sighs and her hot squirming body.

I followed Mrs. Lindstrom down a long dim hall with high ceilings, listening to the echoing slap of my sandals on the concrete floor. She opened the door to the last room on the left.

"I see Natana has already brought your trunk in, so I'll leave you to unpack. Supper is at five-thirty sharp," she added, already halfway down the hall.

The room was narrow, with high white walls and one screened window. The olive-green bedspread matched the curtains. There was a dresser and a closet, both dark Congolese mahogany. Although the room faced west, no late afternoon sun filtered in. The light was blocked by a tree planted too close to the window, a Madagascar plum tree, and I thought about Makua: "I know a very old story about Madagascar plums."

"I'm Carrie Morris. Who are you?"

A girl with a wispy brown pageboy and pale gold freckles stood in the doorway. She looked like somebody had thrown her together out of Tinkertoys, all skinny arms and legs with big connecting joints. She ambled into my room, plopped down on the bare concrete floor, and leaned back against the dresser. Sticking out one leg for my inspection, she announced she had freckles on her knees and guessed I had none. I said I was Grace Berggren, unfreckled but scarred from a three-month infection. Carrie grudgingly admired my arm, then asked where I came from.

"Boanda Mission," I said proudly. "It's right on the equator, and it's famous. Henry Stanley founded it. And we're only seven kilometers from Coquilhatville."

"Oh, you poor thing. You're from downcountry!" Carrie shook her head. "I'm so sorry for you."

"Well I'm sorry for you!" I returned. "My sister's nanny says this district is full of inferior people, and my father says it has inferior rivers."

"The Ubangi River is terrific," Carrie said. "And it's only ninety-five kilometers away."

I fished around in my pocket for my First Federal Bank of Des Moines coinpurse. "I live right on the edge of the Congo River, and I swim in it every day," I said.

"Well, I live right on the edge of the Ubangi River, and it's bigger." Carrie got up to snoop in my closet. "You haven't started unpacking yet? Mrs. Lindstrom is going to be mad."

"It is not bigger!" I flared. "My father showed me the Ubangi River on the map last night. He said it was just a lousy tributary of the Congo, not a real river all by itself. But it's not even here, so who cares how big it is!"

"How nice, you girls are getting acquainted," said Mrs. Lindstrom, poking her head in the door. "Don't you think you'd better start unpacking, Grace? Supper is in thirty-five minutes."

I found the Yale key, unlocked my trunk, and emptied it in several big armloads. I separated my belongings into a dozen little piles and scattered them all over the floor, the trunk lid, the dresser top. That done, I snatched my stuffed dog from one of the piles and sat down cross-legged on the bed. The mattress was hard, much harder than my mattress at home.

"I'm finished," I said.

"What!" Carrie looked shocked. "You're supposed to put all your things in your dresser or closet. And everything better be tidy too, or you'll flunk room inspection. Me, I know. I'm in the third grade."

I wrapped my arms around my plush dog and hugged it tight.

"I won't know it's my room if I can't see my things. I can't put them away."

"Of course you'll know it's your room! Just remember it's the last one on the left side."

"I'd rather see than remember."

Carrie said it was easy to tell I didn't come from the Ubangi district. I said good. She said I was a weird down-country dodo bird. I said good. Then she took me to the back yard and showed me the girls' outhouse, a skinny building made of dull pink corrugated roofing with an un-painted wooden door and a tin roof. Shiny green clumps of bird-of-paradise with bright orange crests hid it from view.

"Here's how you find an outhouse in the Ubangi. You look for extra-tall bird-of-paradise bushes. My mother says the you-know-what makes them grow like crazy."

Carrie took a Bic pen from the pocket of her shorts, and we wrote our initials on the door. She pointed out a tiny round hole halfway up the back wall. If you squinted you could see who was inside, Carrie said, adding that she would tell me if she remembered other important things I ought to know. I was grateful. We returned to the girls' wing of the dormitory by way of the squeaky-hinged back door. I stopped to admire a fantastically long centipede on the screen, but up close it wasn't a centipede after all, just a tear badly mended with heavy black thread. We walked down to my door, the last one on the left side.

"I'm going to finish fixing up my room," Carrie an-nounced. "And if I were you, I'd get started on yours. You have to live in it until June, you know."

"I hate this place. I think it's horrible. And I'll always want to go home no matter what any stupid people say!"

The words sprang from my mouth like ugly toads and snakes from a nasty fairy-tale older sister. I wasn't surprised. I realized that I must be a dreadfully toad-and-snake kind of person. Otherwise I wouldn't deserve to live away from my family in this riverless place. I wouldn't deserve a bedspread the color of leaves at the end of a long hot dry season.

A heavy clanging sound made me jump, but Carrie looked relieved. She said oh-good-that's-the-supper-bell and dragged me down to the dining room. Afterwards we showered in slimy gray cubicles. I shut my eyes and pretended I was at Boanda, bathing in the river at sunset and watching the water flow fiery orange across my arms and shoulders. Then another bell rang. Carrie said this one was for evening devotions, and we'd have to hurry.

"I don't," I said, wrapping my wet bath towel around me sarong-style, like a Congolese *liputa*. "I'm not going."

"You'll get in trouble."

"I'm going to put my things away instead."

Carrie agreed I was in trouble for one or the other, so she dashed off to devotions and left me alone. I sat on the olive bedspread and studied the clothes-strewn room. There was my red-flowered dress with white rickrack trim. Faith had one exactly like it. My mother had made them last spring. On top of the trunk lay "Josephina's Coat of Many Colors," my mother's special name for the multistriped dress my grandparents in America sent me for my seventh birthday. I hung both dresses in the closet but left the door open.

Picture hanging was next, and I had two: a print of The Good Shepherd and His Flock and a tiny plastic-framed snapshot of Faith under the rose-apple tree with Mama Malia and Kitoko, taken the day after Christmas. Mama Malia was trying out a spiky Congolese hairdo on Faith's wispy blond curls, and Kitoko was sleeping in the grass, her little pink tongue hanging out. I wished I had a picture of my mother and father. What if I forgot how they looked before Easter? What if I forgot how they looked by next week?

I panicked suddenly, wondering if I had already forgotten, and squeezed my eyes shut. The blood surged against my skin as I struggled to put my mother's image before my closed lids. I had seen my mother every day for seven years, and I knew she had long legs, a blond widow's peak, and a hesitant smile. I knew she smelled of Avon's White Lilac cologne and strong Swedish coffee, and had a way of laughing softly behind her hand like a Congolese. Yet somehow I couldn't picture her in any complete and immediate way. My memory produced only a fractured, black-and-white translation, the formal family photograph that the Mission Board distributed to American churches for their Sunday School bulletin boards. Just above our heads it said "Pray for the Berggrens in the Congo" in black letters. In that picture my mother was smiling stiffly because she had on those Congolese malachite clip-on earrings that pinched her ears, and she couldn't wait to take them off. ("Serves me right for being so vain and unchristian," she sighed later, unhappy with the proofs.) My father looked stern in his dark suit, as if braced for one of his weekly debates with Mr. Frykman about Agricultural Missionaries Who Mess With Soybeans versus Real Missionaries Who Save Souls. Faith and I wore our matching red dresses, but she looked much nicer in hers than I did. My pageboy was perfectly straight, even after a night in pink sponge rollers and bobby pins, and I'd forgotten to smile. Faith had curls and dimples, and smiled without being reminded. Faith was the right kind of sister, the fairy-tale younger kind, beautiful and lovable and good. People laughed and hugged her when she talked. They saw jewels in her mouth, not nasty reptiles. Faith was only three and too young for boarding school, but she probably deserved to stay at home forever, Mama Malia fixing her hair and Makua telling her stories and singing old songs:

If only my mother,
If only my father,
Had taken care of me . . .

"Grace, you need help with your unpacking if you find you have to skip devotions to do it."

I hadn't seen Mrs. Lindstrom come in, but there she was, arms folded, staring at me. She picked up a stack of my underwear and plopped it briskly in the top dresser drawer.

"No!" I leaped off the bed, clutching my wet towel *liputa*. "Let me do it, please!"

"You've had several chances, and that's enough. I'll do it." Her blue plaid skirt swished as she hurried from trunk to bed to dresser, handling my clothes with efficient bony hands. "I think you need a few things explained to you, Grace. Otherwise I can see you're going to be an attitude problem, and the Evangelical Swedish-American Mission school does not need attitude problems."

Swish, plop, slam. Swish, plop, slam.

"Your parents are missionaries because that is what Jesus wants them to do. You are at a boarding school for missionary children because that is what Jesus wants you to do."

Mrs. Lindstrom shoved my empty Air-Congo-stickered trunk under the bed. She shut my closet door firmly, turned, and gave me a quick bright smile.

"Now do you understand?"

I thought I did. I also thought Jesus got His own way even more than my sister Faith. But at least it wasn't my parents' fault I was stuck here all alone. It was His fault—and Soeur Godwine's, for all those tuberculosis inoculations. When I got home for Easter, I would ask Mama Malia to buy a curse from the witch doctor, a curse powerful enough to kill Soeur Godwine instantly. I would save my spending money for the next three months, every single franc. Maybe I would save my church offering money as well.

"I understand," I said. "Is it all right if I go to bed early?"

"Of course. I'll tuck you in," she said. "Have you brushed your teeth?"

"Yes," I lied, stripping off my towel and yanking my nightgown over my head. Mrs. Lindstrom stood by the bed as I crawled between the sheets. When she leaned over, I realized she intended to kiss me good night. Tiny dark hairs sprouted like weeds from her chin. She smelled of Omo detergent and tonight's vegetable soup, not White Lilac cologne. There was a coldness in her smile, and I shrank at the twisted pale reflections of myself in her glasses.

"I don't kiss people good night," I said. "But I'll shake hands if you want."

Mrs. Lindstrom stared at my outstretched hand. Then she laughed, ignored my hand, and kissed me quickly, dryly, on the cheek. She turned out the light and left, shutting the door behind her. The room seemed less bare in the dark, I thought, but no less strange. I decided to try singing my night prayers like I did at home. I pulled the sheet up to my chin and sang quietly into the blackness:

> "Jesus, Tender Shepherd hear me,
> Bless thy little lamb tonight.
> Through the darkness be Thou near me,
> Keep me safe 'til morning light."

The door opened a crack, then wider. Carrie's brown head glinted in the light of the hallway. I sat up.

"Were you singing, Grace?"

"No."

Kitoko slept by my feet at home. She always barked to let me know someone was coming.

"Do you want to hear a terrible story? A really, really terrible story?"

"Yes."

Kitoko would sleep on Faith's side of the bed from now on. She liked warm places, and Faith was warm all over, even her feet.

"The night sentry from the hospital just came by and told this to our night sentry, Kamu. A pregnant Belgian lady from Coquilhatville flew up here today because her baby wasn't moving. Dr. Berg decided to cut the lady open and take the baby out, and when he did, the baby was dead. Stone dead. And the lady is awfully sick. Tomorrow she might be dead too." Carrie paused, then added, "Did you know you can get from the door of this room all the way over to the windowsill without ever touching the floor? You jump from the dresser to the bed to—oops! That bell means 'Lights out.' I'll show you tomorrow."

She dashed out. I lay down again, remembering Madame Van de Steen's Jeanne-d'Arc face, her thin straight nose and lovely white smile, the worry in her dark eyes. How strange that I could picture every tiny detail of Madame Van de Steen's outfit, even her square white buttons and black stiletto heels, yet couldn't remember my mother's face. I recalled the steward perfectly too, his white Nehru collar and anxious-to-please manner, his blank expression as those dreadful words fell from the Madame's beautiful red lips. I wasn't surprised about Madame Van de Steen's baby. Toad-and-snake people got what they deserved. But I remembered her wave at the Gemena airport and wished I had waved back.

> "Jesus, Tender Shepherd hear me,
> Bless thy little lamb tonight."

This was the wrong song for an older sister to sing. I wasn't a little lamb, and I wasn't getting a blessing.

"Through the darkness be Thou near me
Keep me safe—"

A squeezing pain stopped up my throat and left me voiceless. I scrambled out of bed, fumbling in the unfamiliar darkness until I found the picture. I turned the Good Shepherd and His Flock to the wall and crawled back under the clammy top sheet. I lay still, my eyes wide, listening to the dry scrape of the plum tree's branches against the window screen. The threatening hiss and cackle in the murky leaves made my fingers stiffen and curl. Hostile spirits, I was certain. Spirits unseen but watchful, dangerous and impatient, ready to rise up from the shadows and crush the life out of me.

Oh, I shall surely die!
Oh, I shall surely die!

Foolish Virgins

M Y FATHER had heard you couldn't get any fertilizer or chicken feed in the Ubangi, so he called it "the back of beyond." The Frykmans' cook, who came from Léopoldville and once worked for the French ambassador, called it "the *sauvage* north country." The Belgians called it *"le coin perdu,"* the forgotten corner. And I called it "the riverless roadless boondocks."

Of course I knew that was unfair. The Ubangi did have roads. The map in our science classroom showed a fine brown network linking lots of remote places—Bozene and Banzyville, Zongo and Wasolo—but most of these roads were in such terrible condition that people rarely used them. And after Boanda's constant road and river traffic, I was disheartened by the day-in-day-out sameness and isolation of the Evangelical Swedish-American Mission. "There's never anyone new here," I'd complain to Carrie. "Same teachers and dorm parents. Same hospital staff and Congolese cooks. Nobody wants to visit the Ubangi!"

Some afternoons I'd sit in the frangipani tree by the boarding school veranda and watch the road slip unevenly down into the gray-green savanna. I'd watch and wait, hoping for exotic strangers but willing to settle for less—even someone I knew and wasn't fond of, like Mrs. Frykman. When it got dark, I'd go inside for supper, my appetite ruined by disappointment and my temper tried by Carrie's mocking laughter.

In December of my second year at school, just as rainy season came to a soggy end, strange travelers suddenly began streaming through the mission. Unfamiliar engines labored up the hill at least several times a week, and Carrie quit jeering, racing me out to the road instead.

One day it was a beat-up Land Rover crammed with jolly swordfish-tattooed Australians on their way from Marrakech to Cape Town. The Australians asked to borrow our dorm father's truck tools, because the Land Rover was leaking both gasoline and oil and they had given their tools to a Nigerian merchant in exchange for six cases of African palm beer.

Another day it was a dramatic feverish Frenchman stuffed full of parasites and curses and horrid tales of his malarial nightmares. Africa had ruined his health, he told us, and his last wish was to die in Provence with the scent of lavender fields in his nostrils. Mr. Lindstrom, our dorm father, got him on an Air Congo flight to Léopoldville, where he could catch the next Air Afrique to Paris.

On the second Sunday in Advent, a Canadian couple showed up in a camper made from a London fire truck. The Canadians told us they'd planned to drive only across Europe, but then they looked across the Straits of Gibraltar, and the wife had said, "Wow, there's a whole continent out there!" So they had ferried across to Tangier and headed south. Now, six months later, they were out of money. They stayed in the mission guest house while they waited for their family to wire more.

I thought all these people were wonderful, but Mr. Lindstrom said they were going to be the death of him.

"Trading tools for alcohol! Racketing around Africa without money, boiled water, or antimalarial pills!" His blond pompadour bobbed as he gave his head a disapproving shake. "How is it possible for people to be so foolish? And why in the world are they all coming to the Ubangi? I can't figure this out, I really can't."

Nobody else could either—until Mr. Scott arrived, red with sun and outrage, his horn blaring and his brakes screeching, gravel flying everywhere. We abandoned our Friday recess soccer game to crowd around while he furiously shoved the explanation into Mr. Lindstrom's hands. It was a little blue paperback called *The New Best-Ever Guide to the Roads of Central Africa.*

"Look at this sorry rotten lousy trashy no-good piece of *junk!*" Mr. Scott shouted. "I bought it in New York three weeks ago, and I'm gonna ask for my money back. This screwball writer says this road is *tarmacked!* There it is— page thirty-four! He wouldn't know the difference between old buffalo tracks and the New Jersey Turnpike."

Mr. Scott was a photographer from an American television show called "Wild Kingdom." He'd brought along three mud-splashed Jeeps filled with assistants and fancy equipment, and he wanted someone from the mission to guide him to the Baya River, a shallow river famous for its hippos.

Mr. Lindstrom started to tell him that he didn't really need a guide to the Baya. It was just fifty kilometers away, a straight shot on good road. Mr. Scott interrupted him. "Don't even *think* of telling me I can't miss it!" he roared. "I'm sick of maps drawn by morons, and I've had it with wandering in the bush! Just find me *someone* who knows where this blasted river is before I lose my mind."

Our dorm father got the boarding school night sentry, Kamu, to act as guide. Kamu's village was right next to the hippo river, and he knew all the best times and places for hippo watching. This cheered up Mr. Scott so much that he didn't seem to mind waiting around for a day while Kamu's temporary replacement was arranged. He roamed the mission, taking pictures and talking while we spent our Saturday trailing after him.

"Pictures of hippos *doing* it, that's what I want! Yessirree, that's my life dream, kids. But it won't be easy, not when they're always underwater except for their eyes and ears!" Mr. Scott slapped his thigh and chortled, sweaty jowls wobbling above the collar of his Hawaiian-print shirt. "Eyes and ears, ha! Can't make a hot hippo sex scene out of that now, can I?"

Mr. Scott took pictures of bare-breasted Congolese mothers nursing their babies. He gave us children mystifying lectures on the mating habits of the hippopotamus. ("Male hippos are hung *backwards*, you know! Not awfully convenient for mounting from the rear.") And to our horrified delight, he even cursed in front of our dorm mother.

"Maybe he's some bohemian artist, but it's no excuse for taking the Lord's name in vain," Mrs. Lindstrom said huffily. "And that flowered shirt really is the limit when we've spent years trying to convince the Congolese not to wear gaudy clothing. What a terrible example!"

When Mr. Scott left for the hippo river, Kamu was sitting beside him in the lead Jeep wearing one of Mr. Scott's orange and purple Hawaiian shirts. Kamu was grinning hugely, and Dungu, our school cook, told me why. "Kamu says Mr. Scott is the craziest *mondele*, the craziest white, he has ever seen. Kamu is going along just so he can collect stories of *mondele* foolishness to tell his village."

"Foolishness," said Mr. Lindstrom at devotions that evening. "Sheer unthinking foolishness. That's what our irresponsible travelers are all about, children. They're real-life illustrations of Jesus' parable of the ten virgins and the lamp oil. Five of those ten virgins were wise, you remember. They rationed their lamp oil so it would last far into the night. The other virgins, the foolish ones, burned up all their lamp oil with no thought to the future. Later, when all the shops were closed and midnight was coming on, the foolish virgins needed their lamps, and what did they find? They found their lamps were empty—as empty as our travelers' pockets, as useless as their bad travel guides." Mr. Lindstrom paused, looking soberly at each of us in turn. "Let us *all* make certain, children, that we are never foolish virgins, and that our faithful missionary lamps never run out of oil."

"Yes, Mr. Lindstrom," we chorused dutifully.

Along with the usual dry Sahara winds, the second week of December brought Jonathan Miles. Jonathan was a quick slender Englishman with amused blue eyes and the darkest, silkiest moustache I'd ever seen. He arrived late one afternoon, singing "A Maiden Did A-Bathing Go" as he pushed his black Triumph motorcycle up the hill. The Triumph had survived the Atlas mountains as well as the North African desert, Jonathan told us, but the back roads of the Ubangi had bested it forever.

"I can't say I blame it for giving up," Jonathan said with a good-natured shrug. "The Triumph had a hard life. I could try writing a requiem for it, poor thing, but I don't believe I'll bother. Requiems are too religious for my taste."

Both Carrie and I noticed how bleak and extra-Swedish Mr. Lindstrom suddenly looked, so we sprinted off to the school library and looked up "requiem," and Carrie said, "Well, no wonder! It's a Catholic thing!"

Dr. Hjalmar Berg, the whiskery old mission surgeon who played the recorder in his spare time, rushed over right in the middle of supper to tell Mr. Lindstrom everything he knew about Jonathan. "The man's got a string of Decca recordings as long as your arm," he said. "And a degree from the Royal College of Music to boot! I can't believe he's actually here in *le coin perdu!*"

Dr. Berg wanted Jonathan to sign his albums and talk about how it felt to perform at the Royal Albert Hall, but Jonathan didn't care to discuss his credentials. He wasn't really a performer, Jonathan said, he just liked to sing, just *needed* to sing.

Jonathan called himself a variety of strange-sounding things: a simple minstrel, a wandering purveyor of Elizabethan love songs, a troubadour whose times were out of joint. "Too much I once lamented, while love my heart tormented," he sang plaintively, his curly head bent toward the narrow blond waist of his battered guitar, his long fingers tenderly plucking the strings.

The high school boys thought Jonathan's melancholy tenor was bad enough, but when they heard him sing "Take O Take Those Lips Away" in a high flutelike falsetto, they were completely disgusted. I heard Daniel tell the other forwards on the soccer team that Jonathan was such a sickening fag it made him puke. Since Carrie was in the fourth grade, I asked her if she knew what a sickening fag was. She didn't, but we agreed it couldn't be too horrid or the boys wouldn't be so desperate to get their hands on his motorcycle. And the boys were desperate, we could tell; they hovered over that crippled black Triumph just like Jonathan hovered over his guitar.

Jonathan told them to go ahead and take it apart if they wanted to. "It's done for, so you can't hurt anything," he said carelessly, returning to the second verse of "Cherry Ripe."

"Never heard such caterwauling about a fruit salad before!" our dorm father snorted, his bleak look firmly in place. "Effete, that's what I call it. Why can't the man sing a good hymn like 'Come, Every Soul By Sin Oppressed?'"

"Cherry ripe, cherry ripe, rrr-ripe I crrrry!" Jonathan sang. "Full and fair ones, come and buy!"

From my special branch halfway up the frangipani tree, I watched Jonathan richly roll his *r*'s, raising his lush eyebrows in time to the music. None of the missionary men I knew sang with such reckless enjoyment. They always stood straight and stiff, like Congolese soldiers at flag raising. They always held hymnals at right angles to their chests while they ploughed expressionlessly through verse after verse of "Crown Him with Many Crowns" or "Far, Far Away, in Heathen Darkness Dwelling." They would never think of lounging for hours on the boarding school veranda cradling a blond guitar. They would never dream of singing ballads about tormented hearts and cruel mistresses, ripe cherries and sweet lovers loving the spring.

Jonathan had a ticket for Sabena's Christmas Eve flight from Léopoldville to Brussels. This left him two full weeks to explore the Congo, but Jonathan said he was as travel-weary as his motorcycle. He decided to stay upcountry with us until the last possible moment, giving free guitar lessons to Dr. Berg. He also gave guitar lessons to the high school girls, who suddenly began to dress "fancy American" in spite of the dry Sahara winds sweeping down from Chad and Niger.

"Louise's face has turned the ugliest color," Carrie observed. "It's orange. Up close it even looks like an orange skin. Thick, you know, with lots of bumpy shiny pores. I think she's wearing Pan-Cake makeup!"

"That's nothing," I said. "Carol's got nylon stockings on! Did you see those sweaty dark spots on the backs of her knees?"

Carrie folded her skinny freckled arms across her chest and looked superior. "She must be awfully miserable in those things. My mother met the French ambassador's wife once, and she wore a yellow silk dress with sleeves, but even she wasn't dumb enough to wear nylon stockings in the Congo!"

"My mother has a pair in case we have to go to America someday," I said, and then lowered my voice to a whisper. "I've seen the package, and the color is called 'nude!'"

"Oh, Grace!"

We snickered as Carol and Louise walked by, gently radiating heat, sweat, and Avon Here's My Heart cologne. We were certain Jonathan preferred us to all the high school girls. I wouldn't turn nine for several months yet, and Carrie was just barely ten, but our thin brown legs didn't need nylons, and our skin was smooth without any nasty orange Pan-Cake makeup.

Mrs. Lindstrom finally decided she liked Jonathan when she discovered he knew how to tune pianos. The mission had piano-tuning tools, but nobody knew how to use them, and an extra-humid rainy season had all but ruined the boarding school's piano. Mrs. Lindstrom, who missed playing "Hela varlden frojdes Herran," her favorite Swedish hymn, begged Jonathan to fix it right away.

"I'd be delighted," Jonathan said.

Carrie and I watched Jonathan set to work, his right ear tilting toward the piano frame as he struck a note, then listened, his eyes so tightly closed that the lids quivered. We scowled when several of the high school girls joined us. Louise had shortened her skirt at least two inches, and she wore green eye shadow that was bright as a rain-wet banana leaf. I was shocked. Did she really think Mrs. Lindstrom wouldn't notice?

"Would you teach us some English folk songs?" Janice asked in a breathy voice. "We'd love to learn some, wouldn't we, girls?"

"I'd be delighted," Jonathan said again, his sleek moustache lifting at the corners.

He gave them their first lesson that afternoon while Carrie and I sat in the frangipani tree and listened. He didn't teach them any of the embarrassing ones about coy mistresses with swanlike necks and violets on their white bosoms, so we decided it would be all right if we quietly learned a few folk songs ourselves.

"Sing fa la la la, it's a lovely day. Sing fa la la la layyyy-oh!" the high school girls warbled, "John Barleycorn" having quickly become their favorite.

But Jonathan laughed at their singing style, his blue eyes crinkling at the corners. "Come now, girls, let yourselves go a little," he pleaded with his sweet heart-stopping smile. "This is a lusty pub song, for pity's sake, not 'The Old Rugged Cross.' Don't be so prim!"

Behind the blooming frangipani, my face burned at the very idea of any song being lusty. I knew all about lust. There was a lot of it in the Old Testament. Lust was what King David's son Amnon had for his sister Tamar, so he forced her to stay with him in his bedroom. Afterwards he hated her, and poor Tamar cried and tore her clothes and put ashes on her head. I thought lust was a sad wicked thing. If "John Barleycorn" was meant to be lusty, I probably shouldn't sing that song. I would practice the one about the oak and the ash and the bonny ivy tree instead.

The singing of English folk songs came to a sudden end when we got a new visitor, an evangelist from Missouri. The

Reverend Hadley Wilson arrived in the Ubangi on the third Sunday in Advent, five days before Christmas vacation. He had conducted several dozen revival services in the Central African Republic with the help of a Sangho interpreter, Reverend Wilson said, but now he felt God calling him to the Ubangi, the forgotten corner.

"And can you guess why I won't need an interpreter here?" he asked. Before any of us could reply, Reverend Wilson told us. "Because I'm going to be preaching to *you* and *you* and *you!*" he said, stabbing the air with his thick forefinger. "All too often you missionary children think you'll be grandfathered into the Kingdom of Heaven. You think you can ride to Glory clutching your parents' coat-tails. Well, God won't let you get away with that, and neither will Hadley Wilson. Hadley Wilson has arrived at the Evangelical Swedish-American Mission by the grace of God, and he means to tell you *the truth!*"

Mrs. Lindstrom told Reverend Wilson that we'd all been needing this. "Yes indeed, it's that old story of the cobbler's children going barefoot," she said, and shooed us down to our rooms to get ready.

My stomach tightened at the very thought of attending Reverend Wilson's evangelistic services. I knew exactly what would happen. I would sit there feeling more and more guilty and miserable and panicky until finally I'd go forward during Reverend Wilson's altar call and accept the Lord Jesus into my heart yet again. Just thinking about it made me tired. Tired enough to crawl under my cotton quilt this very minute.

"How many times have you been saved, Grace?" Carrie asked.

"Ten times," I said.

Then I remembered Mr. Frykman's revival service last summer, the one he'd held at Miss Judith's elementary school for Congolese girls. Mr. Frykman had had a way of looking fearsome, spiritual, and deeply grieved all at the same time, and I just couldn't *not* go forward. And afterwards it was almost worth it, because gentle Miss Judith said, "What a brave girl you are!" and hugged me tight while my father patted my shoulder and my mother blew her nose, smiling.

"Oops! Eleven."

"Is that all?" Carrie tossed her head with an air of virtuous suffering. "I've been saved twenty-four times!"

I was impressed in spite of myself.

"I bet you've been saved only half as many times because your father is just an agriculture teacher. If he was a minister like mine, you'd probably be saved twenty-four times too."

I supposed Carrie was right. My father didn't preach very often, and when he did he never gave altar calls. He just talked about Jesus providing food for hungry people, or God sending ravens to feed Elijah in the wilderness. "The Lord called me to be a raven, not an Elijah," he would say. "Evangelism is vitally important, I know, but I'm proud and blessed to teach agronomy, and I'd like to see anyone in the whole of Equateur province beat my students at soybean farming!" I wished—oh how I wished!—that our latest exotic stranger had been my father and not Reverend Hadley Wilson.

"Carrie, I don't want to get saved again. Really I don't. Shouldn't eleven times be enough?"

Carrie shrugged.

"Oh well, at least we get to wear our Sunday dresses," she said. "Plus we can stay up late."

Boarding-school bedtime was seven-thirty, so we usually jumped at any excuse to stay up later. And I did love to wear my new Sunday dress, a pale green cotton print with tiny pink petunias all over it. I had a pink velvet hair bow and

SWIMMING IN THE CONGO

pink anklets to match, sent from America by my aunt. I polished my white sandals, gave my blond pageboy a good brushing, and wished Jonathan could see how nice I looked all dressed up. It was too bad the service was only for us missionary children.

The boarding-school living room had been rearranged to look churchlike, and Reverend Wilson stood by the newly tuned piano, his back to the wide picture window. He had sunburned skin, bushy bleached eyebrows, and a square face topped with a white-blond crew cut. He wore a white dress shirt, and I thought either his collar was too tight or his neck was too thick. While Reverend Wilson arranged his sheaf of notes on the lectern, we sang one of my favorite hymns, "Years I Spent in Vanity and Pride." After we had sung the last verse, he opened his King James Bible and cleared his throat in a commanding way.

"Kindly turn with me to the thirty-ninth chapter of the Book of Genesis."

I found Genesis 39 before Carrie did, so I nudged her hard with my elbow and whispered, "Slowpoke preacher's girl."

"Smarty-pants soybean girl," she hissed, nudging me back, and I tossed my pageboy smugly.

Then Reverend Wilson began to preach about poor Joseph in exile in Egypt, and we settled down fast. Reverend Wilson was exciting to watch, waving his Bible in the air and pacing heavily back and forth. His voice sounded hoarse and hollow, as if it came from a huge cavern behind his mouth.

"So here we have Joseph, a good hardworking respectful young man doing his best for his employer, Potiphar. Then what should happen but this clean virtuous lad is accosted by Madam Potiphar, an evil-minded harlot overflowing with feverish lust! Madam Potiphar practices her wanton wiles

86

on him, making up her eyes with kohl, scenting herself with exotic sandalwood perfume, and wearing low-cut gowns to expose her tempting breasts. But her seductive efforts are wasted—yes, wasted!—on this pure young man. He has no intention of betraying his employer by giving in to Madam Potiphar's sensuality. Finally this shameless woman, made bold by her unconquerable lust, demands that Joseph lie with her. She pulls him down beside her on the perfumed linens, grasping at him with lewd little hands. Joseph flees, his virtue intact but his clothing torn from his body by the foul Madam Potiphar."

Bright droplets of sweat beaded Reverend Wilson's brow and trickled down near his reddened ears. It was not a hot evening, but I understood. My father often said preaching was one of the hardest jobs in the world, every bit as hard as teaching plant pathology or growing soybeans. I supposed it was extra tiring to preach about an extra sinful woman like Madam Potiphar, and as the sermon progressed, I quit noticing such unimportant details as Reverend Wilson's tendency to sweat. I was much too worried about my own evil and provocative nature: How *could* I want to wear shorts and short dresses when Reverend Wilson said it was every Christian girl's duty to wear ankle-length clothing?

"A bared leg may tempt even a godly man to lust," he explained, looking straight at the row of high school girls. "No Christian female wants that on her conscience. The unshakable purity of Joseph ought to be your example, and the girl who refuses to do her part is herself given over to lust, which is depravity of the worst kind."

I glanced down, unhappy with my pink petunia dress for the very first time.

"The downward pull of lust lurks in the forgotten corner of every feminine soul, however young, moral, and modest," Reverend Wilson said sternly. "She enjoys her power as the potential ruin of an otherwise godly man. In thrall to her lust, the modern female wears makeup and short skirts, delightedly enticing men to fleshly desire."

I drew the full skirt of my petunia dress over my skinned knees and arranged the fabric with care, relieved that Reverend Wilson seemed to be looking at Louise's legs, not mine. I noticed Carrie tugging at the narrow hem of her blue seersucker skirt, trying to make it longer. She wasn't having much luck, because the skirt showed too much of her skinny freckled legs to begin with. (Mrs. Lindstrom said Carrie was growing like a weed and must ask her mother to put six-inch hems in all her clothes.) Carrie yanked the skirt down as far as it would go, then pinned it in place with the heavy green hymnal.

"America has become a sinful and corrupt country," Reverend Wilson told us. "The beaches are crowded with bikini-clad female bodies drinking and smoking and listening to rock and roll. American women are just like Madam Potiphar: they beg for trouble, but they always cry rape, and perfectly innocent men are jailed for life. If God hadn't intervened, Joseph—the sole hope of Israel—would have died in an Egyptian prison!"

My chest cramped like I'd gone swimming too soon after lunch, and my whole body felt stiff and cold. I couldn't seem to get enough air through my nose, so I tried breathing through my mouth instead. Did Jonathan Miles think I was a Madam Potiphar because I liked watching him tune pianos and sing songs? Worse yet, did God think so? My ears and cheekbones prickled with the red heat of shame. I shouldn't have primped, wearing my too-short pink petunia dress and my velvet hair bow and my Sunday sandals.

"These are desperate days, make no mistake," Reverend Wilson declared. "Purify your minds and prepare your souls, for the End Times are at hand!"

I had thought I knew all about the End Times, but Reverend Wilson told us things I'd never heard before. The Pope was the Antichrist, he said, and the European Economic Community was the "Ten Horns of the Beast" from the Book of Daniel. There was even another whore, the greatest, most terrible whore of all: the Whore of Babylon.

"Every sign tells us of the imminence of the Second Coming, the return of the Lord Jesus Christ to collect all His Believers and judge this sinful earth. Will *you* be ready to meet Him? And *you?* And *you?*"

Reverend Wilson's booming voice sank to a hoarse whisper, and he leaned heavily against the lectern. Great splotches of sweat darkened his dress shirt and slicked his forearms. He looked worn out by the spiritual struggle for souls—except for his fearsome eyes. They were live blue flames that scorched my heart, for he seemed to be looking only at me. "Will *you* be ready?"

"Please, dear Jesus," I prayed silently, "Don't let it be the End Times yet. Can't your Second Coming wait until I get home for vacation? I want to see everybody and go swimming one last time. Please, please, dear Jesus!"

Yet what if I made it home and saw everyone after all? What if I had my swim—the very best orange-dimpled sunset kind—and the four of us were sitting down to supper when Jesus' Second Coming happened? Jesus would collect my parents and my little sister, of course; maybe He would even scoop up Kitoko, since Faith was so fond of her. But what if there was a dreadful mistake, and Jesus didn't take me too? What if He just left me sitting there all by myself at the dining-room table? I knew Jesus could do that if He thought I wasn't really a Christian, and then, on the Day of the Last Judgment, I would be sent to Hell. I would never see my parents and Faith again. I would never have another chance to repent. I would be stuck in Hell for all eternity, absolutely forever, time never ending.

Probably I had just imagined my conversions those other times. Probably I hadn't really asked Jesus to take away my sins and save me. This was one of Satan's wicked tricks, making me believe I was saved when actually I wasn't. A true Christian wouldn't be so worried—or *would* she?

My head started to ache. I pulled the pink velvet bow out of my hair and stuffed it in my dress pocket. My legs were numb from dangling two inches above the floor, and my swollen feet pressed against the straps of my Sunday sandals. I wiggled my toes cautiously, wincing as a hundred tiny needles prickled beneath the skin. A shakiness in my stomach reminded me that I hadn't liked the vegetable soup at supper. What if I threw up during the altar call? Worse yet, what if my dress slid above my knees and showed my bare legs while I was throwing up?

I glanced sideways at Carrie. She sat hunched forward, her elbows braced on the green hymnal and her chin propped on her knuckles. Under the freckles her face was a pure startling white, like the inside of a freshly cracked coconut. She was sick too.

Although my palms were hot and sweaty, a long chill shivered down my backbone. I closed my eyes and imagined myself in bed beneath my blue cotton quilt, hugging my clammy knees to my stomach. I saw my favorite quilt squares, the misty blue-green plaid and the fancy one with blue cabbage roses and pink ribbons. I traced the embroidered words in one blue corner, "Gift of the Des Moines Ladies' Missionary Society."

"Everyone will please stand for the closing hymn," Reverend Wilson announced. "'Just as I Am, without One Plea.' That's page two hundred and fifty in your hymnal."

My feet were numb and clumsy, but at least I could stand on them. I clutched my unopened hymnal to my chest, not bothering to find page two hundred and fifty. I knew all five verses of "Just as I Am" by heart. I was grateful we didn't have to sing page two hundred and forty-eight, "I Bow My Forehead to the Dust."

"Young people, are there those among you who do not know the Lord? Are there those among you who cannot say with *confidence* that they will spend eternity in Heaven with Him?"

Reverend Wilson's probing blue eyes stared into mine. Stared twice as fiercely as Mr. Frykman's had last summer at Miss Judith's school revival. I knew Reverend Wilson saw the dreadful uncertainty in my soul.

"Some of you are callused and unresponsive to the call of God. Some of you don't even believe you're all that sinful. Well, tonight I'm here to tell you *the truth!* Tonight I'm here to tell you that *all* have sinned and come short of God's glory. That means *every* single one of you, *no exceptions!* As we lift our voices to God in song, come forward and be *saved!* Come forward and be *certain* of your place in God's kingdom!"

Reverend Wilson paused, raising his right arm for a powerful downbeat. "All together now, everybody, *sing!*"

> "Just as I am, without one plea
> But that Thy blood was shed for me."

Yesterday I had been singing "John Barleycorn." How strange it seemed. How lusty and immoral. I hoped I had smoothed down my too-short skirt when I stood up, but I couldn't remember and I didn't dare look.

Halfway through the first verse, Carrie's shaky alto stopped. She closed her hymnal and headed toward Reverend Wilson's lectern. I heard the quick slap of her thongs on the bare concrete floor, but my own sleep-stung feet wouldn't move. I started singing the second verse:

> "Just as I am, and waiting not
> To rid my soul of one dark blot.
> To thee whose blood can cleanse each spot . . ."

Reverend Wilson picked up the tempo with a gigantic sweep of his fist, and my heart pounded in time.

> "Just as I am, Thou wilt receive,
> Wilt welcome, pardon, cleanse, relieve."

Night moths thumped and thrashed against the picture window as they strained toward the light. I winced for their frail, battered wings.

> "Just as I am, thy love unknown
> Has broken ev'ry barrier down . . ."

This was it, the final verse, the last invitation to forgiveness, yet my body moved forward with the terrible slowness of a one-person pirogue battling the Congo current.

> "Now to be Thine, yea, Thine alone
> O Lamb of God, I come, I come!"

With a sudden spurt of energy, I rushed headlong down the aisle, desperate to join Carrie and all the others awaiting pardon and comfort.

Later, in a tired virtuous glow, I returned to my room. Carrie and I had promised each other on our King James Bibles to read the entire book of Romans before Christmas, and tomorrow we planned to take Reverend Wilson's advice and pound a stake into the rich soil under the bird-of-paradise bushes. "Whenever you see that stake," he told us, "you will remember you have formally and publicly buried your favorite sins and lusts *forever!* It will be a reminder to you that you are new creatures in Christ, just as the Apostle Paul promised in the fifth chapter of Second Corinthians."

I crawled into bed and pulled the Des Moines Ladies' quilt up to my neck. Squeezing my eyes shut, I sorted out the Congo night sounds. Balua village is having a party, I thought as I listened to the rhythmic beat of drums, the faint sounds of laughter and women singing. A frog croaked hollowly from the depths of the rain barrel by the cookhouse. The ascending scream of a tree hyrax rose above the slow rustle of mango leaves in the early dry-season wind. The night sentry's wooden lazy chair squeaked, and I heard a scraping deep-throated laugh. That was Kamu, back from the hippo river with lots of stories of *mondele* foolishness.

The darkness lay on top of me, a soft, drowsy weight. I was fading into sleep, lulled and warmed by the familiar, when I heard a sound I had almost forgotten. I slid out of bed and went to the window.

Two shadowy forms sat beside the night sentry's fire. In the light of the flames, I recognized Kamu in his lazy chair hunched over a tin mug of smoky tea. He was wearing his Hawaiian shirt with the big orange and purple flowers. Beside him on a Congolese footstool sat Jonathan Miles. Jonathan was singing, the words clear and tender:

> "To see, to hear, to touch, to kiss, to die,
> with thee again, in sweetest sympathy . . ."

On Thursday Jonathan Miles would leave the Ubangi, taking his blond guitar and romantic troubadour songs with him. He would fly one thousand kilometers downcountry to Léopoldville, then catch his Christmas Eve flight to Belgium. I would never see him again.

But there were still four days. Ninety-six whole hours. Didn't I have a Christian duty to evangelize the lost? Wasn't it my job, regardless of any inconvenience to myself? I would have to spend every possible moment with him until he got on that plane.

Miss Adela's Garden

"SINCE TODAY is Makua's day off, you may do the dishes, Grace. A little soap and hot water might cure your sulks."

That was the last straw. I cleared the table and dumped Grandma Berggren's blue-flowered plates in the dishpan, careless of the fine Swedish porcelain. My mother's lips clamped together, tight and white.

"If you broke any of those, you've lost your swimming privileges for the next three days," she said.

I peered at the blue jumble of dishes in the soapy water, dismayed to find I'd chipped one—badly. After dreaming of the river during twelve weeks of boarding school, I couldn't believe I'd just robbed myself of three precious swimming days. Easter vacation was off to a terrible start.

"At school I never have to help with the dishes," I said. "At school we have kitchen help even on Sundays."

My mother scraped leftover rice and gravy into Kitoko's food bowl and plunked it down on the concrete floor with a gritty clatter, but Kitoko didn't come. Kitoko never abandoned Faith during her afternoon siesta, not even for scraps.

"At school we have Melmac plates that don't break," I went on. "And Mrs. Lindstrom—"

My mother interrupted me. "The way you talk, I really think you'd rather spend your vacations at school than home with us." Her voice had a reproachful little catch in it.

I watched my mother spoon cold Sunday meatballs into a Tupperware container. It was soft and shapeless with humidity, like all our Tupperware, and she frowned as she struggled with the lid. Maybe if I made her laugh she wouldn't mind about the chipped plate.

I tried Makua's favorite excuse. "But Madame, the dishes won't let me hold them. They *want* to break themselves," I said.

My mother glared at me. She put the Tupperware on the top shelf of the refrigerator and slammed the door shut. I sagged against the counter, wondering why I spent the first few days of every vacation feeling cross and getting into trouble. I trailed one hand idly through the dishwater, glanced out the kitchen window, and groaned. The day was about to deteriorate even further.

"Oh please, no! The Can Man is coming!"

I knew my mother didn't like the Can Man, so I figured my own dislike of him was justified, and I didn't bother to hide it.

"Well, if that isn't the absolute limit," my mother sighed, rubbing her forehead with the back of her hand. "I've already put up with a three-hour church service today. I don't think I can put up with him too. I'm hiding in the office."

I retreated to my bedroom before she could suggest I go out and be nice to him. I wasn't the missionary. She couldn't treat me like a nine-year-old with the "sulks" and then expect me to do her job for her.

The Can Man lived in the village just outside Boanda Mission. The rains had washed most of the mud from the walls of his hut, exposing rough posts and rotting elephant grass and crumbling red termite trails. The thatched roof, all gray-green with age and mold, had at least as many bare patches as the walls. The Can Man himself was very old for a Congolese, his beard white and scraggly. He was so thin his chest looked like a cheap flimsy birdcage, the kind with brittle spokes that cave in when you touch them. He always wore the same clothes: a blue T-shirt that said "Property of Alcatraz" and a pair of filthy oversized shorts that sagged from his tiny hipbones. His shorts were secured by a large rusted diaper pin with a pink plastic head.

"Mbote na yo!" the Can Man called in his piercing quavery voice. "I give you greeting! Is anyone here?"

He had no one to garden and cook for him, because his wife had died. He had no one to care for him in his old age, because his wife had had no children. Each week he earned a few francs by selling cans at the Boanda market

Since missionaries used a lot of cans—even more cans than Alain Fougère, who ordered tinned chestnut puree, anchovies, and rum babas from France—the Can Man spent a lot of time on the mission collecting stock. He trudged from house to house with a little wooden stool tucked under his right armpit and a burlap sack thrown over his left shoulder. He always placed his stool directly under the kitchen window, settling himself upon it with pitiful groans and sighs. Then he dropped his head in his hands and began to pray in loud mournful Lingala: "*O Tata Njambe na Likolo,* Father God in Heaven, you know of my many sorrows, my great troubles. I call upon you, *Tata Njambe,* because I know you are a merciful God who loves and cares for the poor. You have seen that I am *mpaka,* old, and my wife is dead. You have seen that I have no children and my limbs have no *makasi,* no strength. You have looked inside my hut and found that what I tell you is true: I have no tea, no corn, no sugar, no manioc. I have nothing but two green plantains."

The Can Man's voice seemed extra loud today. My bedroom door was shut tight, but I heard him anyway. I knew my mother could hear him too. "Because you are great and wise, *O Tata Njambe*, you know everything there is to be known. You know all the riches inside this house, all the food and clothing and furniture. Because you are just and kind, O Father God, I beg you to soften the heart of Madame Berggren, she who has so much while I have nothing, she whom I saw buying more new shoes in Coquilhatville only last week. Fill the Madame with a spirit of Christian generosity instead of a vain love of shoes. May she become like your son, *Yesu Klisto*, merciful and unselfish. May she give me many, many cans, O God, as many as the generous Mademoiselle Adela gave me last week. And lay it on the Madame's heart that I especially need tins with lids on them, like the Nescafé and Ovaltine cans. They sell at a much better price."

The office door squeaked open, and I heard the quick tap of my mother's pretty new high-heeled sandals in the hallway. She hadn't held out very long today. Now she would give him some cans, and the Can Man would insist she pray with him. "The Mademoiselle Adela always prays with me for a long long time," he'd say. "She is a real Christian *mpenza*, kind and unselfish."

So my mother would sit down on the kitchen step while the Can Man started in on one of his long prayers of thanksgiving. In his prayer he would ask God to increase the Madame's generosity in the future. He would suggest that God tell her he needed new clothes, some soap, some sardines, and maybe a few tins of sweetened condensed milk. Then my mother would ask God to suggest to the Can Man that he plant a garden so he would have plenty of food to eat, maybe even some leftovers to sell. The Can Man would heave a sorrowful sigh and beg God to explain to the ignorant Madame that a Congolese man does not do women's work.

It was time to escape, and I knew exactly where to go. The Can Man's prayer had reminded me that I hadn't been up to visit Miss Adela Duncan and Miss Judith Pedersen since I got home. I knew they missed me when I was up-country at school, so I usually visited them right away—and always by myself. ("Why should I go, when you're their favorite?" Davina wanted to know.)

Miss Adela and Miss Judith lived on top of the hill behind the agricultural school in an orange brick house with green shutters, a thatched roof, and a veranda overflowing with orchid plants. I was sorry for them because they lived such a long way from the river, but Miss Judith liked quiet and Miss Adela said the soil up there was better for her roses.

Miss Adela's perfectly square garden was divided into tidy, weedless rows of flowers and vegetables. Some flowers I recognized, but many of the vegetables were strange, leafy, and European-looking. Miss Adela was from Salisbury. ("That's a city in Wiltshire, Grace, and Wiltshire is a county in England.") Miss Adela had come out with the British Baptist Mission in 1935. She told me how she'd arrived in Léopoldville with flower seeds and a Waterford crystal vase in her handbag. "God called me to be a missionary in the Congo," she said, "Not one of those expatriate barbarians who leaves every vestige of civilization behind."

She brought other things too: rose cuttings, twelve silver teaspoons with the initials A. D. on them, a set of Prince Albert Old Country Roses china, and a teapot shaped like a flower-covered cottage. And tea. Lots of tea, in pretty colored tins. She had Gunpowder tea, Assam tea, Irish Breakfast tea,

Prince of Wales tea, Darjeeling tea, even a nasty tea called Earl Grey, which smelled like musty old-lady perfume. Her sister in Harrowgate ("That's a city in Yorkshire, dear, and Yorkshire is another county in England.") had sent Miss Adela tea and sugar cubes every other month for thirty years, except during the war.

I liked the soft plop of sugar cubes dropping from Miss Adela's engraved silver pincers into my teacup. I enjoyed sipping from gold-rimmed bone china that blossomed with deep red and yellow roses. Best of all, I loved leaning back against Miss Judith's fancy embroidered cushions and listening to Miss Adela talk about the Old Days.

Miss Adela knew a lot about the Old Days. She lived here during them, back when the Congolese were still grateful for missionaries, back when everybody used mosquito nets and wore pith helmets against the equatorial sun. In the Old Days, Miss Adela gave people injections for yaws, a disease that caused hideous open sores. She pulled rotten teeth and set broken bones and ran an orphanage for abandoned children. She argued with witch doctors, hunted waterbuck and giant forest hogs, and rode around in a tepoy chair carried by Congolese porters.

Today Miss Adela fixed a pot of tea—Darjeeling, from the lavender tin—and talked about music in the Old Days. "My Victrola was one of the first in the Ubangi district of the Congo," Miss Adela said. "The Congolese crowded onto my veranda to listen to the magic box. After two months my records were all worn out. My opera records were very popular, I remember, especially Puccini. My first convert came just to listen to *Madama Butterfly*."

Miss Judith began humming a tune I didn't recognize, and Miss Adela smiled. "Those were the days!" she said. "The Congolese had a natural good taste in music then, even if they were ignorant. Now all they listen to is jazz from Radio South Africa."

"How long ago was that?" I asked, between careful grown-up sips of Darjeeling. "Your first convert?"

"August of 1936. I lived upcountry then, at the Bolala British Baptist Mission right across the river from French Equatorial Africa. Three years later that same man—Petelo was his name—came by to tell me that England was at war with Germany. He had heard it on the talking drums and thought I would want to know."

Miss Adela got up and walked over to the bookcase, her torso stiff from the corset she wore beneath her flowered housedress. She pulled out a green leather album and showed me a photograph of a stocky dark-haired man. He had a straight mouth, an even straighter nose, and eyebrows that looked like pasted-on rectangles of black velvet. Miss Adela looked just like him, except that she had a large drooping bosom and half-glasses dangling from a fancy silver chain.

"That's my brother Clive. He was killed in France the next spring, the spring of 1940. Very young he was too. Only twenty." Miss Adela pulled a handkerchief from her pocket and blew her nose hard. "Such a good decent boy."

I stared at Clive's picture, searching for goodness and decency in the fine shadings of black and white. Miss Judith reached across the coffee table and gave Miss Adela a brisk pat on the shoulder. "Don't depress yourself, Adela. This isn't like you."

"Good heavens, Grace! Why do you get me started?" Miss Adela sounded cross, and she yanked the album out of my hand and put it back on the bottom shelf. "Judith, you shouldn't let me!"

Miss Judith merely smiled. Like me, she hadn't lived here

in the Old Days. I could tell she liked to sit back and listen to Miss Adela almost as much as I did. Miss Judith had come to the Congo from Minneapolis after the war. During the war she was principal of an elementary school, but when it was over, she had to give up her job to an ex-soldier. Miss Judith liked to say that coming to the Congo was the most practical decision of her life. "I decided if America didn't want my administration skills, I'd find a country that did. And here I was, less than a year later, setting up a Christian elementary school for Congolese girls."

Miss Judith had a pale round Swedish face with a dimple set low in her right cheek. I thought she was still pretty and young looking. So did my mother, who said she'd kill for Miss Judith's beautiful hair and delicate skin. "Though it's beyond me why Judith wears those ugly black lace-up shoes," she remarked to my father. "And those shapeless navy house-dresses haven't been in style since the Depression!"

My father thought it wasn't too late for Miss Judith to land a man, if she would only get a modern hairdo and wear a little lipstick. He agreed with my mother that Miss Judith had lots of potential. "It annoys me to see her wasted," he said. "Where's her initiative anyway?"

Today, having left the dishes, the Can Man, and my mother's white-lipped aggravation behind, I sipped my Darjeeling tea and studied Miss Judith's blond coronet of braids. "Do you ever think of cutting your hair, Miss Judith?" I asked.

"Do you think I should?"

"Well, I don't know," I fumbled, abashed. "My mother and Davina's mother have short hair. So does Mrs. Frykman. I guess it's fashionable."

"I guess it is."

Miss Judith smiled as she rocked gently back and forth in the creaky wooden rocker. She had eyes like a Siamese kitten: clear, sweet, and blue. "Long hair is a lot of trouble," Miss Judith admitted. She lifted one hand to the shining braids wound around her head. They were fixed firmly in place with countless hairpins and black plastic combs decorated with rhinestones. "And that reminds me, I've got to wash it tonight," she said. "I couldn't do it last night because I had a meeting, and it takes ages to dry."

I'd wanted to see Miss Judith's hair down since the very first time I read about Rapunzel. I thought Miss Judith belonged in a fairy-tale castle window, her soft Swedish face framed by thick, silver-blond braids that would reach to the ground, providing Prince Charming with a gorgeous ladder to happily-ever-after. My favorite fairy-tale book had a picture of the Prince grasping that beautiful hair, climbing hand over hand until he reached Rapunzel's window. The Prince was tall, with dashing thigh-high boots, dark wavy hair, and a handsome nose. I always wondered exactly what happened after he got to the top, after he made an elegant bow and promised to love her forever. My cheeks prickled with embarrassed heat as I imagined his strong hands loosening Rapunzel's smooth braids until her hair floated around them like a graceful golden cape. I pictured him burying his princely face in her neck, breathing in the scent of her hair, sifting the satiny strands through his slender fingers.

"Because You are great and wise, *O Tata Njambe na Likolo*, all the secrets of our hearts are known to You. You are like a great hunter, for Your eyes see the smallest movement in the jungle, the faintest track in the grassland. No one can hide from You, and no sin goes unnoticed." The Can Man's loud sorrowful prayer floated in through the open dining-room window.

I groaned, slumping lower in the embroidered cushions. Miss Adela and Miss Judith exchanged a quick glance. Miss

Adela set down her Old Country Roses teacup and headed for the kitchen.

"Though my poverty is great, *O Tata Njambe*, I am not ashamed. You know that the good are not always rich, for *Yesu Klisto*, Your Holy Son, was also a poor man. You know too that the rich are not always good, but that many sins are forgiven the rich who are generous. Soften the hearts of these Mademoiselles who live in this house large enough for twenty Congolese. May you give the Mademoiselles understanding, *O Tata Njambe*, so they know what is wise for them to do. Tell them I need food as well as cans. And remind Mademoiselle Adela that I cannot stomach the strange things she grows in that garden. I want corn and spinach greens only."

"Grace, how about helping me cut out my new flannelgraph pictures?" Miss Judith asked, her voice louder than usual. "They're fresh off yesterday's boat from Léopoldville, and I want to use them in my Bible class tomorrow."

"Oh yes!" I said, promptly forgetting the Can Man outside the kitchen window. "Did you get any really good ones?"

Miss Judith pulled out a big manila folder and two pairs of scissors. "Come have a look," she offered.

Flannelgraph pictures came in thick paper sheets with a special adhesive backing. Some of the pictures were biblical characters dressed in flowing robes, and others were scenery: houses and synagogues, date palms and sycamores, sheep and camels. All the missionary ladies used these pictures to tell Bible stories to the Congolese children. They would stick the pictures onto a little flannel-covered chalkboard and move the characters about as they talked. My mother had a great one about Samson and the riddle of the honey-filled lion, but even she couldn't tell a story as well as Miss Judith.

Miss Judith could sound like a shaky-voiced old lady one minute and a whiny little boy the next. She waved her hands around as she put on different dramatic voices, and her cheeks turned pink as Miss Adela's Queen of Denmark roses. Miss Judith's stories were so exciting that I watched and listened like any Congolese girl who didn't know what came next. She could tell about the princess of Egypt plotting with Miriam to save the life of baby Moses so that goose bumps covered your arms and stood your hair on end. She could make you sorry for Rachel and Leah, the unhappy sisters who spent their lives fighting over the same man. She could make you cheer for brave and beautiful Queen Esther, for faithful friends Naomi and Ruth, for Judge Deborah, prophetess and ruler of Israel.

"This one about the captive Hebrew girl is my favorite," Miss Judith said. "You know about her, don't you? She was a house slave of Naaman, the powerful Assyrian military man. He was ill with leprosy, but her faith found him a cure."

We sat down at the dining-room table and cut out the new flannelgraph pictures. I did one of Naaman standing in his golden chariot wearing crimson robes, and one of the prophet Elisha with a long white beard and wise dark eyes. Miss Judith did one of Naaman washing in the River Jordan and one of Elisha's greedy servant, Gehazi. We argued over the barefoot Hebrew slave girl, who wore an ugly brown tunic and didn't have any name, but Miss Judith finally let me have her since I was company.

I remembered the Can Man when Miss Adela came in to collect the tea things. "He didn't stay very long," I said. "Generally he prays with my mother for at least an hour."

"That's because your mother is more patient than I am," she said briskly. "Besides that, I'm foolish enough to give him everything he wants right away."

"He always wants corn," Miss Judith remarked, carefully cutting out a flannel-backed pomegranate tree. "Did you give him some?"

"Every last ear," she replied. "And the spinach as well. I'm off to the garden now, if you girls will excuse me. I must pick those string beans today."

String beans were one of Miss Adela's few ordinary vegetables. Otherwise her garden was mostly made up of exotic things my father said had no business doing so well in sandy tropical rain forest soil. She grew melons, peas, and brussels sprouts, as well as zucchini, endive, and swiss chard. She even managed to grow a few stalks of asparagus. When my father first heard about Miss Adela's asparagus, he went berserk.

"Those dratted English!" he raged to my mother. "I know they can grow anything, but *asparagus? Here?* Why did I waste my time getting a degree in agricultural science? I really needed an English birth certificate!"

Whenever I visited them, Miss Adela would send me home with a huge tomato or zucchini, maybe even a bag of extra-fancy lettuce with frilly red edges. My father, who called his own garden "Home of the Twelve Plagues of Egypt," would spread Miss Adela's vegetables out on the dining-room table and examine them with his magnifying glass.

"Adela's got a nerve, sending me her picture-perfect produce. Just look at this lettuce, will you?—Not a single hole or black spot! Even though I used fertilizer and DDT, the bugs ate every last one of my lettuce leaves before they were an inch high. That woman's got a nasty streak, Junie, she really does!"

Miss Judith and I finished cutting out all the flannel-graph pictures just as it got dark. She leaned back in her chair, patting her rhinestone hair combs to make sure they were still in place, and told me I had done a beautiful job.

"I know I can always rely on you, Grace," she said. "Your mother must miss her good little helper when you're away at school. I certainly do!"

The cold sulky knot eased in my chest for the first time since my parents picked me up at the Coquilhatville airport two days ago. I used to have a place in my family. Maybe tonight I would remember what it was. I told Miss Judith I had to hurry home and help my mother start supper. "I don't think she can manage it without me," I said, and Miss Judith nodded approvingly.

Miss Adela came inside, a white enamel basin filled with string beans balanced on her hip. Red Congo dirt streaked her hands and housedress, but she was beaming. "I haven't had such lovely string beans in years," she said. "It must be all that papaya rind in my new compost recipe. Take some home with you, Grace dear. I know how much your mother likes string beans. Wait a minute while I find a plastic bag."

I worried about my father's reaction. Although his sweet corn and squash were doing well, every last one of his string beans had withered to nothing.

"Thank you for coming by," said Miss Judith with her comfortable smile. "We always love to have you."

"And I always love to come."

I hugged both of them, enjoying the brush of soft dry cheeks and cushiony breasts, the smell of Pond's cold cream and Yardley's English Lavender cologne. Miss Judith and Miss Adela's affection filled me with a deep secret gratitude. I didn't have to sulk away my unease, chip Grandma Berggren's dinner plates, or be rude about the Can Man. I didn't need to stumble around in a blind panic, trying to retrieve my special family place. Miss Judith and Miss Adela weren't family.

I was halfway home before it dawned on me that tonight was my chance—tonight Miss Judith planned to wash her hair. Maybe she was unraveling those heavy golden braids this very instant. Maybe, like Rapunzel in my fairy-tale book, she was singing a tender love song as she combed her fingers through her rippling locks. I turned and ran back up the hill, my plastic thongs slapping against the uneven dirt path. I slowed to a trot as I neared the house, out of breath and wondering what excuse I could give for my return. I hovered impatiently by the front door, ready to knock as soon as some reasonable explanation popped into my mind. None did. After a moment I decided to scout around and check the windows.

Except for six or seven flannelgraph Bible characters, the dining room was empty. I jumped off the orchid-laden veranda and hurried to the back of the house, careful not to trip over the bulging roots of the mango tree. Inhaling the humid darkness, rose-sweet and mango-spicy, I paused at Miss Judith's bedroom window, staring. The curtains were not fully drawn, leaving an inch-wide strip of brightness down the center of the window. Mesmerized, I picked my way through Miss Adela's well-tended shrubs until I stood directly under that golden spill of interior light. I strained upwards, all my weight on my toes, and my body pressed flat as a lizard against the evening-cool bricks. Hooking my chin over the top of the high sill, I peered cautiously into the room.

A tin of Cashmere Bouquet powder stood on the dresser alongside a jewelry box made of Congolese ebony with ivory inlays. A neat row of Avon perfume bottles shimmered gently in the light of a pale blue lamp. Pictures of Miss Judith's students had been fitted into the edges of the mirror, as well as a postcard that said "Welcome to Beautiful Lake Minnetonka." Two of Miss Adela's Fantin-Latour rosebuds trembled in a slim porcelain vase with Swedish linnea flowers painted on it. Miss Judith sat on the edge of the bed wearing only a white cotton slip. The slip was perfectly plain, not a scrap of embroidery or lace trimming anywhere, but Miss Judith's arms and shoulders were softly rounded, and her skin had the pink-veined creaminess of a frangipani blossom.

Miss Judith was not alone. Miss Adela sat close beside her on the bed, completely engrossed in unraveling Miss Judith's blond braids. She touched the shining hair with her tough gardener's hands, tenderly stroking and smoothing, gazing at Miss Judith like she was the finest, most beautiful rose in the world. Miss Judith tilted her head back with a tiny choked moan, and her loosened hair tumbled past her hips to the bedspread. The feathery tresses swirled like golden surf on a blue fabric sea, daytime silver threads erased by the soft yellow lamplight. Miss Judith looked as welcoming and lovely as Rapunzel in her tower, except it was Miss Adela, not the Prince, who buried her face in Miss Judith's fairy-tale hair and kissed her.

"Because You are great and wise, O Tata Njambe na Likolo, all the secrets of our hearts are known to You."

I backed away from the windowsill, retreating until my trembling legs met the coarse scratchy bark of the mango tree.

"And remind Mademoiselle Adela I cannot stomach the strange things she grows in that garden."

Twisting my head from side to side, I searched the deep Congo twilight for the Can Man. There was nothing but shrubs and a blurred mass of vegetables, bordered by tall spiky sweet corn. Sweet corn without any ears.

I crept down the dark path toward home, clutching Miss Adela's plastic bag of string beans to my chest, whispering prayers to the shadows behind the rustling breadfruit trees. "O Mister Can Man, please, please—just leave them alone."

No Carrots in the Congo

THE SUMMER I was nine, the days melted together in a blur of humid sunlight and the river simmered brightly beneath a hot blue sky. My father's brown leather wing tips developed a jungle green mold that was as fuzzy and yielding as a worn sponge. The Toll House chocolate chips that my aunt sent from Michigan fused into a solid lump the same week they arrived. And Mrs. Frykman said that the sticky heat, so unusual for rainy season, proved beyond a shadow of a doubt that the Return of the Lord was at hand.

"You might have a point," my mother said, pulling a hanky from the belt of her dress and wiping her damp forehead.

"A point! Floods, famine, worldwide changes in the weather—those are our Lord's own words, June! Haven't you read Matthew 24?" Mrs. Frykman took another sip of coffee and leaned forward, her round cheeks flattening with disapproval. "Oh, speaking of famine, that reminds me. Have you heard the latest on Emma Owen?"

My mother gave me an uneasy look. She and Mrs. Frykman were having afternoon coffee on the back veranda since it was so hot indoors, and I knew she was afraid Mrs. Frykman would talk too much in front of Mama

Malia, Faith, and me. My mother wouldn't ask us to leave, because the back veranda was Mama Malia and Faith's special early-afternoon nap place. Mama Malia liked to sit on the cool concrete floor, her straight back pressed against one of the brick pillars, while Faith and Kitoko slept in a golden-blond jumble on her wide lap. I sat beside Mama Malia, pretending to be too busy with my ballet scrapbook to bother about my mother and Mrs. Frykman's conversation.

"Just that she threw out all her dining-room furniture," my mother said evenly, like it was something missionary ladies did all the time.

"Gracious, that was days ago! Anyway, Captain Owen rescued it all. Crammed it in the spare room, I believe," Mrs. Frykman said, clucking. "But that's old stuff. I heard this from Dawena, who got it from Alphonse only today. Alphonse is related to Polycarp, you know, the Owens' new yard boy."

I glanced at Mama Malia, since I knew she was related to both Alphonse and Polycarp, but she wasn't paying any attention. She was making a dried-corn necklace for Faith and humming her favorite hymn, "Fairest Lord Jesus," fancying it up with little bits from the Bantu national anthem.

"Emma is all upset because she can't get carrots. Carrots! Can you imagine? With that terrible drought in East Africa this summer, Kenya doesn't have any carrots to export. Emma had ordered forty kilos, and she threw a hissy fit when she heard she wouldn't be able to get them."

The idea of the calm, controlled Emma Owen throwing a hissy fit rattled me so much that I spilled glue all over the male dancer I was pasting in my scrapbook. I sponged frantically at the glue, moaning softly as the wet paper tore, severing poor Yuri Vladimirov's leg at the knee. Mama Malia leaned over to watch.

"Forty kilos of carrots?" my mother echoed. "What on earth would she want with so many? And at the awful price of imports too!"

"Polycarp told Alphonse that Emma doesn't eat red meat or starchy foods. She only likes vegetables." Mrs. Frykman took a large bite of my mother's nutmeg feather cake, chewed comfortably, and swallowed. "Especially carrots. They were her staple food in New York, I gather. She's going to try growing some herself."

Mama Malia stared at the *National Geographic* I was cutting ballet photographs from and began to laugh silently, air hissing through the space between the points of her filed-down front teeth.

"Oh, poor Emma!" my mother exclaimed. "Didn't you tell her that carrots need colder temperatures and better topsoil? Why, even our Miss Adela can't grow them here!"

"No, I didn't," Mrs. Frykman snapped. "And you know why? Because she wasn't asking me for any advice. She'll scarcely speak to me, or anyone else at Boanda, much less ask for anything!"

Mama Malia gave my arm such a powerful nudge that I almost fell over. "*Nakamwi!* Look at this ugly *mwasi!*" she exclaimed, pointing at a ballerina who had made the Voice of America broadcast by defecting from the Soviet Union. "Look at her hair, so flat and plain! And she needs some palm oil to shine up that dull skin of hers. So thin, too, thin as a child. I suppose she must be very poor."

"Poor?" I was taken aback. "*Nayebi te.* Maybe she is. She's a Communist from Russia."

"She must be poor," Mama Malia said firmly. "Rich people always have more *mafuta,* more fatness."

I tried to explain that dancers were supposed to be skinny, but Mama Malia started laughing again, her chin, bosom, and hips all jiggling at once—jiggling so much that

Faith and Kitoko nearly tumbled off her lap. "*Wapi*, that's foolishness!" she said. "Everyone knows the best dancers are always women with plenty of *mafuta*."

I turned away from her, straining to hear what my mother was saying about Emma. Pale slender Emma with her smooth black bun so heavy it dragged her head back and gave her chin a proud tilt. Sleek strange Emma, her face wide at the eyes and cheekbones, like Davina's pet cat, Lumumba.

"Her reasons for being antisocial might be pretty good ones," my mother was saying, her forehead puckered up in long wavy lines. "I'm not sure the mission board did right in renting the Clare house to the State Department without telling them, without telling them—oh, you know!"

Of course Mrs. Frykman knew, and so did I.

The Clare house had been built around 1910 by a British Baptist missionary named Nigel Clare, who died a horrible death from blackwater fever. The next person to live there, a young American nurse, was fatally bitten by a green mamba during her evening shower. The house hadn't been lived in since 1934, when a pregnant missionary wife cut her finger while slicing an avocado and got blood poisoning. It took her two weeks to die, and by that time her whole body had turned completely black and she had been out of her head for days. Her husband performed the funeral, then drowned himself in the river. Mr. Frykman said the Clare house stayed empty after that because it wasn't needed. My mother said fiddlesticks, no missionary who knew the history of the house was willing to live there, and that included her.

I liked the Clare house myself. Jungle flanked it on one side, and the mission cemetery on the other, so it was perfect for playing hide-and-go-seek or sardines. Cannas with pink and white stripes grew in the front yard, the only ones that color in all of Equateur province. The sweetest, biggest, yellowest guavas in Boanda grew there as well, and the overgrown gardenia bushes were always in bloom. I knew my mother had to be wrong about Emma Owen and the Clare house, just as Mrs. Frykman was wrong about Emma Owen never asking for anything. Only two weeks before, Emma Owen had asked Davina and me for something important—our bodies.

That day had been our first day together in three months. We were both home for the summer, me from my upcountry boarding school, and Davina from her downcountry one, where Davina's father said she'd have more opportunities. ("Opportunities for what, I'd like to know!" Davina grumbled. "Léopoldville is noisy and dirty and full of stupid white people who can't speak Lingala, and all I get out of it is flute lessons.") The two of us sat on a fallen palm tree by the edge of the river, worn out from swimming, talking, and maybe some first-day strangeness as well—at least on my part, as Davina was suddenly several inches taller and wore aqua cat's-eye glasses just like her mother's, with rhinestone flowers in the corners.

We dangled our feet in the muddy shallows and watched Mama Malia hike her *liputa* up around her sturdy thighs before wading into the water with my little sister. Faith squealed and laughed as Mama Malia rubbed her all over with strong-smelling Congolese lye soap, even her fine pale hair, and dunked her underwater. The two of them began a splashing contest just as the sun slid behind a narrow strip of island, casting sizzling orange shadows across the river. Davina and I squinted and frowned against the glare, our noses and cheekbones tight with sunburn, our still-damp bathing suits clinging to our sweaty skin.

"I don't think I've met you girls, have I?"

A strange woman had come up behind us, quick and silent as a genet, one of those tiny spotted jungle cats with the long, long tails. She was thin, terribly thin, with the whitest skin I had ever seen and straight dark hair drawn tightly away from her face instead of a short motherly cut curled with a home permanent. I thought she looked sternly beautiful, like the ivory and ebony statues that Wamba down in the village carved and sold at the tourist market in Coquilhatville.

She looked us over slowly, deliberately, the way my mother did Nile perch the local fishermen brought to our door. I half expected her to flip me upside down and give me a good shake.

"Excellent. You both look strong and wiry," she said. "I'm Emma Owen. My husband and I moved here just a few weeks ago. We live in the Clare house. Would you like to take ballet lessons from me?"

Davina and I stared at her, joyfully dumb.

"I wouldn't charge you anything, of course," she added quickly, a tinge of pink on her white cheeks.

"Real ballet? Like in *National Geographic?*" I squeaked. "With the fancy clothes and the long Russian names?"

Mrs. Owen smiled for the first time, a small pretty crease appearing above her upper lip. "Yes, although I don't think any of us will ever dance with the Bolshoi," she said, a dry edge to her voice. "We'll do it just for fun."

"Oh yes, please!" we said.

"Good. Wednesdays and Fridays, I think. Be at my house on Wednesday afternoon at two-thirty. Bring your imaginations with you. And plenty of energy. Dancing is fun, but it's hard work too."

She turned away and climbed the riverbank, her narrow shoulders thrown back, her long white cotton skirt swaying gracefully. Davina and I looked at each other, then jumped up and down, shrieking.

"*Nyoka ejali?*" Mama Malia cried, running out of the river clutching Faith, the two of them streaming water.

"No. No snake," I said. "We're going to learn how to dance! Madame Owen said she'd teach us!"

The sun behind her lit up Mama Malia's skin, and she glowed with a black-orange fire from the top of her spiky Congolese hairdo all the way down to her fat bare toes. She sat Faith on the sandy bank and began dancing in little circles, stamping her muddy feet, clapping her hands, and swishing her wide yellow-flowered hips. She shut her eyes and started to sing in a loud wailing voice, her head thrown back so far I thought she might overbalance into a handstand. Davina and I stared first at her, then at each other.

"Come on, children!" Mama Malia called over her fiery shoulder. "No white Madame can teach you as well as I can!"

"But we're going to learn a different kind of dancing," I said.

Mama Malia was making so much noise that she didn't hear. "*Olobi nini?*" she shouted.

"I *said*, we're going to learn a *different* kind of dancing, Mama Malia!"

The breath whistled out through the chiseled points of her teeth as she came to a dead stop. All her flaming sunset color slid away and sank deep in the river. "White people dancing!" she said mournfully, tightening her loosened *liputa*. "*Mawa monene!* I've never known a *mondele* who really knew how to dance."

She started up the hill with Faith while Davina and I ran on ahead, anxious to tell our mothers about Mrs. Owen's wonderful offer.

Our mothers did not think ballet lessons were at all

wonderful. Mrs. Carlson said no daughter of hers was going to learn anything so downright sinful and decadent as ballet, but for once Mr. Carlson disagreed with her. "You're wrong, Irma," he said coolly. "That's a different kind of dancing. Besides, ballet takes discipline. It might be very good for the girls." Mrs. Carlson was so shocked that she backed down right away.

While my mother liked the word discipline, she was still uneasy. She asked Mrs. Palmquist for her opinion. Mrs. Palmquist had been a missionary in the Congo since 1932, so she was a real authority on what was proper for a missionary to do. She told my mother and me that ballet lessons could be a good practical opportunity to Bear Christian Witness to the nonmissionary expatriates. "What with the heavy drinking, smoking, carousing, and goodness-only-knows-what-all down at those Embassy parties in Léopoldville, I'd say they're every bit as Lost In Sin as the Congolese," she said. "Captain Owen is just a military attaché, but it's a foot in the door all the same."

"All right." My mother sighed. "But I'm never going to hear the end of this from Hilda Frykman."

Two weeks and four lessons later, I was starting to think my mother was right.

"It's not just the dancing, June, it's her attitude!" Mrs. Frykman said, dumping another teaspoon of sugar in her coffee and fanning her large yellow-checked bosom with an old issue of *Evangelical Witness* magazine. "Artistic posturing comes naturally to someone like her, I suppose, but you would think she'd at least try to adjust. She has no consideration for her poor husband."

I carefully trimmed the *National Geographic* photo of prima ballerina Maya Plisetskaya as the Black Swan and pretended I was cutting Mrs. Frykman to bits instead.

"I feel sorry for her," my mother replied. "Naturally she's doing the right thing, following her husband where his job takes him, but it can't easy for her."

"Easy or not, it's her responsibility as a wife. And I'll tell you this: I would never have permitted my daughter, Carol, to spend so much time with non-Christian people, whatever the reason. Young girls are easily influenced."

"Not your lovely Carol," my mother said. "She was always as principled as she was pretty. I doubt that has changed, even though she's going to Bible college in Chicago, do you?"

Mrs. Frykman's pursed lips suddenly relaxed into a soft, proud smile. "Well, I must say our Carol has never caused us a moment's anxiety," she said. "Perhaps she's an exception. But you can't count on Grace being one, you know!"

I sucked my breath deep inside my chest and held it tight while I prayed Mrs. Frykman would catch leprosy and die. Or cholera. There was a cholera epidemic upriver in Stanleyville. I had heard it was a nasty way to go.

"I think Mrs. Owen is beautiful and wonderful," I burst out, dropping my scissors on the veranda floor. "And so is ballet. And I've never, ever heard her say she doesn't want to be here. Of course she does! She loves Boanda. Who wouldn't?"

Mrs. Frykman raised her eyebrows at me, then gave my mother one of those superior adult looks.

"You see, June?"

"Hmmm, yes. But what I don't see is how I can possibly change my mind at this point," my mother said. "Besides, I suspect it gives Emma something to look forward to."

"Just getting out of New York would give me something to look forward to," Mrs. Frykman sniffed. "Elmer and I were there once, speaking at the Madison Avenue Mission to the Unredeemed. What a filthy city! I wouldn't dream of being in a ballet corps if I had to live there, not for a minute."

I tried to imagine plump Mrs. Frykman in a tutu and nearly laughed out loud. She had no waist or neck, and lumps of fat sagged from her upper arms like wax dripping from a candle. Even the old lady who sold smoked eels at the Boanda market, whose body was horribly deformed with elephantiasis, was more graceful than Mrs. Frykman.

"And Captain Owen is such a nice man," Mrs. Frykman continued. "It's a crying shame. He doesn't deserve a wife who has to be different."

Mrs. Owen *was* different, I realized. Her hairstyle was different, and so were the long flowing clothes she wore over her thin body. She spoke in quick pruned-back sentences that never rambled from mission work to children to household help. She rarely smiled and never laughed, yet there was something fascinating about her face when she discussed ballet, something fierce and loving in her eyes. I'd seen missionaries with that same look when they prayed or read the Bible, but I didn't say so. I would never be allowed to go to her house again.

I loved Mrs. Owen's house almost as much as the lessons. It was the most naked house I'd ever seen, all cool bare lines and angles without a single crocheted doily, lace tablecloth, or ruffled curtain. Posters of leaping dancers and twirling ballerinas decorated the whitewashed walls instead of sad still paintings of Jesus blessing the little children or praying in the Garden of Gethsemane. There wasn't a stick of furniture in the dining room now, not even a rug or woven mat on the concrete floor. Just a long barre, which the mission carpenter had installed against one wall according to Mrs. Owen's instructions, a battery-operated record player, and a stack of records.

"*Mwana,* do you hear my words?" Mama Malia asked, giving me another of her bruising nudges. "I think it's almost time."

I carried my scrapbook supplies indoors and looked at the kitchen clock. Mama Malia was right. It was nearly two-fifteen. I crammed a pair of sandals on my feet, making a face as the hot flabby plastic stuck to my skin. Then I slipped out the back door to find Mama Malia putting Faith in the Radio Flyer wagon my parents had mail-ordered from Montgomery Ward in America.

"The child woke up," Mama Malia announced. "She wants to go for a wagon ride to the cemetery by the dancing white Madame's house."

I sighed. I knew exactly what came next. Mama Malia would take Faith to the cemetery, but not for long. A few minutes into our lesson we'd see Mama Malia watching us through the Owens' curtainless dining-room window. She'd be laughing herself sick, her face all crumpled up and her chin wobbling. Faith would peer down at us from her perch on Mama Malia's wide shoulders, laughing just because Mama Malia was laughing. Mrs. Owen, Davina, and I always ignored them.

We walked slowly down the road to the Clare house, blinking in the sleepy yellow glare of early afternoon. The gravel crunched noisily under the wagon tires, and Faith sang "Jesus Wants Me for a Sunbeam" to her doll, Thumbelina. Since she was still groggy, she slurred the words together. "Sunbeam" turned into "shunbeam," and I snickered.

"Tell me, what is that food the dancing white Madame wants so much?" Mama Malia asked.

"Oh that. Carrots," I said. "I have eaten tinned ones. They are a vegetable, an underground one like the *libenge*, the sweet potato. And the same color too, but not rounded. Long and skinny instead."

"I see. Like the Madame," she said. "I think the Madame is a child."

I stopped walking. "Why?" I asked, staring at Mama Malia.

"Because she has no breasts," she said calmly. "And because she has a child's worries. She worries about what she herself will eat. A grown woman worries about what she will feed other people."

Mama Malia shook her head, her long brass earrings sweeping across her dark shoulders like shiny brooms.

"She does not want any grown-woman worries, I see that, but she is about to have some anyway. I could have helped her. I could have gotten her some good *kisi* from the witch doctor, only she never asked me. She is foolish, that one, and filled with *ntembe*, fear. She thinks she's alone in the world."

The idea of wonderful Mrs. Owen needing anyone's help bewildered me. "Why would she want witch-doctor *kisi?*" I asked.

"Because she swallows a lot," Mama Malia said, grinning. "Your eyes are *mpamba*, useless!"

I was still puzzling this over as I turned up the brick walkway to the Clare house, noting the browned gardenia petals, the tall cannas slumped in the heat. Davina was waiting by the front door. The roof's deep thatched overhang shaded her face, but I knew she was nervous by the way she knotted her fingers together. I hurried up the steps and she grabbed my arm, pulling me against the wall.

"They're fighting in there," she whispered. "I don't know what to do. Should we go home?"

Captain Owen's bass voice rumbled through the screen door.

"Emma, I'm only asking for a week! I want a dining room for one lousy week! As soon as the government people go back to Léopoldville you can have your goddamn studio again, I promise."

There was a long silence, then an impatient sigh.

"I don't know any way to host several dinners for ten people without a proper dining room. Can't you be reasonable?"

"No," Mrs. Owen said.

I let my breath out, relieved to hear her say something. Anything.

"Why?"

"Because I know what will happen. Somehow you'll convince me I don't really need this room all to myself, that I can practice in a clutter of furniture." Mrs. Owen's voice had a wild high wobble. "Well, I can't, Allan. I do need it. You don't know how much."

I moved my head just a little and peeked in the window. Mrs. Owen stood in the center of the naked dining room, her thin white arms wrapped tightly around herself, her shoulders hunched forward. She looked like a picture I'd seen in a North African newspaper, a black-and-white photo of some poor Tuareg lady caught in a Sahara sandstorm. The lady had suffocated all alone, my father had told me, and yet she was on the edge of the village, just a few feet from her home.

"Oh, for God's sake, Emma. It's such a little thing to ask!"

I didn't have to see Captain Owen to know he was furious, and my stomach twisted up with sick fright. My parents sometimes had "small disagreements," but then they both turned politely and excruciatingly silent. That was the Swedish way, my father said.

"No, it's not. You want more. So much more. We both know it."

Mrs. Owen's words sounded like stones thrown one by one against a window. The hairs on the back of my neck prickled.

"I don't give a *damn* for those pompous idiots from Léopoldville. They can eat green goat meat at some filthy native restaurant in Coquilhatville for all I care, but you can't have my studio. It's all I've got to keep me sane in this hellish banana republic—and pretty soon it might not be enough. I can feel the misery and craziness in these walls. It's seeping into my bones like the heat. I feel it even in my sleep!"

"Don't be dramatic, Emma."

"Don't be patronizing, Allan," she snapped. "Because of this pregnancy I've given up everything. Everything from my job in the ballet corps to carrots. I'll be damned if I'm giving up my studio!"

Mrs. Owen had sworn twice in the last two minutes. I had never heard a lady say "damn" before, not even a tourist or a Peace Corps volunteer or an embassy wife. I drew away from the window and stared at Davina. She stared back, her brown eyes round behind her cat's-eye glasses. If we told our mothers about Mrs. Owen's swearing, we would never have another ballet lesson.

"Bullshit. You gave up everything because you knew you'd never be another Galina Ulanova, and you couldn't face it. You wanted an excuse to quit, so you hand-picked me to give you one. Maybe I'm patronizing, but you're a coward and a cheat. Don't ask me to give you credit for self-sacrifice."

My legs felt weak, my head light and hollow. I hoped I wasn't coming down with malaria. The screen door burst open and banged against the wall as Captain Owen shot out of the house. He was in such a hurry that he nearly knocked Davina over, but I didn't think he had seen us. He sprinted down the brick walkway, one hand gripping his attaché case and the other jamming the visor of his military cap down over his eyes. I stared dumbly at the screen door, watching it quiver and shudder. The wooden frame had stuck wide open, swollen with heat and humidity. I wondered if we should close it and go away, but it was too late. Mrs. Owen appeared in the doorway. She stared at us, her face stiff and frowning, her dark brows swooped together above her straight nose.

"How long have you girls been here?"

"We just came," I lied.

"I see." Her voice softened, and she took a deep, shaky breath. "Well, come on in. We'd better get started. We've got a lot of ground to cover today."

Toes out, Mrs. Owen walked over to the barre. I stared at her body in the tight black leotard with my usual embarrassed admiration—and something more. Curiosity. Her breasts looked the same as ever, two tiny high mounds above a narrow waist. Her hips still swelled only slightly above her long, muscular thighs. The difference I noticed was in her belly, a small outward curve. I knew how much Mrs. Owen liked making her body do exactly what she told it to. At the beginning of every lesson she'd say, "Ballet is about discipline, girls. About controlling all the parts of your body." I also knew how pregnant ladies looked, since missionaries and Congolese ladies had new babies all the time. What would Mrs. Owen do when that curve got bigger and her body wouldn't obey her anymore?

Mrs. Owen stood directly beneath a black-and-white poster of a male dancer lifting a ballerina high over his head. The dancer held the ballerina's crotch in his palm. I had seen photos like this one before—the *National Geographic* article had several—but I couldn't get used to them. I puzzled over those crotches and hands like a dog worrying over a bone. Wasn't it terribly, horribly embarrassing for a ballerina to have a man's hand right there in that exact spot? Had Mrs. Owen ever allowed a man to hold her this way? Did she like it or hate it? Was this somehow connected to Mrs. Owen losing control of her body parts?

We followed Mrs. Owen to the barre and waited for instructions. She didn't give any. She moved over to the window and stared out, her white fingers clenching the rough mahogany sill. Davina and I joined her, expecting to see some unusual activity on the river, but we were disappointed. There were no pirogues or steamboats on the water, no voices singing or calling greetings in Lingala and Lokundo, no fishermen announcing a catch. Clumps of lavender-blossomed water hyacinth drifted slowly downstream, bobbing gently beneath the hot sun. That was all.

"Aren't we going to have a lesson, Mrs. Owen?" I asked timidly.

The silence stretched long and deep as the river. Finally Mrs. Owen spoke, still facing the window. "Don't you wonder how you ended up here? Don't you wish you could be someplace—anyplace—else? Don't you feel your mind evaporating in this goddamn heat?"

She spun around and studied us like we were two of my father's tropical insect specimens waiting for tidy white labels and formaldehyde. Then she shrugged. It was the only careless sloppy movement I had ever seen her make. "No. Of course you don't. You're just like your mothers. How could you not be?" She turned her narrow back to us, stretched, and sighed. "Never mind. Let's get to work."

A furious lump swelled in my throat. Why shouldn't Davina and I be just like our mothers? I wondered. What was wrong with Boanda? And why was Mrs. Owen's voice so rude, her smile so strange?

We wouldn't take ballet lessons anymore, I decided. We wouldn't come back on Friday, and we wouldn't bother to explain why. Mrs. Owen (Didn't her very own husband call her a coward and a cheat?) could think whatever she liked.

Then again, maybe we would explain. Maybe we'd come by and announce we were quitting ballet lessons. "We like ladies who think it's nice to have company for dinner," we would say, giving Mrs. Owen a tropical-insect-specimen stare. "We like ladies who have dining-room tables and short home-permed curls and eat Swedish meatballs. We don't like ladies who have a horrid seeping in their bones and eat fancy American carrots. We like our mothers, and we don't like you."

Why wasn't Mama Malia peering in the window, rescuing us with her hissing laughter? Maybe she was finally bored with ballet and had taken Faith down to the water instead. Maybe she was dancing for Faith right this minute, singing, stamping, and clapping, glowing blue and green like the river at midday. I saw myself on the other side of Mrs. Owen's window with Mama Malia and Faith, my limbs jiggling and bouncing, laughter whistling between my teeth. "Your kind of dancing isn't the only kind, Mrs. Owen," I would shout. "Mama Malia is going to give me lessons from now on. I'm going to dance her way, all happy noise and bright river colors. My body parts are going to do whatever they like!"

"I am a coward." Mrs. Owen's voice sounded dull brown and overflowing, like the river on a sunless day in rainy season. Her heavy knot of hair had loosened, and several damp strands clung to the back of her neck. Sweat had soaked her leotard, leaving dark uneven blotches all over the black spandex that was too warm for the Congo. She gripped the barre with both hands and stretched in one long smooth motion, every lengthened muscle following her unspoken orders. I could feel that discipline Mr. Carlson valued so highly in the careful arc of her neck and torso, legs and toes. I admired the strength behind her taut arms and wrists, the tension in her white knuckles. And then I saw her face.

Tears squeezed from her closed lids, painful and shocking as blood. They trickled slowly down her cheeks even while she pressed her lips firmly together so she wouldn't make a sound. And as I watched, Mrs. Owen sniffed. It wasn't the discreet little sniff of a missionary lady. It was the kind of sniff Davina or I made when we felt upcountry lonely or downcountry strange and didn't have a hanky.

Wonderful Mrs. Owen, so cowardly and lost.

Strong Mrs. Owen, frail as any paper dancer in my scrapbook.

Beautiful Mrs. Owen, with her tiny breasts, flat hair, and dull skin.

I stared at my ballet teacher, at her lifeless expression and her pale closed eyelids. Her face, wet and smooth, seemed to float beneath a film of water. I had a blurred impression of river hyacinths tangled in her arched feet, her pointed toes.

Maybe next year I could learn Mama Malia's kind of dancing, but for now I would keep on taking ballet lessons. I would make sure Davina did too. We would both take ballet lessons from Emma Owen for as long as she was here, living carrotless in the crazy Clare house, where she could feel misery in the walls.

Sea of Iniquity

FINALLY there was just one sheet of gold construction paper left. I measured the sheet carefully, then cut it up in three-inch squares. I stacked all the gold squares in a tidy pile, the last of five piles neatly lined up on Mrs. Frykman's dining-room table. Each paper stack was a different color, and each was in proper order for the quick assembly of Protestant Five-Color Salvation Books.

Most Boanda missionary ladies used these books, but Mrs. Frykman was especially fond of them. ("Such a terrific child-evangelism tool. Something the Congolese children can keep, and so simple to make. One square from each stack, two staples on the left, and it's done!") I even knew Mrs. Frykman's explanation for each wordless page by heart—mostly because her Lingala was bad, and she liked to practice aloud while she did other things. "The black page comes first, children, because black is the color of the wicked human heart," she would say as she beat the spice-cake batter. "The red page is next, since red is the color of Jesus' blood, spilled for the sins of all the world. And this white page, children, represents the clean pure hearts of those who accept Jesus' sacrifice on their behalf and promise to forsake their evil ways." After color number three, she might stop beating to sample the batter with a teaspoon. "Now this green page stands for growth— growth in the sanctified Protestant Christian life. And the gold page is last, children, because gold is the color of the heavenly city where Protestant Christians will live forever with Jesus." And then she would pour the batter into a cake pan and stick it in the oven.

"This is very helpful, Grace," Mrs. Frykman said, coming in from the kitchen to peer over my shoulder. "Now I'm all set for my visit to the new Sunday School at Mobaya village. And you've had something to keep you busy. Working is much better than sitting around moping, isn't it?"

She backed away, smiling brightly and ruffling her pudgy fingers through dark newly-permed curls so tight and sepa- rate that her pale scalp shone between them. Her head looked like a checkerboard, I thought. Or maybe a patch- work quilt in black and white.

I said, "Yes, Mrs. Frykman."

"Good, good. Now how about running down to the market for me? I need fresh fruit, and there's no one else to send."

I said yes again. Both Mrs. Frykman's cook and gardener took vacation the last two weeks of December, so Mrs. Frykman was shorthanded. Besides, I liked Boanda's little market, and I had nothing better to do. Davina and her fam- ily had flown to Nairobi last week so Mr. Carlson could attend an education conference. Miss Adela and Miss Judith were away at the same conference—or at least Miss Judith was. Miss Adela had gone on safari to the Northern Frontier District, since Mr. Frykman had told her it was a rugged trip through desolate country and she was much too old for such shenanigans. ("No tarmac for hun- dreds of miles, not to mention that little border war with

Somalia," Mr. Frykman said gloomily. "And all Adela said was, 'I'm younger than Louis Leakey, and he still traipses around the Kenya backcountry. Anyway, this might be my last chance to see an oryx.'")

I went to my bedroom—pretty Carol Frykman's old pastel-pink bedroom, actually—to collect my shoes and a pair of ankle socks. When I returned, Mrs. Frykman handed me some coins and a white string shopping bag.

"Off with you now," she said. "And don't forget you absolutely may *not* go to your house. Not even the yard. You can wave from the road, Dr. Birgie said, but no closer."

I nodded yes. I was growing just as wordless as those Protestant Five-Color Salvation Books. Ever since Wednesday, when I'd arrived at the Coquilhatville airport and heard the news, my throat had been so tight that I could squeeze out only a few words at a time. Something painful had lodged halfway down it, something I wanted to cough up like Davina's cat, Lumumba, coughed up hairballs and lizards.

I took the river road and kicked the gravel with my faded blue Keds until red dust billowed up, blurring even the broad white-painted trunks of the royal palms. When I reached my own house, I crossed the yard to the Madagascar plum tree beside the dining-room window. I paced around and around the decorative orange bricks that circled the tree, hoping my mother would notice me. As long as she had time to look out the window, wave, and smile, I figured my father couldn't be too terribly sick.

But of course I knew he was.

Last night Dr. Birgie (whose full name was Birgitta Sabina Dagny Lundquist, only nobody used it much) had stopped by the Frykmans'. "No time to spare," she'd said, all brisk and disinfected, even her voice. So we had stood on the porch while she told us she was still waiting for Father

Antoine Girard of the Redemptorist Mission to bring word from the Centers for Disease Control in Atlanta, Georgia. "I used to think Father Antoine's passion for ham radio was a bit crazy," she'd said, "but now I'm grateful. He's calling a French doctor he knows in the Central African Republic who's calling another in Algiers and another in Tripoli. And up north they've got phone access to Europe, thank God!"

Mr. Frykman had said what a shame it was to have to rely on a Catholic priest, especially one of those fanatical Redemptorists who called us "the Accursed Boandan Prots," but Dr. Birgie had shrugged impatiently. "I'm too practical to care," she'd told him. "And speaking of practicalities, Elmer, would you please line up medical evac plans? If Robert doesn't start improving in the next two days, we've got to fly him out. Johannesburg is quicker, but Brussels is better. Plan for both." Dr. Birgie had jabbed at the ivory hairpins in her gray-blond bun. "I'm completely mystified. And I only hope this . . . this *thing* doesn't turn out to be infectious, because I'm getting worried about June. She's not a big hearty type like me."

I had walked away to stare up under the roofline, where two fruit bats squeaked and blinked, and to pretend this conversation was about strangers I would never meet.

"At least those blood samples I sent downcountry this morning should be on tonight's Léopoldville-Brussels flight, Lord willing."

Mr. and Mrs. Frykman had both echoed "Lord willing" as Dr. Birgie climbed back on her bicycle, switched on her single headlamp, and rattled back down the road in a moving pool of light. I had watched her heavy legs pumping fast and hard, her lab coat billowing behind her like a fat white ghost, and hadn't laughed.

"Thirty-eight . . . thirty-nine . . ." I paced the orange herringbone bricks around the Madagascar plum tree one more time. "Forty," I said and sagged against the tree trunk until my head quit spinning. Then I swung on the lower branches until they rattled, and still no one appeared at the dining-room window. There wasn't much more I could do except call or shout, and Dr. Birgie had absolutely forbidden noise—not that there was any, with both Mama Malia and Makua on paid leave and my little sister Faith staying in Coquilhatville with a Mennonite missionary family who had a girl her age. ("Safely out of the way for the duration," said Mrs. Frykman. Mr. Frykman had replied, "This isn't the *War*, for pity's sake!")

I abandoned my forbidden yard and headed down the road. Boanda's market wasn't much if you compared it to Coquilhatville's, which covered several city blocks and had a dozen expensive stores run by North African men in loose white robes and turbans. Except for one small shop made of tin roofing, Boanda's market was just a bunch of ladies squatting on the hard-packed ground behind shallow enamel tubs of squirming eels, orange palm wine, and tiny dried fish with staring eyes. But you could take your time looking at things—maybe dare yourself to buy roasted grasshoppers or fried ants—and no one shoved you out of the way or picked your pocket.

Nothing caught my eye today. I bought as many tangerines and grapefruit as my money would buy, which wasn't a lot, because I had never learned to haggle properly. Then I wandered over to the tin shop beneath the jacaranda tree at the far end of the market, hoping to find something interesting. Tinned beans from China, maybe, or Roget et Gallet sandalwood soap from France.

"*Mbote*, Mademoiselle. *Ojali?*" The shopkeeper's face was round as the grapefruit in my bag, and thick beads of sweat peppered his nose like transparent freckles.

Since he'd called me "Mademoiselle" even though I was

just ten and not really a young lady, I decided I liked him. "*Malamu mingi te,*" I said. "Not well at all. My father is very sick."

"Oh, so the teacher of soybean planting is your *tata?*" He shook his head gravely. "I have met him. A nice man for a *missionaire.* He should have stayed away from those inland swamps. They are full of strange fevers that are *mabe mpenza*—even for us Congolese. What was he doing back in there anyway?"

I didn't want to admit my father had made a special pirogue trip deep into the murky green swamp country just to look for butterflies. Even rare butterflies. The shopkeeper would get that "*mindele*-are-crazy" expression, and I would know he was laughing even while he looked perfectly serious and said kind things. Some Congolese already thought my father was funny about his Rhode Island Reds and soybeans, and I knew butterflies were worse. I remembered the first time Makua saw my father tiptoeing after a butterfly and making delicate swoops with his white net. Makua laughed so hard he cried.

"Wild pig," I said. "My father was hunting wild pig. With his .375 Winchester."

"Ah." The shopkeeper nodded, impressed. "But it is still too bad. There are better places to hunt wild pig. Places without so many dangers."

I said yes and looked away, studying his merchandise. The counter was a confusion of Vaseline jars, plastic hand mirrors, tins of Spam and Ovaltine, and green rolls of English Trebor Mints, Extra Strong. The shop walls were lined with rickety shelves bearing liter jugs of kerosene, blue-speckled enamel dishes, and tall narrow bottles of red grenadine syrup. A triangular tower of tinned milk rose to the low ceiling, and sacks of flour were stacked against one wall. Square black letters spelled "United States Government Surplus—

Not For Resale" on both the milk tins and flour sacks. A pile of blue Chicago Cubs baseball caps reminded me of my father's green DeKalb Seed Corn cap, and the hairball in my throat grew bigger.

"*Nkombo na ngai* Jokamba," the shopkeeper said, holding his hand out over the jumbled counter.

"*Nkombo na ngai* Grace," I replied.

As I shook his hand, I noticed the elephant-hair bracelet on his wrist. Two oddly-shaped wooden beads and an animal tooth (leopard?) dangled from it. Although I had never seen such a bracelet up close before, I suspected what it was and knew it by many names. According to Mama Malia and Makua, it was "a very special *kisi*." According to my father, it was "sad evidence of the enduring power of witchcraft." But it was Mrs. Frykman's name that sent horrified shivers down my spine: "Pagan jewelry for the Prince of Darkness."

I had to know for certain. "Your—your bracelet, Jokamba," I began hesitantly. "It is beautiful, I think, only—"

A sudden wandering ray of sunlight illuminated the rack of used clothing behind Jokamba's head. I wouldn't have let my mouth drop open—lots of market shops had used clothing—but I found myself staring at Miss Adela's favorite housedress, the green paisley one with maroon piping. Beside it was the aqua nylon shell with the back zipper that had disappeared from Mrs. Nordstrom's clothesline last summer. The pale pink blouse with embroidered daisies surely belonged to Mrs. Carlson, and hadn't I seen my very own sister wear that red-striped Buster Brown T-shirt?

Bright orange suns floated behind my eyelids as Jokamba's grapefruit face slipped out of focus. My feet stayed coldly rooted to the ground while my head lightened, lifting upward. All the market noise of cackling chickens and laughing women and crying babies faded away. Then I heard

Jokamba saying "Mademoiselle? Mademoiselle?" and I was back to normal—except that my forehead was sweating and my bag of fruit very heavy.

"Do you have the swamp fever too, Mademoiselle?" Jokamba's hand was on my arm. It was the hand with the elephant-hair bracelet, and the brownish tooth and wooden beads lightly brushed my skin. There was a kindness in his voice that I didn't expect from a thief—or a *fetichiste*.

"Special witch-doctor *kisi, boye te?*" I asked, keeping my eyes lowered on his bracelet.

Jokamba jerked back his hand and plunged it in his pocket. "Very special, yes," he said with an embarrassed frown. "But fetishes are not talked about with *mindele*, Mademoiselle Grace."

I nodded coolly, feigning indifference.

"*Mindele* find fetishes too *sauvage*," Jokamba explained, his hand still hidden. "And I myself am not really a *fetichiste*, you must understand. I just need more protection from evil than most people. I was a twin, but my brother died—and my mother died as well."

My arm began to tingle where Jokamba's fetish had touched me. I suddenly wanted to escape this shop of stolen goods, this person of pagan wickedness and dead family. I said, "Yes, yes, I understand," in a panicky voice and took to my heels, the bulging bag of fruit bouncing against my knees. It wasn't until I passed my own home, off-limits and strangely quiet, that I admitted to a real sympathy with Jokamba. I thought I might need more protection from evil than most people too.

Mrs. Frykman was listening to the Léopoldville news, but she turned the volume down when I walked in the door.

"Of all the ridiculous things!" she exclaimed. "President Mobutu is changing the names of Congo's biggest cities. 'Africanization,' he calls it. *Authenticité!* Léopoldville is going to be 'Kinshasa,' and rumor has it Stanleyville will be renamed 'Kisangani.'"

"What about us?" I asked.

"Coquilhatville is probably going to be called 'Mbandaka,' but it isn't settled."

Mbandaka. What an ugly flat word. Why did President Mobutu want to get rid of Coquilhatville anyway? Didn't he know names meant something, that you couldn't just change them?

"We'd better get at the housework," Mrs. Frykman said, snapping off the radio. "We're having an emergency mission prayer meeting here this evening."

I'd never attended an emergency mission prayer meeting—they were serious, for adults only—but I remembered they had held one last summer for Miss Renquist, who taught English at the Protestant Secondary School. She was sick with malaria and pneumonia combined, but the day after the prayer meeting she began to get better, and two weeks later she was perfectly well. The tightness in my throat eased ever so slightly, and I asked who the meeting was for, just to hear Mrs. Frykman say it.

"Why, for your father, of course." She handed me a dust-cloth. "The Apostle Paul said we should persevere in prayer, our mightiest weapon against Satan and the darkness of this world. And remember, too, that Jesus said, 'Ask anything in my name, and it shall be done.' So we'll do both tonight. All of us."

We dusted and swept, sprayed ant spray, and put out fresh cockroach poison. Afterwards Mrs. Frykman asked if I would help her sort and pack all the things Carol had left behind when she went to America to attend Moody Bible

Institute in Chicago. It needed to be done right away, she said. Carol had been gone for three years already, and I wondered why the sudden hurry. I was staying in Carol's room, and I honestly didn't mind having all her leftover things around. Not even the heat-ruined bottles of Avon liquid makeup and Chantilly cologne or the torn Sabena travel poster with pictures of the 1958 Brussels World's Fair.

"I should have done this ages ago," Mrs. Frykman said, handing me a stack of beautifully kept clothing from the bottom drawer. "But I always thought she'd be back sometime and want to do it herself. And now she's getting married."

This was news. "She *is?*"

"Yes." Mrs. Frykman looked sternly cheerful as she emptied a drawer filled with old exams and notebooks into a wastebasket. "In June."

"What's his name?" I asked. "The man she's marrying."

"John O'Brien." She punched down hard on the papers so she could fit more into the wastebasket.

"I never heard of anyone named O'Brien before," I said.

"He's a Chicago Irishman," Mrs. Frykman replied. "A Catholic."

A Catholic. Sweet, lovely, good Carol Frykman was going to marry a Catholic. I sank down on the pink vanity stool with Carol's ratty old teddy bear and watched Mrs. Frykman start in on Carol's well-filled closet, energetically sweeping lace-trimmed dresses from their hangers and dumping them in a pastel pile on the bed. There was a hurt look around her eyes that I'd noticed only once before, when the Congolese ladies at church patted her fleshy arms and complimented her on being a woman of such amazing *mafuta,* such great fatness.

After a minute Mrs. Frykman poked me in the ribs with an empty clothes hanger. She looked so terribly bright and jolly that I knew she was sorry she had told me. "Now, now, back to work!" she said. "It's much better than lying around moping."

"We pray, O Lord, for Robert and June in this time of illness and anxiety. We know that even the falling sparrow is worth Your notice, Your compassion. And so we entreat Your divine mercy on Robert, who is worth so much more." Mr. Frykman paused to clear his throat. "We remember Your promise that whatever we ask in Your name shall be done, and we believe in Your healing power."

Mr. Frykman leaned forward in the squeaky cane rocker and began to remind the Lord very firmly of all His miracles, particularly dwelling on the raising of Lazarus, the raising of Jairus' daughter, and the healing of the Roman centurion's servant. I sat in the corner on Mrs. Frykman's embroidered ottoman and worried about Mr. Frykman's choice of miracle ex-amples. All these people were dead or drastically ill. Why didn't he mention any of the folks who were just lame or blind?

Finally Mr. Frykman finished his prayer, and it was Mrs. Frykman's turn. "We struggle with You, O God, like Jacob of old, for the life of our brother Robert. But we wage war through prayer, not the physical weapons of this world. We pray that evil and death will not have the dominion, that Robert will be spared to continue Your work as a witness against Satan in this sinful and superstitious land."

The Frykman living room was crowded—all Boanda's missionaries were here tonight—and a squeezing ache began to build in my chest. The ache grew worse as Mrs. Frykman prayed fiercely on, telling God He should think of my father as His battleground against the spiritual forces of the Evil One. Why wasn't it enough for God that my father was sick, I wondered? Couldn't God heal my father just because He *liked* him?

Mrs. Frykman concluded with a verse from Ephesians about the Apostle Paul wrestling against principalities, against powers, against the rulers of the darkness of this world. I thought my chest ache was as dreadful as it could get, but then Mrs. Palmquist, whose husband died of sunstroke thirty years ago and was buried in the Boanda cemetery, began to pray. She sniffed and wiped her eyes while she told God that our times were in His hands and we were reconciled to His divine will. I slid off the embroidered ottoman, tiptoed through the kitchen, and crept out the back door.

After the lamp-bright living room, the darkness was as solid and overwhelmingly black as the first page of a Protestant Five-Color Salvation Book. I stood very still on the brick veranda until the blackness lifted and I could make out the steep back steps, the square outline of the cookhouse, and the dark bulk of Mr. Frykman's green Terrot motorcycle parked next to the hibiscus bush. I sat down on the bottom step, curled my toes in the cold dewy grass, and watched the faint glow of the rising moon through the breadfruit trees.

Breadfruit. My father's favorite food. ("*Artocarpus incisa*, technically speaking, but I call it 'Manna from Heaven' myself.") My father liked to roast a whole breadfruit in a campfire until the thick green skin was nothing but flaky ash. Then he'd crack it open, cover the steaming white flesh with butter and salt, and eat it with his fingers. "Junie," he'd say, his eyes closed and butter dripping from his chin, "even if all my Rhode Island Reds die of sleeping sickness, even if soybean farming never catches on, we're going to stay here forever. I'd die of breadfruit deficiency anywhere else."

I wrapped my arms around my cold knees and prayed he wouldn't die of a strange swamp fever first, but my own prayer discouraged me. I didn't sound nearly so accomplished and authoritative as Mr. Frykman, with his miracle list and deep evangelist voice. Besides, those two fruit bats squeaking under the eaves ruined my concentration. Not that I was afraid of them—I'd heard my father's Official Bat Lecture many times, how disease-carrying insects would overwhelm the world if it weren't for bats. "They're valuable animals," he'd say. "Just be smart enough to leave them alone." I only hoped the bats had left my father a few good butterflies, and that he had found them before he came down with the terrible swamp fever.

Back in the living room, quavery-voiced Mrs. Palmquist started singing a Swedish hymn, *"Tryggare kan ingen vara,"* and pretty soon everyone joined in. I listened from my chilly step, alarmed. What if they didn't quit before they got to verse six? It wasn't practical of them to sing "Though He giveth or He taketh, God His own He ne'er forsaketh." God might misunderstand and think "taketh" was as good an option as "giveth."

And just as I was wishing I could do something for my father besides worry about the missionary adults and their prayers and hymns, I had an idea. An idea I instantly determined to carry out. No missionary could do it better—no missionary could do it at *all*—but I had sources. And even while gooseflesh prickled my skin, I allowed myself no second thoughts. My father was ill, and Mrs. Frykman was right about the evil powers abroad in our sinful world: this was war, and it must be waged on every spiritual front.

The moon surged above the breadfruit trees with only a slight flatness on one white-gold side. Tomorrow night it would be completely full. I stared at the moon and wondered if that dark irregular shadow expanded and shrank with the moon's waxing and waning. The moon shadow had a name. From half attending to yet another of my father's one-minute science lectures, I knew what it was: the Sea of Iniquity.

Mrs. Frykman left right after breakfast for Coquilhatville. She wanted to get supplies for making more Protestant Five-Color Salvation Books to give away to the Congolese children.

"I've decided I need to keep about fifty in the glove compartment of the Ford at all times!" she told me. "Ten more stashed in my handbag, I think. And maybe fifteen or twenty in my bicycle bags."

I waited until I couldn't hear the Ford anymore, then left the house carrying a bulky cotton flour sack that I'd packed late the night before and hidden under my bed. The sack was heavy enough that I had to stop and rest every so often, but I passed my own home quickly; I wanted to do more for my father than wave, and I wanted my efforts to go unnoticed, unquestioned.

I found Jokamba sitting cross-legged on a cleared spot on his shop counter. He was listening to his transistor radio and singing along with a Lingala advertisement for Omo dish detergent.

"Omo-o-o-o-o! *Ejali malamu mingi* o-o-oh!" he sang, twisting his torso and drumming his fingers on the flimsy tin wall of his shop.

"*Mbote*," I said.

"It's the little Mademoiselle Grace!" he cried, slapping his leg. "*Mbote mingi!* Have you heard the news about the new names? Today I heard Elisabethville is now Lubumbashi, and Lake Léopold II might be changed to Lake Mai-Ndombe."

"I don't mind about those," I said. "But Mbandaka is a very ugly name compared to Coquilhatville."

Jokamba grinned, his wide face growing even wider.

"Mama na ngai!" he exclaimed. "Only a child, but already a *mondele,* a white! African *authenticité* finds no favor with you! You should understand that names tell important truths."

"I *do,* and Coquilhatville is beautiful," I protested.

"To your ears, perhaps, but my Congolese ears find Mbandaka both truer and more beautiful," Jokamba said. "Ah well. What can I do for you today?"

I heaved the cotton flour bag up on the counter and pushed it toward him. My fingers were trembling all of a sudden, my palms wet. I put my hands behind my back and drew a deep breath.

"Yesterday I noticed you sell clothes," I said, striving for my mother's cool haggling voice. "And yesterday I think you did good business. Madame Nordstrom's *elamba* is gone, I see, and so is Mademoiselle Adela's dress."

Jokamba switched off his transistor radio without saying a word.

"I have brought you more clothes to sell," I went on. "Lots of them. Dresses, blouses, and skirts. Even shoes."

The pupils of Jokamba's eyes were small cold dots. He didn't touch the bag.

"I don't need money for them," I added quickly. "I need a fetish. A really good fetish to protect my father."

Jokamba sat perfectly still for a moment, then slowly straightened his legs and slid off the counter. He reached into a wooden crate and pulled out a bottle of Coca-Cola. After he'd pried off the cap with his teeth, he put the bottle in my hand. It was warm, but I didn't mind. I didn't have Coca-Cola very often.

"A fetish for a *missionaire,*" he said softly.

I decided I had better try to explain.

"You see, there are more dangers and evils than I realized," I said and suddenly thought of Davina, whose Air Congo flight might very well crash in the jungled Ruwenzori Mountains of East Congo on her way home from Nairobi. Planes lost in the Ruwenzoris were seldom found. I thought of Miss Adela too. She was probably driving a rented Land Rover to the arid north of Kenya this very minute, her corset and flowered housedress her only protection from Somali snipers and ivory poachers. And what about my mother? What if my father's swamp fever turned out to be infectious, and she caught it? Dr. Birgie said my mother wasn't the hearty robust type.

"You must get me a fetish strong enough to take care of my friends as well," I told him. "And my mother. I want everyone to be safe."

Jokamba muttered something in Lokundo—or maybe Mongo. I couldn't tell.

"Oyoki ngai?" I asked.

"Yes, I heard. But I warn you this will be a very *very* expensive fetish!"

"But these are very *very* nice clothes," I said, upending the bag on the counter.

Mrs. Frykman had sewn Carol's clothes from high quality fabrics and trimmings ordered from Belgium, and size five Junior Miss patterns ordered from an American dry-goods catalog. They were lovely—perhaps a little too lovely, according to my mother. ("I'm afraid the Congolese see all that Swiss embroidery and Brussels lace and get the wrong idea about missionary salaries. But I understand the temptation. An only child, and such a pretty girl.") Carol's clothes were very little worn, maybe because she had so many. Jokamba's eyes widened as he touched the *broderie anglaise* insets on a white blouse that looked brand new.

"I need that fetish soon," I said. "I'll come back for it tomorrow morning."

Jokamba glanced quickly around the market, as if making certain no missionaries were watching from behind a palm or jacaranda tree, but he and I both knew it was unlikely. Missionary ladies didn't visit the Boanda market; they sent their Congolese help or else drove to the big one in Coquilhatville.

"*Early* tomorrow morning," I amended.

Jokamba swept all the clothing back into the bag and set it on the dirt floor behind the counter. Then he stared at me, his round face suddenly all hard edges and sharp angles.

"Finish that Coca-Cola and give me the bottle," he snapped. "I pay a deposit on those."

As I drained the last drops of Coca-Cola, strange and horrible scenes flashed into my mind: Davina still buckled into her moss-covered Air Congo seat, vines and papaya trees growing out the broken windows. Miss Adela slumped over the wheel of the Land Rover, still holding her binoculars while blood pumped from her chest. And my father, my own father, overcome by the evils of swamp country, floating facedown in thick black water while ugly wet reptiles chewed first on his DeKalb Seed Corn cap, and then—

"Get me that fetish right now!" I commanded, thumping the empty Coca-Cola bottle down on the counter. "I'll wait. Tomorrow is *mpamba*, no good at all."

I knew I sounded exactly like Mrs. Palmquist, who summoned her cook with a miniature Swiss cowbell she carried in her skirt pocket. Mrs. Palmquist alternated between barking orders and talking very patiently and sweetly, as if to a small child, a child younger and far more stupid than my six-year-old sister Faith. ("Old school," my mother called her, but my father snorted, "Old harridan, if you ask me. I had a drill sergeant just like her at boot camp.")

Jokamba silently emptied the cash box into his pocket and began closing the shop windows. He didn't look at me, but I could see the alarming straightness of his spine and the rigidity of his neck. "Go outside," he ordered over his shoulder.

I obeyed, but I didn't go far. I hovered beside the door until Jokamba came out. He gave the door a good hard slam and padlocked it. Then he buckled on his plastic sandals, leaning against the door for balance, and told me he would be back as soon as possible.

"Wait right here," he said curtly and turned away before I could nod agreement.

I watched him disappear down the kudzu-choked path to the village. As soon as he was out of sight, I began waiting for him to reappear. (And surely he will, I told myself. He has to—doesn't he?) I watched and waited, waited and watched, my knees locking up with a painful tightness and my eyes squinting in the bright sun. My scalp grew hot and my T-shirt damp, but I didn't think of sitting down in the shade of the jacaranda, or even leaning against the tin-shop wall. I just stared at the trampled red earth and bold green kudzu until at last—at long last—he was coming, walking fast, his right hand swinging free but his left curled into a fist.

"Your fetish," Jokamba said, opening his fingers and dropping something into my outstretched hand.

It was a piece of light, weathered wood. Everyday wood, the same kind I saw scattering the soggy banks of the river or dried and tied in bundles for firewood. It was soft, porous, and gray, and there was a hole bored through the center. I liked the feel of it in my hand: smooth as soap when all the sharp new edges are water-worn and wash-cloth-rubbed away. I decided to hang it on a string around my neck. Under my shirt, of course, where no one could possibly see it.

"I think I will not tell you how I got this so quickly," he said, jamming his hands in his pockets. "But this fetish is a good one. Powerful *kisi*, medicine, against the evils of the world."

Now that I'd won, I wanted to make Jokamba happy with me again. I said *merci mingi* and smiled gratefully, as if he had made the fetish a voluntary gift, as if neither of us knew the wickedness of the other.

Jokamba did not smile back. "I must say one thing," he said, "especially since this is the very first week of President Mobutu's program for African *authenticité*. It is not well done of you to grab our Congolese *kisi*, Mademoiselle Grace. Not when you already have so much powerful white-people *kisi* of your own."

I nodded miserably, clutching my fetish, desperate to escape before I found myself offering to return it. Once I was away from the market, I would be glad I had kept it, glad I hadn't contented myself with missionary *kisi*. And perhaps it was already taking effect. Perhaps my father was sitting up in bed this very moment, irritable and fever free, asking for something to eat. My father wouldn't behave nearly so well as Lazarus or the Roman centurion's servant after they were healed. "Junie, I'm *hungry!*" he would bellow. "And I won't eat any of that sloppy milk-toast stuff, you hear? I want *real* food!" I backed away from Jokamba, half silly with eagerness, dreaming of my father's cranky convalescent roar.

"Thank you," I repeated. "I'll never bother you again. Truly."

I turned and ran the one-kilometer length of the palm lane, ran so fast that the palms and the river blurred together, green flowing into blue, the smooth gray fetish tucked securely in my white fist.

Dr. Birgie beamed, waving her fork in the air and spilling mango pie filling on the tablecloth, undismayed by Mrs. Frykman's pained frown.

"No question about it!" she said. "Robert's on the mend. His fever is gone. His pulse is stronger. Even that rash is beginning to fade."

"Thank God!" Mr. Frykman said.

"Prayer wins mighty battles," Mrs. Frykman said, then turned to me. "Well, Grace, what do you say? Aren't you happy?"

I nodded, keeping my eyes on my plate and pretending to be occupied with my dessert. My head seemed to run fluid and hot with relief. Any moment my eyes and nose would begin streaming.

"Of course she's happy," Dr. Birgie said matter-of-factly, taking a last swallow of coffee and pushing back her chair. "Lovely pie, but I must run."

Dr. Birgie trotted out to her bicycle, the rest of us trailing after her. She parked her black medical kit in the wicker basket attached to the handlebars, sat down on the worn vinyl seat, and gazed up at the sky.

"Just look at that moon!" she exclaimed. "I don't even need my headlamp tonight."

She pedaled away, kicking up a dark spray of gravel.

"Well, well, well," Mr. Frykman said. "There's nothing quite so wonderful as answered prayer."

I fumbled under my shirt for my fetish and stroked its soft worn edges.

"I bought up every last sheet of colored construction paper in Coquil—Oops!—Mbandaka today," Mrs. Frykman announced. "Enough for another four hundred Protestant Five-Color Salvation Books. I'm going to start on them right away. I think I'll store a few dozen in the pantry, and the rest in Carol's room, now that Grace has helped me pack Carol's things away."

"Four hundred! Why so many?" Mr. Frykman asked.

"I want to build up a big reserve," she said. "To save these people from sin and superstition."

She went inside, leaving Mr. Frykman and me to stare at the moon balanced delicately on the topmost branches of the tallest breadfruit tree.

"It was very nice of you to help Mrs. Frykman pack away Carol's things," Mr. Frykman said. "We've enjoyed having you with us, Grace. Enjoyed it a lot, even under the anxious circumstances."

Mr. Frykman's voice was earnest and kind, his "altar call" voice, the voice responsible for my eleventh revival-service conversion. I leaned against the cookhouse wall, studying the Sea of Iniquity with extraordinary care. The sprawling darkness took up more pale gold moon space than usual tonight, I was certain.

"I'm sorry about all those boxes cluttering up your room," he went on. "I'll haul them up to the attic first thing in the morning."

I wondered if they would ever realize I had taken several pieces of clothing from each box. I thought not. "That's okay," I muttered.

Tiny spots scattered the broad shadowy sea like pock-marks leftover from a disease. I had never noticed those spots before. Perhaps they were brand-new.

"Why, Grace, look how distinct the Sea of Tranquility is! Because the moon's so bright, I suppose—but your father would know a more scientific explanation." Mr. Frykman gave my shoulder a cautious pat. "And soon you can ask him."

He walked back to the house. I stayed where I was, drenched in guilt and moonlight. Mr. Frykman might know a different name—even a surprisingly reassuring one—but I didn't fool myself. How could I accept such handy comfort when the name I knew told an important truth?

I huddled against the rough concrete wall and watched the dark Sea of Iniquity press beyond its normal boundaries, expanding into uncorrupted territory, spreading dangers and evils in every direction.

Blaspheming the Holy Spirit

"I'M BIKING OUT to Esengo," I said.

My father looked up from his new Burpee seed catalog fresh off the steamboat from Kinshasa. "Are you biting your nails again, Grace? Please don't."

I glanced down. The skin around my thumbnail was ragged and bleeding, but I didn't remember chewing on it. I stuck my thumbtip in my mouth and sucked the blood away. My father marked his place in the tomato-seed section, closed the catalog, and volunteered to put some air in my bike tires. "I thought they looked a bit low when you got back yesterday," he said.

We went out to the cookhouse where I stored my bike at night and examined the tires. They were perfectly fine, but my father couldn't resist adding some air as well as giving me his lecture on compression. Although I'd heard about the Beautiful Simplicity of the Bicycle Pump any number of times, I knew better than to try to speed him up. I shifted my feet impatiently and pretended to listen. Finally he was finished, and I clambered over the bar of my old black Raleigh. Even then I couldn't leave, because my father held onto my back tire, his forehead puckered up as if he were grading an extra-bad set of plant pathology exams.

"Your mother and I think it's pretty generous of you to spend so much of your summer vacation helping Dr. Birgie," he said. "Just make sure you have enough time for fun. Ten-year-olds ought to have fun."

He gave me a push like he used to do when I was little and just learning. I waved at him. He waved back, smiling, and I turned north on the corduroy road to Esengo.

I had never been to Esengo before this vacation. If I had not committed the unforgivable sin, I wouldn't be going there today. But I had committed it, and my whole life was different. More than different: my whole life was *ruined*, both now and forever. In the *now*, a fun summer vacation was out of the question because I didn't deserve fun of any kind. In the *forever*, I was condemned to the Lake of Fire, and the rest of my earthly life was just a matter of marking time until I got there.

Three months ago I hadn't known the unforgivable sin existed. I'd only known about the ordinary kind, the kind God forgave if you repented, although my boarding-school dorm father often reminded us that we took unfair advantage if we sinned too frequently. ("Remember the words of the Apostle Paul in the sixth chapter of Romans," Mr. Lindstrom would say. "'Shall we sin that grace may abound? Heaven forbid!'") But then on the first Sunday in May, the pastor of the local Congolese church had preached a seventy-minute Lingala sermon on the unforgivable sin— a terrifying sermon that left me hollow bellied and weak in the knees, like I had dysentery. And the very next day Mr. Lindstrom expounded on it during boarding-school evening devotions. Pastor Malako Mokili and Mr. Lindstrom had used the same Gospel text, Matthew 12:31–32: "Blasphemy against the Spirit will not be forgiven," Jesus said. "Anyone who speaks against the Holy Spirit will not be forgiven, either in this age or in the age to come."

These words of Jesus had echoed in my brain, a weighty, horrifying formula for everlasting damnation. An invitation—no, a passport—to Hell. Why had Jesus invented something so fatally wicked, I wondered? And why did He have to tell us about it? Didn't He realize the very awfulness of it would tempt us to think about it? I tried to resist, tried *hard*, but dire and dizzy thoughts of blasphemy teased my mind constantly. I thought about it during math class and choir practice, after-school games with Carrie and evening prayers. I even dreamed about trying not to think about it. So when I lost my special wooden fetish in a recess soccer match the following Friday, the dreadful formula sprang immediately into my head. I couldn't resist trying it out mentally, silently, in proper Bible English: *Holy Spirit, I hereby blaspheme You.* Only afterwards did I remember that thinking a sinful thought was just as bad as actually doing a sinful deed— Jesus had said that too—and my heart iced over with terror. I was eternally damned. I had committed the unforgivable sin.

What was worse, I kept committing it over and over again. Once I'd started, I couldn't seem to stop. Within a week of my initial blasphemy, I had several versions of it repeating endlessly in my mind: *Holy Spirit, I hereby blaspheme You* and *I, Grace Linnea Berggren, curse You, Holy Spirit.* Even *Curses upon You, O Holy Spirit.* Within a month, these ruinous phrases seemed more natural to my ear and instinctive to my heart than the familiar formula for salvation. More powerful as well, because any one of my blasphemies was enough to cancel out all twelve of my conversions over the past five years. And the shame of being a Holy-Spirit Blasphemer was so terrible that I could tell no one—not Carrie in the Ubangi, not Davina at Boanda.

My front tire hit a rock, jarring the bike so that I almost crashed into the roadside bamboo. I worried I might have a puncture. The tire would be ruined if I kept on riding with a puncture, but if I walked the bike all the way to Esengo, I would be late. Dr. Birgie would think I wasn't coming. Why hadn't God protected me from that rock? I had given up all my summer swimming time in order to help out at Esengo. I had given up all my play time with Davina, all my visiting time with Alain, Miss Adela, and Miss Judith. I was being useful instead of having fun. Couldn't God have taken just a little trouble, even if I was hopelessly hell-bound?

Yes, I decided. Yes, He could!—And there it was, yet another occasion to curse the Holy Spirit in spite of my good intentions. "I, Grace Linnea Berggren, curse You, Holy Spirit." I pounded the handlebar with my fist. "I blaspheme You!"

Sweat slimed my hands, and my mouth dried up like I'd stumbled on a nest of cobras in the woodpile. Was there any way to undo even a tiny portion of the damage? True atonement was impossible, that I knew, but God might feel some small mercy if He heard me recite a verse of Psalm 51, the Repentance Psalm. And I might feel scoured clean, the way I did when I said "gosh" or "darn" and my mother washed my mouth out with soap. Fatty, foul-tasting Congolese soap always convinced me I'd properly paid up for my sins.

"Have mercy upon me, O God, after Thy great goodness," I said fervently. "According to the multitudes of Thy mercies, do away mine offenses."

"*Mbote*, Mademoiselle Grace," Fiakona called.

I slammed on the hand brake, surprised to find I had arrived so quickly. Fiakona was sitting cross-legged in the sparse shade of the flamboyant tree marking the entrance to Esengo. The flamboyant tree was in bloom, tiny red-orange flowers spattering Fiakona's woven grass mat. I got off my bike, walked over to him, and shook his bandaged hand carefully, striving for just the right amount of pressure. If I squeezed too hard, I might damage what was left of Fiakona's stumpy fingers. If I squeezed too lightly, too gingerly, he might think I was afraid of shaking hands with a leper. ("Leprosy isn't half so catching as people used to think," Dr. Birgie had told me. "You need close and prolonged contact to get it.") So I tried to shake Fiakona's hand up near his wrist where the skin was still healthy and I could shake firmly.

"*Sango nini?*" I asked.

"Oh, Luta's baby is cutting a new tooth with much unhappiness."

I nodded. Luta's baby had the cutest little white teeth I had ever seen, but not very many of them. Dr. Birgie said she really ought to have more by now.

"Otherwise *sango ejali te.*" Fiakona wiped sweat from his balding head with a scrap of cloth held awkwardly between his swollen knuckles. "There is no news. Just Esengo."

"*Malamu,*" I said and walked my bike into the village center.

Esengo was a leper colony. Sister Fatima, a Belgian Catholic nurse, founded it just before the Second World War—or the Second German War, as Miss Adela sometimes called it. Sister Fatima and her staff left in 1960, when the Congo became independent of Belgium. They never returned, so Dr. Birgie finally took charge of it. My mother said she didn't know how Dr. Birgie managed to give so much time to Esengo when she already had heavy responsibilities with the mission's public health program. My father said she managed by having endless willpower, a genuine fascination with the disease, and no personal life whatsoever. "You notice she doesn't even take Sundays off, most of the time," he said. "I don't remember the last time I saw her in church!"

From Esengo, there was no view of the river. The leper colony hid out in the swamp country like a wounded animal seeking shelter, the nearest village at least five kilometers away. Esengo was crudely carved right out of deep jungle, an extra-shabby village hemmed in by enormous vine-strung trees that shut out both sunrise and sunset. Many of the two dozen smoke-blackened huts needed repair, and the untidy plots of corn and manioc were very small. The village center was a windowless two-room clinic, a square concrete-block building with a front veranda where Dr. Birgie held clinic hours. She was there now, her white lab coat hanging down to her brown Hush Puppies, surrounded by a crowd of people waiting to be seen. I counted thirteen of them, mostly men. They all sat patiently on their little wooden stools except for one old man in a grimy loincloth. He lay flat on the hard ground, toeless feet together and fingerless hands at his sides. A large banana leaf protected his face from the sun and muffled his tuneless singing.

"Oh Grace, child, bless you!" Dr. Birgie cried as I leaned my bike against the wild coffee bush and hurried up the veranda steps. "You're just in time. Can you get the spare bandage rolls out of my knapsack? The extra-wide ones?"

A faint sickly-sweet odor hung in the air. When I first came to Esengo I asked Dr. Birgie what it was, and she said, "Gangrenous flesh." I didn't notice it much anymore.

"How many rolls do you want?" I asked.

"Two for now. The others go in the storeroom when you get a chance."

I always liked rummaging in Dr. Birgie's knapsack. I didn't know her very well—perhaps nobody did—so I never knew what might be in there besides medical supplies. Old issues of the *New England Journal of Medicine*, of course, but also extra-strong Swedish licorice in blue-green boxes, bird-watching books, daggerlike Congolese ivory hairpins, photos of her cocker spaniel, Älskling (Swedish for "darling," Dr. Birgie said), and a rare feather from a lilac-breasted roller, which Dr. Birgie had found and saved.

I put two bandage rolls on the table beside Dr. Birgie and took the rest to the clinic storeroom. As I felt about in the stuffy darkness for the shelves, I stumbled and knocked my forehead against the wall.

"Curses upon You, O Holy Spirit. Lots and lots of curses."

Then as quickly as I could, I started gabbling Psalm 51. "Wash me thoroughly from my wickedness, and cleanse me from my sin. For I acknowledge my faults, and my sin is ever before me."

"Are you okay in there?" Dr. Birgie's large shadowy frame filled the doorway. I could just make out a small shape in her arms, a little head bobbing above her shoulder.

"Yes, I'm fine."

"I need to rebandage Luta's feet. Can you take Esengo?"

Esengo was Luta's baby girl, named for the leper colony. Her soft springy hair was fixed in tiny cornrows, and she wore a special fetish necklace to protect her from leprosy. (All her fetishes were much fancier than the worn gray one I had lost, but I wasn't jealous; I was beyond the help of any fetish now.) Esengo had soft brown-gold skin, round bright eyes like a lemur, and clutching, clinging arms. If Luta couldn't hold her, someone else had to, or Esengo would deafen the whole village with her screams and howls. Not that anybody minded having to cuddle her. Esengo was the only baby around.

"Sure," I said.

I followed Dr. Birgie back outside, and she handed Esengo to me. I parked her on my hip just like Mama Malia used to do with Faith, jiggled her up and down, and sang "Jesus Bids Us Shine with a Clear Pure Light" in Lingala. This was her favorite song, I knew. She giggled and pulled my hair with her skinny little fingers. I moved on to "Nearer My God to Thee" to calm her down.

"Nabelema na Yo, Njambe na ngai—"

Except for twigs in her ear holes and her fetish necklace, Esengo was completely naked. I knew right away when she began to pee. I held her at arm's length over the edge of the veranda, but it was too late. My T-shirt was already soaked through with warm, strong urine. I'd be smelling it all morning, even after it dried. Just my luck.

Holy Spirit, I hereby blaspheme You.

Against Thee only have I sinned, and done this evil in Thy sight.

Curses upon You, O Holy Spirit.

Behold I was shapen in wickedness, and in sin hath my mother conceived me.

"That should do it," Dr. Birgie said from the other end of the veranda, where she was rewrapping Luta's stumpy feet.

"Ejali malamu," Luta replied in that small soft voice that made me think of a shy seven-year-old, not somebody's mother. "It's good. Merci."

Dr. Birgie stood up, her heavy knees cracking, and gave Luta her white-coated arm. Luta struggled to a standing position, swaying a little on her bandaged feet. I carried Esengo over to her, and Luta snatched the baby up and made silly faces. Esengo showed off her tiny white teeth and dimple, then made a grab for her mother's dangling brass earrings. Luta's smile widened even as she rescued her ears and gave Esengo's hand a gentle slap. I thought Luta was very pretty in spite of ulcerated feet, swollen joints, and feverish bloodshot eyes. She said good-bye and walked carefully down the three veranda steps while Dr. Birgie and I watched.

"That baby's got to get out of here," Dr. Birgie said, for once speaking in English. "This place isn't healthy for her, especially since Luta isn't responding to DDS like she should."

"She isn't?" I asked, dismayed. "I thought she was getting better."

Dr. Birgie leaned against one of the veranda's rough wooden pillars. Most of her thick gray-blond hair had escaped her bun and straggled down her neck. Her round cheeks were slack and pale. "It's the side effects," she said flatly. "Drugs are complicated. DDS can cause all kinds of serious health problems—anemia, neuritis, and hepatitis, for starters—and Luta suffers quite terribly from a drug-induced mental pain."

I didn't see how Luta's mental pain would be helped by sending Esengo away, and I said so in my most belligerent voice.

Dr. Birgie was silent for a long moment, her lips compressed. "It isn't supposed to," she said finally. "It's just supposed to protect Esengo."

I could tell Dr. Birgie didn't want to talk about it anymore, but I couldn't let the matter drop. "Where could she go?" I wanted to know. "She's only a baby!"

"Luta's younger sister has offered to take her. She lives near Mabolo Mennonite Mission. I could arrange transportation easily enough."

Luta and Esengo joined a small group of women sitting under the leper colony's only guava tree. One of the women, Luta's neighbor Celestine, held Esengo while Luta lowered herself slowly, slowly onto the skimpy grass.

Dr. Birgie frowned.

"The hard part is convincing Luta that it's necessary. That we can't depend on—on Esengo to have negative skin tests indefinitely. The statistics are against any small child whose parent has leprosy, *particularly* if that parent is the mother."

I stared hard at Dr. Birgie. Maybe the skin-test-and-statistics part was true, but I didn't believe that was what she really meant to say.

"I've wondered how Luta would respond to this new non-sulfone drug I've been reading about," Dr. Birgie went on. "And the unfortunate truth is, I'll never know."

"Why not?"

"The mission can't afford it."

Dr. Birgia pushed herself away from the pillar and exclaimed, "Well, goodness gracious, what a *mess!*" and briskly stuffed all the filthy bandages into a bag to be washed and boiled later. She trotted over to the wash basin, scrubbed her hands and arms up to her elbows with special disinfectant soap, and slapped herself dry with a clean towel. She began stabbing her loosened ivory hairpins back into place. Her blue eyes had the fierce expression that made my father call her "the Valkyrie from Harvard Medical School." ("A term of endearment," he always explained. "I'm convinced that fierceness of hers saved my life last Christmas.")

I started to tell Dr. Birgie I was sure she could beat any silly old statistics, but she turned away, already busy again, and I stopped midsentence.

Poor Luta, having to give Esengo away to her sister. It didn't seem right. It *wasn't* right.

I, Grace Berggren, curse You, Holy Spirit.

Thou shalt purge me with hyssop, and I shall be clean.

You deserve it, Holy Spirit, for making Luta have leprosy and *mental pain. For making the mission too poor for new drugs. And especially for making the statistics against Esengo.*

Thou shalt wash me, and I shall be whiter than snow.

"Grace, have you got a minute to take a picture of Fiakona's right hand? He says it's okay. I need it for that article I'm writing."

Dr. Birgie had taught me to use her old Leica, and I was proud to be trusted with it. I took the camera from her knapsack and asked Fiakona to spread his unbandaged hand flat on the table so I could get a good picture.

"*Monganga* Birgie says this picture will be in an American magazine," Fiakona told me. "She promises to tell the Americans I was a good carpenter with this hand. The best in Equateur province, I think."

I leaned both my elbows on the table and focused carefully on Fiakona's finger stubs. Under his sloughed ashy skin there was a tight shiny layer of bright pink. It looked like any other leprous skin to me, but Dr. Birgie said he had some rare secondary infection.

"Make your fingers flat, as flat as you can. Then hold very still," I said.

Fiakona did. Just as I pressed the shutter release, a mangy yellow village dog brushed by me, jarring my hand. I knew the picture was ruined. I also knew it was the end of the roll, and I hadn't seen any more film in Dr. Birgie's knapsack.

Holy Spirit, I hereby blaspheme You.

Turn Thy face from my sins, and put out all my misdeeds.

Curses upon You, O Holy Spirit.

Make me a clean heart, O God, and renew a right spirit within me.

"Dr. Birgie, do you have a new roll of film somewhere? That horrid dog wrecked my picture, and it was the last one."

Dr. Birgie said oh dear, she'd left it at home, but never mind, she'd get the picture next time. She'd only just started the article, so there wasn't any hurry.

I sat down on the concrete floor of the veranda, relishing the coolness of it. Low-lying swampy Esengo was always hot. Much hotter than Boanda with its bluffs and river breezes.

"If you have to have leprosy, it would be a lot nicer to have it at Boanda than here," I said to Dr. Birgie. "There's less mosquitoes, and a view of the river. I think Boanda's river view would cure anything."

Dr. Birgie smiled and fanned herself with a patient chart.

"Undesirable people get undesirable locations, my dear. This was the best the Catholic Sisters could do, and they tried hard to make it a pleasant place, a cheerful place."

"Is that why they named it Esengo?"

Dr. Birgie's smile slipped. "I can only suppose so," she said dryly. "Although as St. Paul's Fruits of the Spirit go, I think Patience or Kindness would have been a more appropriate choice than Joy. Joy is a tough one."

I said nothing. I had never been good at living out St. Paul's Fruits of the Spirit like I was supposed to, and lately I didn't even try. How could I possibly have Christian Joy when I was going to Hell?

"I don't mind if you bite your fingernails, Grace, but you must wash your hands first. And properly, like I've shown you. Do it now, and you may help yourself to the oatmeal cookies in my knapsack."

I said thank you, hoping I sounded appreciative, knowing those cookies would be tasteless and hard as rocks. Her cook was far and away Boanda's worst, but Dr. Birgie didn't seem to mind. Engrossed in the *Atlas of Leprosy* or one of the tropical medicine books that littered her dining-room table, Dr. Birgie just ate lots of whatever he provided without even looking at it. Mrs. Frykman sometimes tried to get Dr. Birgie to fire him and hire a good cook, but Dr. Birgie always refused. "At least he's a better cook than I am," she would say. "Besides, I like Philippe. Every single Saturday he burns the rye bread, and do you know what he says? 'It was the bite of the gods, *Monganga* Birgie. Lightning struck it!'"

I knew she liked Philippe's father as well, the toeless old man who lay on the hard-packed ground outside the Esengo clinic with a banana leaf over his face, singing.

I washed my hands, ate two cookies that tasted exactly

like sun-dried mud bricks, and began rearranging the windowless clinic storeroom by the light of a hurricane lamp. Dr. Birgie had sulfone drugs I wasn't permitted to touch, but she kept those in her medical kit, not the storeroom. Everything here I handled routinely. I peered at the label on a brown glass liter bottle and read "Rubbing Alcohol." What if I dropped it? It could be disastrous if I didn't find all the glass bits. Little Esengo might crawl into the storeroom unnoticed and get glass in her tiny palms and knees. Worse yet, she might pick up the glass bits and eat them. Or maybe a leper on an errand for Dr. Birgie would step on them. Maybe the leper would cut himself badly and not even realize it because of the damage to his nerves. Maybe he'd lose part or all of his foot.

Holy Spirit, I hereby blaspheme You.

Cast me not away from Thy presence, and take not Thy Holy Spirit from me.

I blaspheme You, Holy Spirit, do You hear?

Deliver me from blood-guiltiness, O God.

I watched my hands set the bottle very slowly, very carefully on the rough wooden shelf. The bottle did not tip over and break. There was no glass scattered across the floor. There were no lepers in the room, and Esengo was outside under the guava tree chewing on her fetish necklace while Luta and two other ladies rebraided her cornrows. I nibbled on my cuticle until blood seeped through the skin. Surely I wasn't blaspheming the Holy Spirit over things that didn't even happen?

Each day the unrelenting voice in my head found new reasons to curse, and the sum total of my blasphemies grew higher. Dr. Birgie and I weighed Esengo and discovered she'd lost half a kilo, and then I washed down the storeroom shelves and found they were eaten through by termites.

Holy Spirit, I hereby blaspheme You.
My tongue shall sing of Thy righteousness.

One night Philippe's father burned himself terribly. He fell asleep by the campfire, and while he slept his toeless right foot somehow slid into the still-glowing coals. Because he had so little feeling left in his foot, he didn't wake up until he heard Fiakona yelling as he emptied a cooking pot filled with water on the charred heel and instep.

"An extra-evil *ndoki* pushed his foot into the fire," said Fiakona.

"It was a rainy night," said Philippe, who had hurried over as soon as he found out about the accident. "There was lightning, I think. The bite of the gods."

"The old man's just plain senile," said Mrs. Frykman, who had driven by to tell Dr. Birgie about the American Labor Day party she was planning and to grumble that Dr. Birgie was never at home.

I, Grace Berggren, curse You, Holy Spirit.
Thou shalt open my lips, O Lord, and my mouth shall show forth Thy praise.

A few days later, Dr. Birgie and I arrived at the clinic to find Celestine sitting on the veranda steps feeding Esengo bread and milky tea. Esengo was swinging her feet and giggling with her mouth full, but Celestine had inky pouches under her worried eyes.

"Luta brought her to me in the middle of the night, *Monganga* Birgie," Celestine said. "There was a *ndoki* in her house, Luta told me. This *ndoki* filled her mind with evil thoughts and she was afraid."

"I see," Dr. Birgie said. "I will talk to her."

While Dr. Birgie talked to Luta, I gave Esengo piggyback rides around the clinic and played peekaboo. The two of them talked so long that I sang Esengo every Lingala hymn I knew. I even rigged up an empty sardine can to collect sap from a wild rubber tree so I could make a ball for her. When Dr. Birgie finally came back, she didn't say much. Just, "Mrs. Frykman's driving to Mabolo Mennonite Mission next week. She's offered to bring Esengo along, and Luta is willing."

Curses upon You, O Holy Spirit.

The sacrifice of God is a troubled spirit; a broken and contrite heart, O God, shalt Thou not despise.

As I bicycled into Esengo on Tuesday, I noticed a green Ford pickup parked under the mango tree by the clinic. The Frykmans' pickup. I coasted to a stop, got off my bike, and leaned it against the wild coffee bush. Dr. Birgie stood by the cab with her arms tightly folded across her hefty bosom. She wore the fierce expression that always accompanied her kindest voice. Beside her was Mrs. Frykman in a navy cotton traveling skirt and blue canvas Keds. The softened lines around her mouth took me by surprise. Her tortoiseshell sunglasses hid the expression in her eyes.

"Birgitta, I hate to say it, but I really must get on the road," Mrs. Frykman said quietly. She sounded troubled, hesitant. I'd never seen Mrs. Frykman like this before.

Dr. Birgie broke off a creamy sprig of wild coffee blossom and held it to her nose, inhaling deeply. "Give her another minute," Dr. Birgie said. "As long as you leave by eleven, you should make it to Mabolo before dark."

"Barring truck trouble." Mrs. Frykman grimaced. "At least Régine is good with babies. With her along, I won't have to worry about Esengo at all."

"Régine. Isn't she your cook's daughter?"

"Yes. Dawena's oldest. She just graduated from Miss Judith's School for Girls."

"Oh, very good," said Dr. Birgie.

"Miss Judith says she's extremely bright. We're sending her to the Protestant Secondary School this fall."

"A fine idea," said Dr. Birgie.

They spoke in absentminded voices, both looking in the direction of the smoke-stained hut where Luta had lived for nearly two years, ever since her illness was discovered and her husband threw her out. Several people sat outside it, leaning silently against the cracked clay walls, swollen knees drawn up to their chins. The sun glared on Luta's tin cooking pot, upturned and drying beside the dead fire. I heard the harsh call of hornbills in the trees and the scratch and peck of chickens beside Luta's doorway. There were no sounds from inside the hut.

"Oh dear. I'm only trying to help, but I feel terrible," Mrs. Frykman said. She frowned, smoothing the wrinkles in her skirt with pudgy palms. "I'm just grateful you know you're doing the right thing."

"I do?"

Dr. Birgie's sad uncertainty stunned me. Mrs. Frykman turned a furious red.

"Dear Lord in Heaven, Birgitta!" she exclaimed. "I should certainly *hope* so! Otherwise—"

Dr. Birgie interrupted her. "Allow things to be complicated, Hilda," she said. "Just this once."

Mrs. Frykman pinched her lips together, and the three of us stood quietly, steeping in the reflected heat of the shiny Ford pickup for what seemed an endless time. At last Luta came through the low doorway of the hut, her narrow shoulders hunched and her head down, Esengo in her arms. She stumped painfully across the hard ground, one foot trailing a fluttery bit of dirty bandage. The people waiting outside fell in behind her as she approached the Ford. Esengo seemed to be half asleep, one pale brown fist curled around her mother's darker neck. Luta's face was a severe wooden triangle with thin slits for the eyes and mouth, like an antique Congolese mask. She gently lifted Esengo's arm from her neck and handed the child to Mrs. Frykman. Mrs. Frykman looked startled and awkward, as if she hadn't held a baby for a very long time, but Esengo didn't cry. Luta handed over a tiny Java-cloth bundle as well, then fumbled in the folds of her faded *liputa* until she found a knotted scrap of fabric. It took a long time for her puffy fingers to untie the knot, but nobody spoke or moved. The silence was as heavy as the dank Esengo air. Finally Luta pulled out three coins and gave them to Mrs. Frykman.

"*Merci,* Madame," she said.

Mrs. Frykman looked unhappily at the coins, then tried to return them. "I must go to Mabolo anyway," she said in her halting Lingala. "It costs me nothing to bring Esengo too."

"Please," Luta said softly. "I am very grateful. Truly."

"Keep them," Dr. Birgie whispered in English. "Give them to her sister."

Mrs. Frykman nodded and put the coins in the pocket of her navy skirt.

Luta turned and walked slowly through the silent crowd. She walked past the clinic, the pineapple patch, the ragged rows of corn and manioc, making straight for the jungle. It took her in, closing green ranks behind her.

"Holy Spirit, I curse You," I choked. "I curse You. I do, I do."

My blasphemy sounded thin and helpless—pitiful, almost—as though I had lost faith in my own wickedness. And then I realized I had spoken my blasphemy in the presence of Mrs. Frykman and Dr. Birgie. Had they heard? I recited a verse of the Repentance Psalm just in case. "Thou shalt make me hear of joy and gladness, that the bones which Thou hast broken may rejoice."

167

I paused, staring at the place where Luta had disappeared. Already the leaves, glossy green in the midmorning sun, were perfectly still. Maybe there was a path, but I couldn't see it for the heavy branches and thick twisted vines. Jungle was complicated too.

Mrs. Frykman cleared her throat. "Well," she said unsteadily, "I'm sure—" and stopped.

Esengo's curly lashes shone wet with tears, but she didn't make a sound. Not even when Mrs. Frykman carried her around to the passenger side of the Ford, opened the door, and handed her to Régine. A moment later the door slammed, then another, and Mrs. Frykman started the motor.

"Dr. Birgie, I haven't committed the unforgivable sin." The words were out before I knew they were coming. I wondered if I meant them, if it was the shaken confidence of missionary adults that allowed me to say them. I looked sideways at Dr. Birgie and waited for her reaction. Her judgment.

At first she seemed unaware that I'd said anything. Her face was closed up mask-tight like Luta's, her eyes trained on the jungle. Finally she said, "No, child. Of course you haven't."

The sweet waxy scent of Dr. Birgie's wild coffee branch gave me a sudden giddy sickness. It must have done the same to Dr. Birgie, for she frowned abruptly and tossed the branch away instead of saving it for her knapsack. "The unforgivable sin is not a human offense," she said.

Mrs. Frykman put the Ford in gear, waved, and drove slowly down the rain-rutted road. Through the back window I could see two adult heads bobbing up and down as the pickup jounced along. I couldn't see little Esengo at all.

Highly Favored Ladies

O N DECEMBER ELEVENTH Ruth Sanderson locked herself in the outhouse. Though none of us saw her do it, the nine-inch gap between the bottom of the door and the concrete floor told us who was inside. Only Ruth wore lime green Keds and pink nylon anklets decorated with yellow happy faces. And only Ruth was stubborn enough to maintain silence while a dozen people begged her to tell them what was wrong. Finally I dropped flat on my stomach and wriggled under the sun-faded mahogany door—a tight cobwebby squeeze—and coaxed her out.

"Grace, I'm pleasantly surprised," my dorm mother said when all the excitement was over. "I admit I've had my doubts, particularly when you came back from summer vacation so glum and edgy. But I think you just might blossom into a fine Christian yet."

"Thank you," I said, astounded by Mrs. Lindstrom's cautious approval.

"I'm pleased you took my suggestion to heart and started reading Galatians in your private devotions," she went on. "Your character is reaping the benefits already. One of the great Fruits of the Spirit is Kindness, as of course you know from Galatians 5:22."

"Yes, Mrs. Lindstrom," I said. But I hadn't intended to be kind. I hadn't been reading Galatians either. Ever since September, when Mrs. Lindstrom told me she thought Galatians would improve my poor attitude no end, I had skipped my private devotions and given up the struggle to be a fine Christian altogether. The only reason I'd gone after Ruth—a frightful snob about downcountry people who couldn't speak Ngbaka dialect—was because I'd often wondered whether I could fit beneath the outhouse door. This had seemed my best chance to find out without having to explain an unusually dirty shirt-front.

Ruth's problem was her brown hair, and most people at the Evangelical Swedish-American Mission School didn't need to be told why. December thirteenth was Santa Lucia Day, the first day of the Christmas season in Sweden. I'd known the story of Santa Lucia as long as I could remember, how this beautiful and kind young maiden of the Roman Empire was martyred for trying to help some persecuted Christians. Lucia was supposed to be burned at the stake, but because she was so pure and good, the flames wouldn't hurt her. She stood right in the middle of the huge crackling bonfire, patient and untouched, wearing her biggest, most forgiving smile. In the end her executioners had to run her through with a sword.

When the people of Sweden heard about Lucia, they started a holiday tradition in her memory, a tradition that our dorm mother never tired of explaining to the few non-Swedish-Americans at school. She'd have to wipe her eyes and blow her nose halfway through Lucia's story, but she always cheered up when she got to the Swedish part. "And now you understand why every December thirteenth is such a very special day," Mrs. Lindstrom would say as she tucked her handkerchief back in her skirt pocket. "It starts early, at dawn, when the oldest daughter in every Swedish household gets up to prepare for the occasion. She dresses in a long white robe with a bright red sash and places a crown of lighted candles on her head. Then she serves her family real Swedish coffee with an egg in it—that's for clarity, of course—and coffee bread filled with raisins and topped with almond frosting. It's a lovely tradition, children, and a privileged role for any girl to play." Mrs. Lindstrom would pause, then casually add, "Any blond girl, that is."

Ruth said all she wanted for Christmas was permission to spend the whole month of December hiding in the outhouse. "I don't even *want* to be Santa Lucia!" she wailed. "I just want to play Mary in the Christmas pageant someday when I'm older. And it's never going to happen."

I couldn't think of anything comforting to say. Ruth was right. At our school, only blonds could hope for Lucia's candle crown and silver coffee pot. Only blonds were chosen for Lucia's retinue of crownless attendants. And in the Christmas pageant traditionally held on the evening of Santa Lucia Day, the part of Mary was always given to the oldest of Lucia's attendants.

Being a blond myself, I thought December was wonderful. I was eleven, and too young to play Santa Lucia or Mary, but not too young to sneak a smug look in the mirror now and then, not too young to feel a trembling in my knees at the red-sashed possibilities. There was a small chance I could be selected as Santa Lucia's most junior attendant. I wouldn't be nearly as important as Lucia herself (an attendant just stood around holding a thin beribboned candle and keeping an eye on Lucia's hair to make sure it didn't catch on fire) but it was still a high honor. Until Ruth's outhouse escapade, I never considered how I might feel if I had dark hair, but it occurred to me now that Carrie was mopish lately too—and her hair was dead-leaf brown.

When I awoke at dawn on December thirteenth to the sound of pillow-muffled sobbing, I wasn't surprised. I crossed the hall to her room. "What's wrong?" I asked.

"Nothing. Go away."

I planted one knee on her mattress and folded my arms across my chest. "If you're homesick, it's only eight more days till vacation."

"Don't be stupid. I'm not a sap."

That was true. I shouldn't have said it. "Homesick" was a word we never used.

"All right then, is it Santa Lucia?"

Carrie buried her face so deep in her pillow that all I could see was her fine brown pageboy. "Shut up," she said.

"*Mama na ngai!*" I was shocked. "That's bad language. If Mrs. Lindstrom heard, you'd be stuck in your room the whole morning and miss all the fun."

Carrie said so what, who cared, and she was sick of Swedish people with blond hair and cousins in Uppsala and Stockholm. Then she bounced up, facing me with a ferocious glare. "I like my brown hair, and Morris is a much better name than Berggren. Besides, I look like Jane Eyre."

"Of course you don't," I said kindly.

Carrie couldn't possibly enjoy looking like that pathetic English babysitter. All the fifth and sixth grade girls were taking turns reading the school library's lone copy of *Jane Eyre,* and while I liked the story as much as anyone, there was no pretending that the picture of Jane on the frontispiece was anything but plain. She looked like an albino mouse with her colorless pointy face, small eyes, and tiny white teeth. Her pale brown hair (true mouse, not albino) was drawn flat over her little ears and arranged in a boring bun at the back of her neck. I wasn't at all surprised Jane ended up marrying a blind man who wouldn't have to look at her.

My own model of female beauty was Kristin Lavrans-datter, the heroine of the Sigrid Undset trilogy, which Miss Judith had loaned me. ("You may take all three volumes up-country if you like, Grace dear," she'd said. "I think you're old enough to appreciate them, and I know you'll take good care of them for me.") The cover of Miss Judith's first volume, *The Bridal Wreath,* showed Kristin with dazzling sun-colored hair that hung in two heavy braids down to her knees. Kristin's medieval robes were embroidered in bright Scandinavian reds, yellows, and blues, and she wore a cir-clet of gold on her head. Her skin had a thick creamy gloss from her smooth forehead down to the tops of her full breasts. Her gold eyebrows curved delicately, like crescent moons, and her wide eyes sparkled deep Baltic blue. If I'd thought I stood to gain Kristin's beauty instead of an im-proved attitude, I would have read Galatians all day long.

I knew I wasn't much to look at, all short and skinny and flat. (Mrs. Lindstrom called me "underdeveloped," while my mother preferred "late bloomer.") I didn't like my crooked bottom teeth, my scarred and bumpy knees, or the way I squinted in strong sunlight. My eyebrows didn't have any arch, and ever since last summer, the Esengo summer, my fingernails were always bitten to the quick, the surrounding skin red and puffy. But at least I was a blond.

"There's bleach in the pantry," I said tentatively. "The Lindstroms won't announce their Santa Lucia choice for at least half an hour, so we've got time. And your hair is fine. It should dry fast."

"Grace!" Carrie's mouth pinched into a governessy Jane Eyre frown. "Don't you know dyeing your hair is a terrible, terrible sin? It's a worse sin than piercing your ears, even."

I pondered. Miss Larson, one of the mission hospital nurses, periodically showed up at church with her gray hair transformed to a rich Congolese ebony. Some of the younger missionary ladies defended her. "It must be awfully hard to go gray in your early thirties," they said. "And it's not like she dyes it red. She's just restoring the natural color of her hair." But most people thought Miss Larson was shockingly vain, not unlike some of the Belgian Catholic ladies in Mbandaka who bleached their dark hair blond, wore low-cut dresses, and painted their toenails. (Of course they didn't know any better: they were Belgian, and they were Catholic—with the exception of Alain Fougère's alarming new girlfriend Nina, who said she was *agnostique* and a true believer only in chain-smoking.)

Mr. Frykman regularly preached on the Fallen Woman from the seventh chapter of Proverbs. "It's a petal-strewn path," he'd warn in his richest deepest evangelist voice. "It seems so easy, that first step, but it's a moral crossroads, and the end of that path is *destruction!*" Could bleaching Carrie's hair for Santa Lucia be that first easy step? Would Carrie become a Democrat and volunteer in the Peace Corps, maybe even convert to Catholicism someday, all because I encouraged her in this first and fatal mistake? Yet how tragic to know you could never be Santa Lucia in a pure white gown, never balance a blazing crown of candles on your head. Surely you would dread the thirteenth of December for the rest of your life.

I thought about Saint Paul's Thorn in the Flesh. The missionary adults liked speculating on the real nature of his Thorn, and all of them had different ideas about it. Mr. Frykman said it was a rare eye disease, and Mr. Lindstrom said it was migraine headaches. My father said it was too bad, whatever it was, and a visiting Swedish-Lutheran theology professor said it was Unnatural Lusts, which seemed to upset everybody terribly. Now I had my own theory: Saint Paul was not a blond.

"My mother likes to quote Micah 6:8, about God loving justice and mercy," I said. "I think He probably allows brown-haired people a few extra sins."

Carrie agreed this seemed only fair, so we tiptoed down the hall to the pantry, where we found a clear glass bottle of Dupree's extra-strong bleach. We brought it back to Carrie's room and pulled out the cork, but the smell was so overpowering that we decided we'd better perform the operation outside. We crept out the back door, careful not to let it slam.

The early morning air smelled of dripping mango leaves and damp moss, but a bright dry-season haze already blurred the hills across the valley. Six-foot poinsettias bloomed against the whitewashed walls of the cookhouse like a church choir in showy Christmas robes. Hungry chickens pecked in the dirt beneath the poinsettias, carefully avoiding the leaves that lay on the ground in poisonous drifts of violent red. We scurried around the back of the cookhouse, our thin cotton nightgowns flapping around our legs. The chickens followed us, cackling hopefully for field corn. "Shoo! Vamoose!" we hissed softly, waving our arms, worrying about the noise.

The night sentry, Kamu, didn't seem to notice the fuss. He sat on his wooden stool by the fire, wearing his much-faded orange and purple Hawaiian shirt and sipping his morning tea from a Campbell's Soup can. Between sips, Kamu sang snatches of "O Bride of Christ, Rejoice." He sang this favorite Swedish Advent carol, I supposed, because the Santa Lucia song hadn't been translated into Lingala yet.

"Grace, we can't go that way," Carrie whispered, pointing. "Elizabeth's sitting under the kapok tree reading her Bible."

Elizabeth always had her private devotions outdoors. She had explained to everyone that the natural world made her feel closer to God, more truly and deeply spiritual. At first Mrs. Lindstrom didn't like it. "Keeping track of people indoors is so much easier," she said. But she did like Elizabeth, reserving for her a special smile that rearranged the tight dry skin around her mouth and warmed her chilly eyes. So every morning Elizabeth read her Bible outdoors, underlining passages in red and purple pen and writing tiny cramped comments in the margins. Her Bible had more underlining and marginalia than any Bible I'd ever seen, even Mrs. Palmquist's much-scribbled-in King James Version, held together by rubber bands and masking tape. (Mrs. Palmquist, Boanda's oldest missionary, often said that young people today were "lazy in the Faith," but I knew she'd consider Elizabeth an exception.)

"I'll bet she isn't reading Galatians," I muttered to Carrie. "Nobody would ever tell her she needs to."

A light breeze ruffled the branches of the kapok tree, releasing a pale shower of cottony fluff that drifted slowly down, slowly down, finally landing softly on Elizabeth's hair, housecoat, and Bible. Elizabeth didn't seem to notice.

"Just look at all that blond hair!" Carrie breathed. "Why does she bother with devotions? She doesn't have anything to pray for."

I stared at the bright hair flowing past Elizabeth's slim waist. Today she wore her royal blue housecoat, the one with gold buttons. Kristin Lavransdatter's medieval robes were exactly that same rich shade of blue. And on the cover of the last volume in the trilogy, *The Cross*, Kristin too held a Bible in her hands.

"We'd better get on with this," I said. I dragged Carrie off in the direction of the girls' outhouse, where we burrowed deep into the bird-of-paradise plants. I was certain we couldn't be seen, although I could still hear Kamu singing:

> "Exultant raise your voice,
>   To hail the day of glory,
>   Foretold in sacred story . . ."

I popped the cork from Mrs. Lindstrom's bottle of Dupree's. "Tilt your head back and shut your eyes," I ordered.

Carrie nodded, holding her nose with her thumb and forefinger, squeezing her eyelids so tightly that they trembled. I poured the bleach on Carrie's Jane Eyre locks, gasping as the fumes eddied and swirled around us. My eyes both flooded and burned while the sky turned deep leafy green and the broad leaves went all hazy blue.

"Stop it!" Carrie shrieked, twisting her drenched head away. "Stop it! You got it in my eyes!"

I tried to calm her down, but she struck out at me with both arms. I dropped the bleach and crashed backwards against the outhouse. Carrie tripped over the bottle and fell into the clustering bird-of-paradise, snapping off several stalks at ground level. I watched the straight orange-crested plants topple and ooze clear green liquid into the red earth. Had anyone heard us? I curled into a horrified ball, my bumpy knees tucked up inside my dirt-streaked nightgown. Carrie huddled beside me, one hand covering her eyes, sniffling and moaning.

"Grace and Carrie! Come out this minute!"

I shut my eyes tighter, my nail-bitten fingers curling with dread as I recognized the voice Elizabeth reserved for all younger girls. It was not the same one she used on dorm parents and high school boys. Elizabeth reached into our bird-of-paradise sanctuary, grabbed our wrists, and hauled us out.

"What is that horrible smell?"

Carrie raised her stinking streaming head and met Elizabeth's Baltic blue eyes. "Bleach," she said in a tiny pleading voice. "I wanted the right kind of hair for Santa Lucia."

Elizabeth tipped her head to one side, and her rippling mass of blond hair shifted and resettled on her right shoulder, her rounded arm, her royal blue bosom. Every ringlet glimmered and shone in the sunrise, and Elizabeth's mouth curved in a tender half smile, her eyes downcast. She looked exactly like Mary in last year's Christmas card from Miss Adela and Miss Judith. The card was a reprint of her favorite painting in the National Gallery, Miss Adela had told us, and she'd ordered fifty of them airmail from London. It showed beautiful demure Mary shrinking back as the Angel Gabriel, magnificently dressed in red brocade robes, offered her a single white lily. Under the picture, in a flowing gold script that exactly matched Mary's waist-length hair, there was a Bible verse: "Hail, thou that art highly favored, the Lord is with thee. Blessed art thou among women."

"Poor Carrie," Elizabeth said softly, her voice pearl-smooth with pity. "Poor, poor Carrie."

Carrie suddenly frowned, brushed the dirt from her knees, and stood very tall. I hadn't realized that her back was so straight before, her bottom lip so prominent. "I've changed my mind," Carrie said. "I want my brown hair. I love my brown hair. I'd hate to be blond if I turned out like you."

Elizabeth's tender expression faded, and her lips puckered white. "I don't think you realize how serious this is," she said. Her slim fingers ticked off our sins. "One, you left your rooms before the rising bell. Two, you stole bleach. Three, you interrupted my private devotions. And four, it's Santa Lucia Day, for pity's sake! Mrs. Lindstrom is going to be very disappointed in you."

Elizabeth was right. And just when Mrs. Lindstrom was beginning to approve of me, thinking I was reading Galatians and learning to be kind. I shut my eyes, but the all-too-familiar and horrible vision of Mrs. Lindstrom's disappointment wouldn't go away. Our dorm mother got angry about small things, but about serious matters, like rules and attitude, she was never "angry," she was "disappointed." This disappointment meant she talked to you for a long endless time, her face grieved and sorrowful. Finally, when you thought you couldn't bear it another moment, your throat sore and thick, tears spurting from your swollen eyes, she would say, "Now remember 1 John 1:9. 'If we confess our sins, God is faithful and just to forgive us our sins and to cleanse us from all unrighteousness.' Let's have a little talk with God, shall we?" And so you would pray, kneeling by the sofa and crushing your face into green-striped cushions that smelled of mildew, salt water, and repentance.

"Elizabeth!" It was Janice, her voice high and breathy with excitement. "Come inside quick! They're ready to announce Santa Lucia."

Elizabeth didn't reply. She stared at Carrie and me as though we were dangerous and ugly jungle bugs she'd discovered under her bed or in her shoes. Tarantulas, maybe, or huge Goliath beetles with bold white stripes and fuzzy ink-black feelers. I was about to scuttle for cover like the disgusting insect she thought I was when Elizabeth turned away.

"I'm coming," she called. "Tell them to wait."

Carrie and I watched Elizabeth head for the door at a ladylike run, long blond curls billowing behind her. We followed at a slower pace, making faces of exaggerated terror at her royal blue back, silly with relief. I showed Carrie the white mark where Elizabeth had grabbed my wrist too hard, and Carrie pushed up her bangs so I could see how the bleach had irritated a tiny open cut on her forehead.

Carrie's eyes had turned a watery rabbit pink from the chlorine fumes, and her nose was running. She looked even worse than Jane Eyre now. At least Jane's eyes had been wide and clear, and she would never have allowed her nose to run in public. Poor, poor Carrie.

While all the other girls gathered around our teachers and dorm parents at the other end of the hall, I hurried Carrie off to the washroom, dunked her head in the sink, and scrubbed her hair with Congolese hand soap that was fatty and yellow with palm oil. I couldn't understand why Carrie's brown pageboy was no lighter than before. All this trouble for nothing, I mourned, twisting her hair up in a towel. We threw housecoats over our grimy nightgowns and hurried to join the others before anyone noticed we weren't there clamoring to know who would be Santa Lucia. I wondered why I had cared in the first place. I was probably still too young to be an attendant.

"All right girls, let's quiet down now," said my dorm father. His expression reminded me of my least favorite hymn, "Immortal, Invisible, God Only Wise."

"We want you to know we had a hard time selecting a Santa Lucia this year. Many of you girls deserve to be chosen." Mr. Lindstrom paused, then slowly smiled. "But finally we, along with your teachers, have decided that our choice is Elizabeth. Janice, Mary, and Sharon will be her attendants."

Everyone screamed except Elizabeth, who dropped her eyes and looked beautifully humble. Then all the hugging started, mixed with laughter and giddy chatter.

"Let me fix your hair for you!"

"Where are the red sashes from last year?"

"How much time do we have to get ready?"

"I'll take charge of the candles."

Carrie and I escaped to her room. I sat on Carrie's bed and watched her remove the towel, shake out her still-brown hair, then part it carefully down the center. I wondered aloud why the bleach hadn't worked, and Carrie said she guessed kitchen bleach was different from real honest-to-goodness sinful hair bleach. "I'm glad it didn't work," she added. "Really I am."

I leaned back against the pillow and thought about Elizabeth's downcast eyes. I was tired of her careful goodness, tired of approval falling on her blond head like a soft radiant shower of kapok. I wished the day was over, not just beginning, and hoped Carrie understood I had never, ever had any Santa Lucia ambitions for myself.

"Santa Lucia Day is silly," I said. "And I don't believe it's Christian to make such a fuss over one person. I think we ought to boycott the Santa Lucia breakfast."

I only intended a little casual heresy, and Carrie's reaction surprised me. "That's a fabulous idea!" she said enthusiastically, turning away from the mirror and throwing down her comb. "We can ask the Lindstroms to give our share to the help. Santa Lucia would like that much better than a breakfast party in her honor, I'm sure. And we'll get some of the others to do it too."

Carrie's eyes were clear again, a bright earnest hazel. I thought she looked even more like Jane Eyre than usual: stubborn, excitable, and pious all at the same time. I realized we'd have to go through with it now and worried she'd gotten the wrong idea.

"All right, but remember it's only a boycott," I cautioned her. "We don't have to get ourselves martyred over it. We'll just refuse to eat that special Santa Lucia coffee bread. Like how my parents won't buy things from South Africa, not even Prince Henry apricot jam, which is absolutely the best!"

181

In a few minutes we had converted several other girls. Rebekah Lundquist didn't like sweet breads anyway, and I promised Rachel Swedberg my after-school snack for three days if she would join our boycott. Ruth Sanderson thought it was a wonderful plan and didn't want a bribe.

"Everybody out to the dining room to wait for Santa Lucia and her attendants," our dorm mother called, shooing us down the hall. "Hurry now!"

We trooped into the dining room and paused, wide eyed. The everyday blue plastic tablecloths were gone, and so were the sun-faded Melmac dishes and sticky Tupperware glasses. Two of the largest tables had been pushed together to make a long buffet, which was covered with white linen and lace. There were flowered china dishes, fat white candles in bright wooden holders, and a dozen hand-carved Swedish Dalarna horses painted red, blue, and orange. And in the middle of all these decorations, perfectly centered on silver platters, were three enormous circlets of Swedish pastry dripping with imported raisins, nuts, and maraschino cherries. The almond frosting was at least half an inch thick, I was sure, and the cherries were the largest I'd ever seen. For one famished moment I wavered—How could I forgo all this?—and then Mrs. Lindstrom said, "All right, here they come. Everybody *sing!*"

> "Night goes with silent steps
> Round house and cottage,
> O'er earth that sun forgot.
> Dark shadows linger."

Mrs. Lindstrom hated to hear Swedish *r*'s rolled improperly, so we all sang in English, our eyes on the girls slowly processing into the dining room. Sharon entered first, gravely smiling as she carried a burning candle decorated with a scarlet ribbon. Mary followed, and then Janice, poinsettia-red sashes fluttering, long white gowns flowing over Sunday-sandalled toes. Last came Elizabeth, pausing modestly in the doorway, her many-candled crown flickering above her golden hair.

> "Then on our threshold stands,
> White clad, in candlelight,
> Santa Lucia, Santa Lucia!"

Elizabeth curtsied while everybody cheered, then took her place behind the fancy silver coffee pot that Mrs. Lindstrom brought out only once a year. Everyone was served large slices of coffee bread by Santa Lucia's attendants. Santa Lucia herself poured each person a cup of coffee rendered clear, pure, and Swedish by the addition of an egg. Students and teachers formed little huddles, everyone talking and laughing as they ate.

Everyone except us. We stood in a silent line against the wall until Santa Lucia noticed. She stared, drew her crescent-moon brows together, and whispered something to Mrs. Lindstrom and her attendants. They all turned, all looked our way, and I decided the time was right. I walked over to the linen-and-lace-draped buffet. "Mrs. Lindstrom," I said, carefully avoiding the suspicious gaze of candle-laden Elizabeth. "Some of us want to follow Santa Lucia's example of generosity this year. We'd like our share of the Santa Lucia breakfast to be given to the help. We'll go without."

Mrs. Lindstrom's eyes widened behind her bifocals.

"We hope that's all right with you," I added quickly.

"Well, what a generous thought!" she said, wiping her hands on her Christmas apron with *"God Jul"* embroidered on it. "You surprise me, Grace. Generosity is another Fruit of the Spirit. I had no idea you were so spiritually mature."

She gave me her Elizabeth smile, the warm approving one. Usually I got her everyday brisk one, if she smiled at all. I felt my cheeks flush with pleasure. Why had no one ever told me it was so rewarding to be saintly?

Mrs. Lindstrom cut five large slices of coffee bread and sent Janice to the kitchen for a serving plate and five plastic cups. "This will be a such a nice treat for them," she told me. "You know how the Congolese are about sweet things."

Janice came back with the plate and cups. Mrs. Lindstrom handed Elizabeth the cups. "Fill these with coffee, Elizabeth dear, and stir in lots of milk and sugar," she said. "And I think it would be lovely if you and the attendants carried them out to the back porch yourselves. I think the help would enjoy that."

Elizabeth stared at me, her eyes freezing slits of blue. I stared back, too elated by my own unfamiliar goodness to feel intimidated. She looked away first. "Of course," she answered graciously and headed for the kitchen door with her retinue. I rejoined Carrie and the others, then leaned against the whitewashed wall and practiced Elizabeth's Madonna smile. I didn't have it quite right, but it would do.

Mrs. Lindstrom was pouring coffee refills and telling our teachers what we'd done. "Such promising girls!" I heard her say. "And I do like to encourage selfless impulses whenever I can."

They all smiled approvingly in our direction, even Miss Holmberg, who always read her students an essay on gluttony the day before Thanksgiving and never approved of anything.

I sucked in my cheeks, trying for a hollow spiritual effect as I studied the red richness of the wooden candlesticks, the shiny maraschino cherries, the rippling sashes of the returning Santa Lucia quartet. (They were back amazingly fast, deep red poinsettias flowering in their cheeks and white candlewax streaming down the length of Lucia's hair.) Who needs almond frosting and Swedish coffee when praise can be had instead, I wondered, sucking the insides of my cheeks even harder.

Mrs. Lindstrom gathered a few people around the piano to sing *"Marias lovsang,"* her favorite Swedish Christmas carol, but everyone else stood around drinking coffee and admiring us, the five foodless boycotters drooping against the wall. Through the dining-room window I could see the help starting in on their Swedish pastry. Kamu popped a maraschino cherry into his mouth and made a terrible face. He spat it into the poinsettia bushes with a shudder, then took a huge swallow of coffee while the other men laughed.

"Everybody together on the last verse!" Mrs. Lindstrom cried.

> "My soul now magnifies the Lord,
> With joy His praise I sing;
> For God, my Savior unto me
> Has done a wondrous thing;"

I sang with the lilting energy the Swedish folk tune required, but my mind was occupied with last year's Christmas card from Miss Adela. I had no quarrel with the Angel Gabriel down on his red brocade knees looking handsome and reverent. When Gabriel said, "Hail, thou that art highly favored," he probably meant it. But the artist had made a mistake with Mary. He should have painted her the way she felt, not how she looked. For Mary really wanted to rush at the angel with all her pastel robes flying. She wanted to snatch that pure white lily right out of his hand before he could change his mind. And as for Lucia, I knew how she felt too. It wasn't in Mrs. Lindstrom's story, but I imagined Lucia hurriedly scavenging loose twigs from her own bonfire and cobbling them together in a flaming crown which she placed firmly on her own blond head, helping herself to martyrdom with both hands. Like Jane Eyre, who married blind Mr. Rochester. Like Kristin Lavransdatter, who left family and property to enter a nunnery.

> "This child of dust He set apart
> For blessedness sublime;"

Carrie elbowed my rib cage. "Elizabeth looks like she swallowed a whole green pineapple," she hissed, and I elbowed her in return.

I wondered if God really chose His own highly favored ladies. What if it was the other way around? What if highly favored ladies chose God to favor them, to make all the sacrifices other people approved of worth something?

> "His answer to my prayer extends
> Beyond the realms of Time."

Mrs. Lindstrom twirled around on the piano stool and gave me a warm, almost loving smile. I smiled back, so anxious to enjoy my full measure of temporary approval that I forgot to lower my lashes and look meek. She started playing another Swedish carol, "How Glad I Am Each Christmas Eve," with lots of extra flourishes and chords. I sang along, gazing out the window to the backyard, where orange sparks and wood smoke gushed from the cookhouse chimney and disappeared into the mango trees. The overgrown poinsettias swayed awkwardly in the breeze while kapok drifted down from Elizabeth's tree like snow on a Christmas card. And on the back veranda, Kamu and the other men grinned and shook their heads as they carefully scraped all the cherries, raisins, nuts, and frosting off their Swedish pastries and fed them to the chickens.

Leopard Curfew

"NO NEWS REALLY, except the mission has a leopard curfew on," my father's letter ran. "Hope it's over by the time you get home for vacation, but there's no telling. It's a nuisance, not being able to go out after dark. I haven't seen the leopard myself, but Elmer Frykman and Nils Carlson caught a glimpse of it. And I'm pretty sure one of my Rhode Island Reds caught more than a glimpse because I'm missing a hen. Elmer calls the leopard a panther. His dictionary says they're the same, but mine says they're not. Wonder what your big school-library dictionary says?"

I looked it up, but our dictionary said only this: "Leopard, noun. A large catlike beast of prey with beautiful spotted skin."

On my first day home for summer vacation, I spent a good eight hours in the river. The sun shone so bright and searing that the surface of the water bubbled hot and golden like percolating coffee. Even the floating hyacinths wilted from lavender to brown. I got such a frightful sunburn that

I had to spend the next three days in bed, feverish and blistered and weepy, wearing only my underpants. My mother fed me salt pills and made me drink a full glass of water every hour. "I don't know what you were thinking of, Grace," she said. "Eleven is plenty old enough to be sensible!" I didn't tell her that I hadn't been thinking at all, just feeling crazy-happy to see the river again, and my river-love left no room for being sensible. "When you're over this, two hours in the water per day is your limit," she told me. "At least until I can mail-order a really good suntan lotion. We're right on the equator, don't forget. This sun can kill."

The day I was finally allowed back in the water, I chose my swimming time carefully, deciding on three to five in the afternoon. Davina, home from her downcountry boarding school, promised me some good reading entertainment to pass the early afternoon hours. We met in the rose-apple tree in our backyard.

"My mother doesn't know I swiped these," she said, pulling up her shirt and extracting two small paperbacks from the elastic waistband of her shorts.

"What are they called?" I asked.

"Harlequin romances," Davina replied, grinning hugely. "My Aunt Doris sends them from Florida."

I settled myself on a rose-apple limb, keeping an eye out for suggestive leaf flutterings or a golden flash of spotted fur. My father had said we should be perfectly safe in the early afternoon, but with leopards you never really knew. Especially leopards who wouldn't observe proper leopard rules.

"What kind of book is a Harlequin romance?" I wanted to know.

Davina laughed, her sunbleached cowlick bobbing, her brown eyes squeezed shut behind her aqua cat's-eye glasses.

"The mushy kind," she said. "Lovey-dovey."

I'd read a lot of different kinds of books over the past year, from the Kristin Lavransdatter trilogy to *National Velvet*, from my mother's worn-out Elsie Dinsmore novels to my own worn-out Nancy Drew mysteries. But I didn't think I'd read anything "lovey-dovey" unless you counted *Jane Eyre*, which nobody could ever laugh about because it was so terribly sad. I liked variety, and there was nothing left to read at our house except my father's biographies of missionary explorers in Africa. Every last one of these biographies had a dull green cover, a title page that said "made during wartime," and black-and-white photos of David Livingstone or Mary Slessor wearing pith helmets and so many clothes that it made me sweat to look at them. Whatever a "lovey-dovey" Harlequin romance was, it had to be more exciting.

Davina handed me a book facedown. "I found a whole stack of these in the back of my mother's closet," she said. "Seventeen of them. Behind the box with her good Sunday sandals."

Where had Mrs. Carlson found the time to read seventeen books? She was forever telling my mother how overworked she was, what with her Bible classes for Congolese ladies, her sewing projects, and her unreliable help. "I've got the most temperamental houseboy in all of Congo," she'd sigh. "And the yardboy is a half-wit."

My mother would say, "Really, Irma! You shouldn't call them boys," and Mrs. Carlson would color up with aggravation.

"Oh, what's the difference!" she'd snap. "In a country where you've got to make your own bread and jam from scratch, there aren't enough hours in a day to worry about such stupid niceties. The Lord only knows what I put up with!"

"Go on, look at it," Davina ordered.

I flipped it over and found a girl wearing a skimpy

sundress printed with pastel flowers. She had big blue eyes, lots of pale blond hair, and a pointed little face. Behind her was a castlelike house, a huge black car, and a handsome man with silver hair and dark glasses. The man wore tight black trousers and a partially unbuttoned shirt that showed off his black chest hair. He looked as sleek as a jungle animal, as strong as his car. I couldn't imagine why Mrs. Carlson, efficient and frowning in her drip-dry Dacron, wanted to read about such a man. Mr. Carlson was nothing like him. Mr. Carlson, who taught biology and chemistry at the Protestant secondary school, had thinning blond hair and kind brown eyes in a long sunburned face. He drove a dusty Chevrolet pickup and wore baggy cotton shirts with oodles of leftover material untidily crammed inside his belt.

"Grace, look at mine."

I peered at Davina's book cover and nearly fell out of the tree. The setting was plainly Africa, but an Africa I didn't know. Another pretty girl, this one wearing a low-cut white blouse, leaned gracefully against a Land Rover. A big tanned man stood beside her, one long arm thrown casually around her shoulders. She looked up at him with full puckered lips while he gazed off in the distance through his binoculars. In the background was an African man wearing an elaborate beaded mask and leaping into the air, waving big wooden rattles. There were also a few huts, gazelles, elephants, leopards, and zebras thrown in.

"Can you believe what he's wearing?"

"He's dressed up for tourists," I said.

"No, not him. The European. He's wearing a safari suit!"

The rose-apple branches quivered as we laughed ourselves sick, pinching our thighs together so we wouldn't wet our pants. American officials sometimes arrived in Mbandaka all rigged out in brand-new tan safari suits, trying to dress like brave explorers although they hadn't exactly paddled up the Congo River in a pirogue. More than likely they'd flown here in one of those elegant white embassy planes with a flag and "United States of America" painted on it. As far as we could tell, their job meant smiling, shaking hands, and pretending they understood Congolese French. They needed ice water, real cream in their coffee, electricity for their razors, and lots of other things we couldn't supply.

"Let's read yours first," I suggested, shifting position so I would have a better view of the jungle bordering the backyard.

The leopard curfew wouldn't be in effect until after five o'clock, late afternoon and early evening being prime hunting time. "No point getting paranoid and staying indoors twenty-four hours a day," my father had said. "But I do want you kids to keep your eyes open. I don't really trust a leopard that hangs around settled areas and hunts domestic animals."

Davina started reading her book, *To Dare My Love,* aloud. The story was set in a game reserve north of Johannesburg where everybody important was rich and white and drank liquor. Lots of liquor. I knew exactly what Mrs. Frykman would say. "Gone to the *dogs,* just like the Belgians. Just like *all* white people in Africa who aren't American Protestants."

As Davina read on, I realized Mrs. Frykman's reaction was the only thing I could safely predict in this puzzling story. There was no mystery for Nancy to solve and no dreadful boarding school for brave little Jane to endure. There were no horses or medieval Norwegians either. There was only Rosamunde, the silly heroine, forever crying over the Safari-Suit Man, Marshall Carter IV, wishing he would talk to her, love her, kiss her. And if she wasn't crying, Rosamunde was trembling. Whenever Safari Suit came around her house, he would catch her wearing her swimsuit, her nightgown, or just her underwear, and then they would exchange long glances and Rosamunde would start trembling again.

"Rosamunde ought to tell Safari Suit to go lose himself in the jungle and get eaten by our leopard," I said. "He'd be a real treat. Much bigger than a chicken or a dog."

Davina skipped ahead to the last page.

"Rosamunde is pitiful," she said, shaking her head. "Safari Suit is kissing her savagely, and she's trembling again. And her bosom is straining the buttons of her low-cut silk blouse."

"Just like that girlfriend Alain had last year," I said disgustedly. "Nina Nieberding, the one from Antwerp who chain-smoked."

A mosquito landed on my leg. I gave it a vicious swat, forgetting my skin was still pink and tender. It hurt, but not as bad as poor Rosamunde seemed to hurt page after page. She wore all her feelings on the outside of her skin, like sunburn.

"Can we look at the other one?"

"Sure." Davina shut the book. "I wish the rose-apples were ripe."

I did too. Rose-apple trees were good for climbing, but even better for their fruit, which were shaped like pears and striped like peppermint candy. They had big pits like avocados and crunched like apples. But their taste was unlike anything save pure rose-apple: sweet, wild, tangy, addicting.

"Remember last summer when your dad's Rhode Island Reds got drunk on rotten rose-apples and ran around in circles cackling like crazy?"

I remembered. I hoped liquor didn't have that effect on Rosamunde and Safari Suit.

"Grace, look!"

Davina pointed toward the jungle path connecting the Protestant secondary school and the agricultural institute.

"It's Miss Renquist—and she's taking the back path!"

"Isn't that the one where your father and Mr. Frykman saw the leopard?" I asked.

She nodded, her face scrunching up with puzzlement. "How funny she doesn't mind using it. My mother won't."

"Mine neither," I said. "Not until the men decide it's OK to lift the leopard curfew."

Davina lowered her voice to a soft hiss. "Miss Renquist borrows these books from my mother sometimes," she told me. "She's always got a few in her bedroom bookcase."

"How do you know?"

"I was in her bedroom once. My mother brought her some Swedish fruit soup and jungle orchids that time she had malaria real bad. I went along."

Plain Miss Renquist reading about lovely Rosamunde trembling in her bikini? Or her underwear? Or her night-gown? Modest Miss Renquist reading about savage kisses behind the bougainvillea at a South African barbecue? Deeply shaken, I peeped through the branches and watched Miss Renquist walk down the leopard path, half expecting this information to alter her appearance.

But no. She looked the same as always, her gray-blond permanent bobbing briskly, her navy cotton dress swishing nearer her ankles than her knees, and the set of her shoulders as prim as the blue-flowered Danish china she used on special occasions.

"My mother says Miss Renquist's life has been a terrible disappointment to her, and we ought to be extra kind," I said. "Her fiancé was killed in the Second German War, like Miss Adela's brother. After that, Miss Renquist dedicated her life to missionary service."

Davina said it was beyond her how reading about Rosamunde and Safari Suit could improve Miss Renquist's disappointing life.

"We must have missed something in your book," I said. "Maybe we better try *The Passionate Strangers.*"

Davina rolled her eyes and picked a hard green rose-apple. She bit it, then spat, her face twisting horribly.

I skimmed through the romantic trials of lovely Alicia Burroughs, secretary to the owner of a Spanish wine-making estate. Ignoring Davina's remark that all these Harlequin people seemed to be absolute drunkards, I read aloud the passage where Count Raoul de Monteña-Silva visits Alicia in her bedroom at the back of the castle. "'Are you really the innocent English rose you pretend to be, Miss Burroughs?' the Count rasped, his heavy black brows drawing together in threatening Satanic points.

"His sensual lips curled sardonically as he stared at the fragile girl standing so quietly before him, sylph-like in her simple dress of virginal white. He pulled her toward him in a sudden, panther-quick movement, his strong fingers digging painfully into the soft skin of her shoulders. Although Alicia knew she would have deep purple bruises in the morning, she was too enthralled to object, reveling in the Count's fierce animal magnetism."

I heard the delicate pick-pick-pick of Davina's fingers worrying the scab on her knee.

"Better quit before it starts bleeding," I said. "Let's find out if it's time to swim yet. I want to build a water-hyacinth fort."

I handed *The Passionate Strangers* back to Davina. She tucked both books inside her waistband, and we shimmied down the rough trunk of the rose-apple tree. I examined the reddened skin on the insides of my legs, wincing. Rose-apple trees had one serious flaw: scratchy bark.

"My father says this leopard is the most beautiful animal he's ever seen," Davina remarked. "In his prime. All sleek and golden."

"I know. My father can't figure it out. He'd thought maybe the leopard was hanging around because he was old and couldn't find food. There isn't much easy prey in the jungle, I guess."

Davina said she only hoped he wouldn't eat her cat, Lumumba, and I resolved to help my little sister Faith keep an eye on Kitoko. (Usually Faith managed fine on her own, but sometimes she was stuck indoors with sore throats and allergies, especially during the early summer rains.)

"I'd like to see that leopard for myself," Davina said. "Wouldn't you?"

"Not if he was hungry," I replied. "Leopards are awfully dangerous."

"Oh, no, girls, not this one. He's just looking for a mate."

We jumped. Miss Renquist stood behind us on the foot-path, her arms filled with blue examination notebooks. The spray of rhinestone flowers in her black cat's-eye glasses glinted in the sun, and a fine veil of sweat clung to the pale hairs on her upper lip. Her patient smile and orthopedic sandals were familiar, but her bright lipstick and strong sweet scent (jasmine? frangipani?) took me by surprise. I'd been mistaken; Miss Renquist did not look the same at all.

"My, it's a hot one! I've got to grade English exams, myself, but I suppose you two plan to spend the rest of the afternoon in the river."

I squared my shoulders, rebelling against her hardworking virtue. "Yes," I said. "From three to five."

"Of course—sunburn or no sunburn," Miss Renquist said, her pale Swedish eyes amused and knowing. "It's understandable you overdid it after several months away, but I heard you were one sick girl!"

"Not so very sick," I muttered.

Miss Renquist often remarked how kind our parents were to allow us so much swimming time. "All you kids—

and especially you, Grace!—are just a bit silly about that river," she'd say, her tone accusing. Or so I believed, for I resented her catching me immersed in my river-passion. Why should Miss Renquist understand how I loved the slow humid days of summer on the Congo, swimming until the water rippled orange from the setting sun and my burned skin wrinkled up like old Mama Marta down at the village? How did she learn I was partial to the glum gray-green intimacy of the river on a rainy day? Did she know other things as well? Had she seen me standing at my bedroom window on moonlit nights, watching the calm silvery sweep of the river? Had she found out my near panic on the rare foggy day when the river was hidden from view? After her first remark of this kind, I avoided Miss Renquist as much as I could. I was afraid of my own transparency and worried that I had given her some subtle advantage.

"I need a coffee break before I get to work." Miss Renquist glanced down at her ladylike Elgin wristwatch. "It's only two-thirty, and Natana has just baked a batch of chocolate-chip cookies. Why don't you girls join me?"

We accepted Miss Renquist's unusual invitation with wide greedy eyes, knowing that her cook, Natana, made wonderful cookies with twice the amount of American chocolate chips our mothers used. (Mrs. Frykman often said it wasn't any wonder Miss Renquist could be so extravagant. "Elsie's one of the lucky ones who doesn't have to spread things out to feed a family," she'd tell my mother, apparently forgetting that Carol was in America now, married even, and not coming back.) I hoped for a chance to peek in Miss Renquist's bedroom and see those Harlequin romances for myself.

Davina and I had just begun to nibble cookies, our ankles crossed like Ladybird Johnson's at a tea party in the latest *Good Housekeeping,* when Natana called Miss Renquist

outside. He wanted her to make an offer on a Nile perch two
fishermen were selling. ("The nicest *kapitani* I have ever seen,
Mademoiselle. And these men are swamp-country fools, so
you can buy it cheap.") We abandoned our cookies on the
coffee table between the spring issue of *Evangelical Mission
Quarterly* and the African violets and dashed down the hall
to her bedroom.

It looked ordinary enough at first. The Sears-catalog bedspread exactly matched the flowered curtains, and two
needlepoint pillows were arranged on the rocker just so. A
green glass kerosene lamp, a box of matches, and a loud-
ticking clock shared the bedside table. And then I noticed
the pictures. While Miss Renquist's living-room pictures du-
plicated ours at home—*Praying Hands* and *Jesus on the Road
to Emmaus*—her bedroom pictures did not. A large picture
of a ruined cathedral overgrown with vines and carpeted
with grass and wildflowers filled the wall behind her rocker.
A Dutch museum poster thumbtacked to the closet door
featured two plump winged cherubs, each embracing the
other's body of warm pink stone. Above the bed was a charcoal sketch of a walled garden with a fountain, lilac bushes,
and one wrought-iron chair. Beside that was a framed poem
by Rainer Maria Rilke, carefully copied in Miss Renquist's
precise handwriting. I read the first two lines and turned
away, shamed, examining the modest jumble on the dresser
with unnecessary attention. Though the lipstick was called
Pink Flamingo Passion and the white Fuller brush trailed
curling strands of gray-blond hair, these toiletries seemed
much less personal than "You who never arrived in my arms,
Beloved, who were lost from the start."

Davina waved me over to an unvarnished mahogany
bookcase by the rocker. I dropped down on my knees,
quickly reviewing the titles. Nearly all were hardcover, including Bibles in Swedish, English, French, and Lingala, and

a well-thumbed Swedish hymnal. I recognized *In His Steps,
The Robe,* and *The Big Fisherman,* as well as a scary new book
everyone was reading about the End Times and Jesus' Second Coming. Dozens of paper markers poked above the
pages of a thick midnight blue book entitled *Poems of Rainer
Maria Rilke.* I passed over thin volumes by Verlaine, Rimbaud,
Herbert, and a water-damaged one by Elizabeth Barrett
Browning that had a cracked spine. And there they were, at
long last, way down on the bottom shelf between a biogra-
phy of missionary Adoniram Judson and a collection of Peter
Marshall's sermons, a row of brightly colored paperbacks
with the black masked-clown trademark. I tilted my head
sideways to read the titles: *Tropical Ecstasy, Remembered
Serenade, A Dangerous Loving.*

Davina and I made it back to the living room just in time,
perching ourselves sedately on the couch beneath *Jesus on
the Road to Emmaus,* trying to look like we had never been
anywhere else. Miss Renquist fed us cookies until we were
forced to refuse, and then we went out on the back veranda
to admire the fish and listen to Natana and Miss Renquist
argue over different methods of preparing it.

"Listen, Mademoiselle, you want to fix it nice and hot,
with good Congolese *pilipili* pepper. You do *not* want that
cold white sauce with the strange green bits."

"But I always have tartar sauce with my fish," Miss
Renquist protested.

"Well, I think even you *mindele* should try new ways
sometimes," Natana said, folding his arms across his chest.
"And a Congolese fish needs hot Congolese peppers."

"Oh, all right," Miss Renquist said, smiling and throwing
up her hands. "I will try it. But just this once, *oyoki ngai?*
And only because I am out of tartar sauce anyway."

"*Nasepeli mingi,* Mademoiselle!" Natana said, grabbing
both her hands and shaking them hard. "This is wonderful!

You will never want that cold white sauce again, not after you have eaten Nile perch fixed the right way. I will send my son down to the market for some palm oil and fresh *pilipili*. It is important to do this properly!"

Miss Renquist was laughing when we left for our swim, her thin cheeks as bright as her Flamingo Passion lipstick. I thought there must be an explanation for her behavior and went looking for one as tactfully as I knew how.

"Miss Renquist looks awfully nice with lipstick," I remarked oh-so-casually to my mother.

"Well, dear, her lipstick is a pretty color, I agree, but it's just a bit bright for my taste," my mother said. She turned to my father, her forehead wrinkling up like a washboard. "Did you hear that, Robert? Even the children are noticing now!"

My father looked at my sister Faith and me, then made a tiny negative motion with his head. My mother was so upset she ignored him and rushed on.

"I really can't bear to watch poor Elsie make a fool of herself! What do we know about Nigel Burton anyway? Just that he's an engineer with a good British firm, and that he's ridiculously handsome, with lovely manners. He could have a wife and six children back in England for all we know!"

"Come now, Junie, we have more on him than that!" my father said with a grin. "He has beautiful French, and he's the only non-African I've ever seen who wears a safari suit well. Don't tell me you haven't noticed how swashbuckling he looks!"

A safari suit! Didn't my parents know that men in safari suits turned women into brainless underclothed dolls who wore their love like a painful sunburn?

"Well, I think he's a menace," my mother snapped. "And this is just the last thing I would have expected from Elsie. She's always been such a spiritual person. Why, she was terribly upset when you men decided to cancel Wednesday night prayer meetings because of the leopard! She said we should trust the Lord to protect His own."

My father's mouth twisted in a peculiar smile. "And you think that suggests a spiritual nature?" he asked. "I think it means she welcomes a certain kind of danger, myself! But don't panic, Junie. There's plenty of time to learn more about him. He won't be done with that feasibility study for weeks yet—you know how government projects are. I'll keep an eye on him."

My father was far too busy with end-of-the-school-year activities at the agricultural institute to keep an eye on Nigel Burton, and I knew it. I decided to do it for him. Spying might be fun. Besides, I was already in the habit of spending my vacations away from my family, swimming or roaming Boanda, sometimes with Davina but most often alone.

I managed several sightings of Nigel Burton. Once I saw him out for an early morning run, his naked chest smooth and golden, his breathing unhurried. Another day I watched him emerge from a late-afternoon swim, shaking river water from his silvery head. One noon he roared up to Miss Renquist's house in a government Jeep and leaped out the doorless vehicle with a box from Madame Vaske's European grocery in his hand. Miss Renquist was waiting on the veranda with a pitcher of limeade, her lips pink with Flamingo Passion and all her feelings sitting right on the outside of her skin. As she ushered him inside, I heard a hearty burst of male laughter and a shocked giggle.

Music suddenly began drifting from Miss Renquist's house at all hours of the day—opera music, a lone soprano voice floating and falling like the scarlet blossoms of a Nandi flame tree in dry season. I tried to follow the words, *"O mio babbino caro, mi piace, e bello, bello,"* stumbling over their lovely strangeness. Miss Renquist's portable record player had been broken for as long as I could remember, but she had evidently managed to get it fixed. And my mother's eyebrows lifted clear up to her hairline when she told my father that Miss Renquist had asked her to buy more batteries for the record player next time she went shopping at the Coquilhatville market.

"She's just having a good time," my father said.

"And where does this good time end, Robert? We don't even know if this Nigel Burton is a Christian!"

That was a truly horrifying thought. If Nigel Burton wasn't a Christian and Miss Renquist married him, she would be Unequally Yoked to an Unbeliever. God thought that was a terrible thing, Saint Paul said so. What if Nigel Burton believed in evolution and supported the Peace Corps? What if Nigel Burton, like Carol Frykman's new husband, was a Catholic? Miss Renquist might as well drink liquor, ride in sleek black cars, and lounge about in her nightgown. I tried to imagine her kissing Nigel Burton. Would her body tremble uncontrollably? Would her breasts strain against the buttons of her blouse? Would he smile sardonically as his fingers dug painfully into her soft skin?

And suddenly Nigel Burton was gone. He took the Wednesday afternoon Air Congo flight to Kinshasa. No one knew if he had finished his feasibility studies. No one knew if he planned to return. My father came home at sundown and told my mother the news just as I walked in from my swim. My mother was sitting on the floor, sorting a sack of boat mail that had arrived for the mission, and she stared at him, dropping an armload of American magazines. For a moment she sat perfectly still, surrounded by a crazy muddle of magazines two months out of date, her upturned hands limp in her blue-flowered lap. Then she began sorting again, adding two back issues of *Christianity Today* to the Frykman pile.

"One other thing," my father said. "Our leopard friend

hasn't been seen or heard of for at least a week now—*and* there've been reports of an unusually handsome leopard up near Bomondo plantation. Elmer, Nils, and I have decided to lift the leopard curfew."

"Thank heaven for small mercies," said my mother.

She picked up a brown paper parcel, studied it carefully, then handed it to me. "Irma Carlson will want this right away, Grace. And since the curfew is over, there's plenty of time for you to deliver it before supper."

I changed out of my swimsuit and set off, my right arm pressing Mrs. Carlson's package to my chest and my free hand swinging the flashlight my mother had forced on me. I had no intention of using it. My first moments of frank black night in several weeks were not to be compromised by a wobbling puddle of artificial yellow light.

The path smelled of damp moss, hidden insects, and overripe papaya, the still-warm shadows softening the pungent impact of the tangerine tree behind the Frykmans' cookhouse. Passing Miss Renquist's clothesline, I was surprised to see a half-dozen pale garments dangling like dispirited ghosts from the wooden pins. By morning they would be soggy and sour smelling, and poor Natana would have to wash them all over again. I knew Miss Renquist ought to be told (plainly she had just forgotten) but her kitchen windows were dark. The bulky thatched roof seemed to press down on the walls, giving the house a crushed deserted air.

I took a few more steps down the path, breathing in the musky sweetness of guavas ripening above my head. Rose-apples too, I realized, sniffing pleasurably—unseen rose-apples with a bold smell, riper than ours at home. But a sudden thought made me turn back: Could it be that Miss Renquist was at home, that her living-room lights couldn't be seen from the back of the house?

The grass, lush and overlong from the early June rains, brushed softly against my ankles as I crossed Miss Renquist's yard. I ducked under the clothesline and made a wide circle around the snake-prone bougainvillea, studying the hollow black windows and aging thatch before pausing beside the frangipani tree that flanked the front veranda. I leaned cautiously against one blooming limb, knowing how brittle a frangipani branch could be, how sudden the crack and fall. The tree trunk seemed to be treading water, struggling to stay upright in a tidal wave of eerie white blossom. I pinched one flower from its stem and savored the shiny stickiness as the sap pooled in my cupped palm. I had always thought of frangipani as greedy, their rich orange-pink centers sucking all the color from the pale petals. Tonight, color invisible, I was newly, strangely aware of the generous dripping and seeping between my fingers.

As I prepared to walk boldly up the worn brick steps and rap on the front door with my sticky knuckle, the full moon slid above the guava and rose-apple trees behind the house, flinging a silver wash across the front lawn, the road, the steep slope down to the river. I paused, transfixed.

The roof's deep overhang offered the veranda no protection from the moon, and gradually there emerged a narrow charcoal-sketch outline of Miss Renquist reclining on her Congolese antelope-skin lazy chair. She was staring at the river, her chin tilted, her finely silvered body as desperately still as my hand on the window frame those nights I watched the river from my bedroom. The expanse of lawn filled in with slow blanched shapes: a crumbling garden wall, a splashing fountain, blooming lilac bushes, and a single wrought-iron chair with dainty curves.

Softly, sweetly, Miss Renquist began to hum. She leaned forward, removing her sensible sandals and lifting her feet to the low veranda wall. Her widespread toes were startlingly chubby, like the pink marble toes in her museum poster of the two Italian cherubs. But she's missing a partner, I thought. She's got only half an embrace.

> "Thy holy wings, dear Savior, spread
> gently over me;
> And through the long night watches,
> I'll rest secure in Thee."

Miss Renquist's humming had gradually taken words and melody, and the gilded night garden echoed with the cheerful Swedish evening hymn. As Miss Renquist wiggled her cherub toes in time, long sleek shapes began slipping out from the bushes and trees, padding silently across the lawn toward the house. They were moon colored, with flicking tails and pale gleaming whiskers. Muscles rippled under their lush fur as they stretched and settled themselves on the grass, the gravel walk, the concrete veranda steps. Miss Renquist smiled and sang on, but I inched carefully backwards, away from the frangipani tree and the listening creatures.

I rounded Miss Renquist's unlit house, shoulders hunched and head lowered, wading through the soft grass on feet that stumbled with surprise. My fingers were curled tightly around my flashlight, my solitary frangipani blossom, my square brown parcel. No, Mrs. Carlson's square brown parcel.

I sat down on Miss Renquist's back step and studied the green customs tag by the light of the moon. The parcel contents were listed in flowing blue script: Jello, Dream Whip, Kool-Aid, and Books.

Books about silly, pretty women like Rosamunde and Alicia. Books about women like Miss Renquist, the *new* Miss Renquist, all Pink Flamingo Passion and *pilipili* pepper.

Women who were not afraid of transparency, women who bravely wore their love outside their timid skin.

Despite my mother's certain anger, I tore off the address label, eliminating Irma Carlson, her sister in Florida, even the Sarasota postmark, and set the parcel flush against the bottom of the kitchen door. I peeled the frangipani from my sticky palm and placed the flower gently over the rough spot where the label had been. Hadn't Rosamunde attended a South African barbecue wearing a frangipani in her long blond hair?

Gazing up at Miss Renquist's shadowy fruit trees, I felt a prickling in my still-tender flesh. The guava branches concealed a dozen watchful animals, I was certain. And the ripening rose-apples and dense dark leaves doubtless hid glowing eyes, twitching ears, soft blunt noses.

I went home by way of the shining, palm-lined river, pondering the mission men's confidence in their own power to impose or lift a leopard curfew. Miss Renquist knew better. Miss Renquist knew that every day was risky. Yet she boldly walked the leopard path.

Bofio

I SAT ON TOP of the woodpile in the far corner of the cookhouse. My throat burned from the smoke, and the backs of my knees were splinter filled and sore, but I refused to cough or scratch. I knew they would throw me out if they remembered I was here.

Bofio refilled his tin mug with tea, poked at the fire, then set the kettle back on the cast-iron range. He poured a thick yellow stream of sweetened condensed milk into his tea and stirred it slowly. My mouth watered all the way back to my itching throat, for I loved tea made the Congolese way. It tasted like strong dark wood smoke with soft milky edges. And though I wished I could drink tea from a tin mug like Bofio's, I couldn't manage it without burning my lips and fingers. My father explained why ("Tin is one of nature's best heat conductors, you see,") but it didn't help. So when Bofio offered me tea, I used a thick china mug that I kept on a shelf in the cookhouse. I would take cautious little sips while Bofio watched and laughed without any sound, his torso shaking up and down, his lips peeled back from square white teeth. Then, eying me triumphantly, he would pick up his tin mug and toss the scalding liquid down his open throat.

"Next week I begin working for Madame of the Hard Words," Bofio announced.

I accidentally knocked a piece of firewood off the pile, I was so surprised, but Bofio didn't notice. He leaned against the smoke-stained wall and grinned at the other two men. Bofio had worked for my mother since last September, when Makua got married and joined his father-in-law's tailoring business in Mbandaka. At first I'd missed Makua, missed him a lot, but I liked Bofio at once. We all did. I was certain my mother hadn't fired him.

Dawena, Mrs. Frykman's longtime cook, clutched at his balding head like it might fall off and roll away. Luke, dozing beside the cookstove, opened his eyes wide and sat up as straight as his bent old bones allowed.

"Eeee, *wapi!*" Dawena cried. "You have gone *kilikili*, Bofio! You should understand how lucky you are to work for Madame Berggren. She has time to talk and laugh, and she gives you extra clothes and food."

"I remember when your son had the cholera," Luke added. "She bought all his medicine and gave you time off with pay, *boye te?*"

I listened eagerly, delighted they were speaking in Lingala today. The men often switched to Lokundo, Mongo, or some other local dialect when they talked among themselves, and then I got bored with eavesdropping—as bored as Davina believed I *should* be. ("Honestly, Grace, downcountry we would never sneak around listening to the help! It's childish!")

"Yes, yes, I know I'm lucky," Bofio said, perching on the heavy worktable and swinging his bare feet. "But I made a bet with Alphonse. He worked for Madame of the Hard Words for three weeks last year, and he says no one, truly no one, can put up with her for a whole month. Of course he's a

Bakumu, so what does he know? A Lokele can prove him wrong."

"Bofio, you do not understand," Dawena groaned, nervously massaging the back of his neck. "But I understand very well! Madame Frykman sent me over there to help a few mornings right after Pekwe quit."

"Oh yes, Pekwe," Bofio said, snapping his fingers. "That bad-tempered Ngbaka from the Ubangi. I forgot about him. He lasted less than a week, I believe."

Dawena's forehead creased, and I watched the wrinkles ripple up to the top of his head. "Three days," he said flatly.

"Well, little can be expected from an ignorant ugly Ngbaka. He spoke only a few words of Lingala, I remember, and no French at all." Bofio rolled his eyes. "As for his balance in a canoe, it was pitiful. He swayed and wobbled like a *mwana* just learning to walk!"

"All that is true," Dawena agreed. "But Pekwe was smart about one important thing, Bofio. He knew better than to work for a hard *mwasi na mondele* with a bitter tongue."

"*Likambo te*," Bofio said with his peeled-back smile. "A woman with a bitter tongue is no problem for a Lokele."

Luke laughed, but Dawena frowned. He took a piece of sugarcane out of his shorts pocket and removed the woody layer with a small handmade knife. "It is not the same when the woman is a *mondele*," he said. "Besides, you know how *mindele* are always so busy? Well, Madame of the Hard Words is ten times busier than the rest of them, even Madame Frykman. She charges around like a maddened pig in the jungle, making fierce noises about everything, even the smallest things."

"Yes, I have heard." Bofio's smile widened. "The wash water is too cold, and there is not enough bluing in the rinse water. The tomatoes are sliced too thick, and the oatmeal has no salt!"

Dawena nodded and popped a chunk of sugarcane in his mouth. "It is foolish to make it a point of honor to endure her, Bofio," he said in a thick voice, chewing vigorously.

"You have endured Madame Frykman for many years," Bofio pointed out.

"Yes," Dawena agreed. "But Monsieur Frykman has always been grateful and given me extra money. And recently Madame Frykman has been very kind to my daughter Régine. Madame Frykman not only pays for her schooling but sews her beautiful clothes. The dress she made for Régine's graduation from Mademoiselle Judith's school was *kitoko mpenza!*"

The men nodded as if they'd all seen Régine's graduation dress.

"And you can ask a high bride price for a girl with a good education," Luke remarked.

Dawena said that had already occurred to him. They all laughed, but I was thoughtful. I'd seen Régine a few times, and I recalled that she was little, pretty, with a soft alto chuckle. Like Carol Frykman.

"But we are talking about Madame of the Hard Words, not Madame Frykman," Dawena said. "And this woman, Bofio, this bitter-tongued woman, she is *not* your *libeli!*"

I sucked in a deep thrilled breath. The missionaries discussed *libeli* only rarely, and then in a whisper, but I'd heard enough to know it was a very terrible thing. A Lokele male rite of passage, the whispers said, that the Congolese government and Protestant missionaries could not control. Even now, in 1969, the Lokele elders took their teenage boys deep in the jungle, dangerously deep, where the daylight was a hushed green darkness. There the boys would stay for three sunless months of illegal *libeli,* building strange bark huts, dressing up like leopards, learning magic curses, and undergoing a mysteriously horrible operation called circumcision to prove their manhood.

Bofio shrugged. "Maybe not, but a challenge is a good thing. I'm no feeble cowardly Ngbaka. My family traps fish, and my father—are you listening?—my father once caught a Nile perch in the Kisangani whitewater that weighed fifty kilos! A Belgian administrator took a picture of it."

"You people from Kisangani," said Dawena, his shiny scalp lifting with his eyebrows. "I think you're all *kilikili!* The mist in the bend of the river makes your heads soft, like rotting breadfruit. And you, Bofio, you are the very worst. You probably laughed when they circumcised you."

"That is so." Bofio drained his tea and tossed the tin mug into a dishpan. "In fact, I asked them to do it again!"

"Kilikili mpenza!" Dawena slapped his knee while Bofio wiped his grinning mouth with the back of his hand.

"Madame Berggren says she'll take me back if I don't like working for Madame of the Hard Words. I do good work, Madame Berggren says. She's hiring my friend Patrice for a month as her temporary cook."

I'd met Patrice, who often came by to drink tea and joke around with Bofio. I wondered if Patrice would throw cookhouse tea parties and make people laugh the way Bofio did. Probably that was too much to hope for, but at least Patrice might have the latest on Miss Renquist's activities since his brother-in-law was her cook, Natana. (Everyone was interested in Miss Renquist, just returned from an impromptu fourteen-day bicycling vacation in Holland, where she'd stayed in castles, visited gardens, and toured museums—"Though I don't suppose that's all she got up to!" Mrs. Frykman said. "I saw some of her photos, and she was wearing shocking-pink pedal pushers!")

"Madame Berggren is a kind fair woman," Bofio remarked. After a moment's pause he asked softly, "What do you suppose Madame Berggren thinks of Madame of the Hard Words?"

I'd thought Luke was napping again. Now I saw he was wide awake, just silent. Dawena's mouth puckered into a smile as sour as a green mango, and he spat a mouthful of sugarcane fibers onto the cookhouse floor.

"You listen well to me," Dawena said. "If Madame Berggren dislikes Madame of the Hard Words, we will never know it. No *mondele* says anything bad about another *mondele* to her Congolese boy. *Mindele* stick together."

If you can't say anything nice, don't say anything at all. My mother lived by this rule, and I'd noticed she never had anything to say about Mrs. Nordstrom. She didn't even comment when she heard me using Bofio's nickname for her, Madame of the Hard Words. I'd decided she enjoyed it.

Last year Mrs. Nordstrom and my mother were in charge of refreshments for the Boanda Mission Christmas party. Mrs. Nordstrom wanted to get a head start, so one night in August my mother went over to her house to help plan the menu. When she came home two hours later, her lips were pinched white, and thin hard cords bulged in her neck. She stalked into my father's office fuming about "people who live in the depths of the Congo and think you can't have Christmas without imported Swedish potato sausage, pickled herring, and lingonberries." But Mrs. Nordstrom came from the same part of America as my mother, the upper peninsula of Michigan, and twice a week they taught a Bible class together for Congolese ladies. They were dreadfully polite to each other most of the time.

"Alphonse says he likes working for the Belgian sisters at the Catholic Mission," Dawena said. "He has to make a great many special sauces, and if there are any lumps, Sister

Polycarp screams at him. But the rest of the sisters are nice for *mindele,* he says, and even Sister Polycarp is better than Madame of the Hard Words."

So Alphonse had gone over to the Catholics. Surely even Mrs. Nordstrom wasn't as bad as that!

Luke rose slowly from his chair beside the stove. His frail back curved out like a bow, and his skin had the ashy blackness of the very old Congolese. Luke had been Miss Adela and Miss Judith's "yardboy" for seventeen years. I'd met his granddaughter, Francine, at church. She had just finished the second grade, like my sister, only she attended Miss Judith's school while Faith went to the Ecole Belgique in Mbandaka. ("I'd rather Faith had an American education," my mother had sighed. "But I don't dare send her upcountry until she grows out of these allergies and throat infections.")

"This is I, *Tata* Luke Kangayani, wishing to say a few serious words." Luke leaned forward, curling both palms around the top of his ebony cane. "And because I am such an old *tata,* because of my white hair, you must listen."

"All right, father, I'm listening," Bofio said. Although he sounded respectful, Bofio's grin was not.

"Work for Madame of the Hard Words if you must, but be sure to quit before she makes your head crazy with anger," Luke said. "Afterwards it is too late. Much too late."

Bofio said, "Yes, father," in a playfully meek voice, and Luke sighed.

"I should get back," he said, dropping his formal tone. "I have to help Mademoiselle Adela plant the strange things Mademoiselle Renquist brought back for her. Tulips, Mademoiselle Adela calls them."

He hobbled toward the cookhouse door, his cane tapping loudly against the concrete, his bare feet silent. At the door, he paused. "That kind of madness, Bofio—it is truly terrible," he said soberly. "A sharp burning thing that takes a man by surprise and fills him up like the strongest palm wine. *Mindele* often have that effect. It's part of being white."

Sometimes listening to the help wasn't so interesting, but today it was well worth the itchy legs and smoke-sore throat. Today I was finding out things. Strange and new things. I tried to imagine either Bofio or Luke filled with a sharp burning madness, acting like crazy palm wine drunkards, and I failed completely. Dawena was often grouchy, but Bofio and Luke were lighthearted laughing men who showed up on time each morning, worked hard, and didn't steal. Miss Judith and my mother were always congratulating themselves on their good help. Bofio made wonderful Swedish rye bread, ironed beautifully, and never broke dishes like Makua used to. Miss Judith said it was a miracle the way Luke, for all his age and frailty, could sniff out a rainstorm and clear the clothesline just in time. "And when it comes to chopping firewood—on my honor as a born-and-bred Minnesotan, June—that man is a Congolese Paul Bunyan!"

Bofio remarked that Luke had more white hair than sense, but I noticed he didn't say so until Luke was well out of earshot.

"Eeee, Bofio!" Dawena nodded his bald head in my direction. "Do you see who is on top of the woodpile listening to our foolish talk?"

Bofio jumped off the worktable and stared at me with such exaggerated surprise that I was suspicious.

"She is very wise to hide where her color will blend with the wood smoke and whitewash, *boye te?*" Dawena asked, poking Bofio in the ribs.

"Very wise," Bofio agreed seriously. "But next time she should wear a white shirt, I think. Not a red one."

Dawena laughed until his chair rattled and squeaked. I

began to slide silently off the firewood. Maybe I'd go play with Davina even though she was a downcountry snob lately.

"No, no, Grace." Bofio gestured me back into place. "We were joking."

Sweat glistened on Bofio's upper lip, and soot from the wood-burning stove streaked his white cook's apron. He stood so still that I could see the faint currents of cookhouse heat and smoke drifting all around him. Then he dropped down on one knee in front of the cast-iron stove, opened the door to the oven compartment, and pulled out a blackened cake pan filled with shelled roasted peanuts.

"I'm going to grind these for peanut butter," he said. "But you may have some first if you like."

"*Merci.*"

I watched Bofio carry the pan over to the worktable with his bare hands. "My mother has lots of potholders," I said. "Nice thick ones too. Why do you never use them?"

"Because I don't need to," he replied. "My hands are *makasi*, tough, and so are my feet. I can walk barefoot on roasted palm nuts fresh out of the fire. I can even stamp out burning coals. You should never try it though!"

"*Mpo na nini?*"

Bofio grinned, faint squinty lines appearing around his eyes. "Because white skin is too *mpamba*, too weak and useless." He dumped a handful of the roasted peanuts into one of my mother's Pyrex custard bowls and handed it to me. "Now don't eat these right away, or they will burn your *mpamba* little white fingers!" he said.

Dawena snickered quietly, gently, shielding his eyes with callused hands. I promptly dumped all the peanuts into my palm, wincing as each one sent a fiery dart into my skin.

"Eeee, *nakamwi!*" Bofio exclaimed. "I am astounded! Why did you never tell me you are so much stronger than other white people? We'll make you an honorary Lokele."

I nodded, knowing he was laughing at me, knowing I looked foolish. Even childish, like Davina said.

"Grace! Come inside right away!"

It was my mother's voice, higher than usual, quivering with excitement—or was it anger? I clambered down from the woodpile and dashed across the backyard to the house. My mother poked her head around the kitchen door, her cheeks bright as the crimson bougainvillea that grew alongside the front veranda. She drummed her fingers impatiently against the rough mahogany doorframe.

"Hurry *up*, Grace! *Quick!* The Voice of America broadcast is on, and American astronauts have landed on the moon! They've actually *walked* on it, *walked* on the *moon!*" Her eyes began to get teary and her chin wobbled. "It's amazing. I can scarcely believe it."

My mother cried often, and always over the strangest things—a letter, a sermon, a bouquet of jungle orchids, a Fanny Crosby hymn. I preferred to keep out of her way when she got emotional, but today I didn't have a choice. She grabbed my arm, saying, "You'll remember this day all your life, Grace," and then pulled me into the dining room, where my father sat at the table with his ear pressed to the radio, a wide smile splitting his face.

"Shhhh!" he whispered, waggling his forefinger at us.

Voice of America reception wasn't always good. Sometimes the static was so frightful you couldn't hear anything except very American Rice-Krispie snaps, crackles, and pops. When President Kennedy was killed six years ago, nobody at Boanda Mission heard about it for three days. The Arab traders at the big Mbandaka market told us while my mother was haggling over the price of eggplants. America must be going to the dogs, the missionary adults had said, or such a terrible thing would never have happened. And Mrs. Nordstrom had told us we ought to count our blessings. "Just think how much worse we'd all feel if President Kennedy had been a Republican."

Today Voice of America's signal was coming in strong, but I'd already missed the part about the moon landing. Now the announcer was talking about Vietnam. I sat across the table from my father and studied the gray speckles in his hair while he hunched over the radio. My mother stood behind him, wiping her eyes with the embroidered handkerchief she tucked into her pocket each morning. Then the newscast was over, and Radio South Africa came on with "Swingin' Safari."

My father switched off the radio and repeated everything the VOA announcer had said about the moon landing. Since he was in a really jolly mood, he went on to explain how radios worked, how all these wonderful sound-carrying waves bounced around in the atmosphere. My mother sniffed and blew her nose. I crunched my cooling peanuts, noticing that the fiery red dots had faded from my palm. When my father was done, I returned to the cookhouse to tell Bofio the news. He stopped feeding peanuts into the meat grinder, rolled his eyes, and grinned. "Those crazy Americans walking on the moon had better be careful, " he said. "Everybody knows the moon is filled with evil spirits."

The next week Bofio began working for Mrs. Nordstrom, and my mother hired Bofio's friend Patrice as our temporary cook. Patrice was nice enough, but he burned an iron-shaped hole in my new white sailor blouse with the red satin ribbon, he kept taking days off without warning us, and he didn't know how to bake. My mother had to do a lot more housework than usual. She wasn't happy about it, so she assigned some of the extra housekeeping chores to me, which I considered unfair. My summer vacation was only ten weeks long, and extra chores meant I had less time to spend swimming and building water-hyacinth forts in the river.

When I complained, my mother made a horrid remark about Bofio saving both my poor skin and the family budget. ("Do you have any idea how much it costs to mail-order American suntan lotion?") I settled for silent resistance after that, doing all my housework slowly and clumsily. Two weeks of this drove my mother crazy, so crazy that she asked my father to straighten me out. "I'm sick of Grace acting like the village idiot about her chores!" I heard her say. "Maybe she doesn't want to wash dishes or dust or shake rugs, but she's nearly twelve. That's life! And I think she'd quit having these so-called accidents if *you* talked to her."

I wanted to tell her I hadn't broken the butter dish on purpose, only the dessert plate. Besides, dusting and shaking rugs honestly did make me sneeze. There was just one thing to be done, I decided. Bofio had to be persuaded to come back right away, before he could ruin any more of my all-too-short summer. With this object in mind, I visited Bofio at his new job, hoping to soften him up with a can of Spam I'd swiped from my mother's pantry. Bofio accepted the Spam but flatly refused to leave Mrs. Nordstrom until the month was up.

"But Bofio, we miss you!" I said, putting on my Nice-Missionary-Girl smile, the one adults always liked whether they were American, Congolese, or Belgian.

Bofio peeked under the lid of a four-gallon kettle of drinking water. He frowned when he saw it wasn't boiling and put more firewood in the stove. I looked out the tiny cookhouse window and sighed. It was a beautiful swimming day, the kind that sparkled even when you were underwater with your eyes closed. I could almost see the sun glowing through the sheer hyacinth petals, almost feel that silly gush of happiness that made me wave and shout *"Mbote! Bonjour! Jambo!* Hello!" to passing boats and pirogues. And here I was, stuck with Bofio's chores while perfect river days went by.

"You have gone *kilikili*, Bofio," I grumbled. "Just like Luke and Dawena said. Otherwise you would never work for Madame of the Hard Words when you could work for us."

Bofio dumped a half dozen sweet potatoes into a basin of water and began cleaning their orange skins with an old nail brush.

"You shut your mouth and listen well to me, Grace," Bofio said, scrubbing ferociously. "I will not leave this job until I have worked here a full month. I have a bet with Alphonse, and it's worth a lot of money. After I collect on my bet, I'll go back to your house again, I swear it, but not before. I was not born to make your life easier."

I started to coax and plead, but he shushed me, cocking his ear toward the house. "Madame of the Hard Words is calling," he sighed, and then he grinned, his lips drawing back from his teeth. "Her voice reminds me of an ill-tempered monkey down by the river at sunset."

I listened to the distant spill of quick nervous chatter and snickered, my own ill temper fading. "Oh, the cranky old colobus monkey!" I said. "The one who lives in the umbrella tree just down the hill."

"*Yango wana!* I don't understand why hunters didn't get her long ago—or that leopard last month. Maybe they all think she's too mean for the belly to digest."

I pictured Mrs. Nordstrom scampering about with a long curling tail, swinging from branch to branch with frantic monkey energy. I pictured her, too, in a greasy monkey stew seasoned with *pilipili* peppers, spinach greens and rice on the side.

I was still laughing when Mrs. Nordstrom appeared in the cookhouse doorway, all crisp blond curls and cool starchy clothes, spurting breathless and angry words. "Bofio, I was speaking to you! I insist you pay attention when I speak to you!"

"*Oui*, Madame," he said politely. "I'm listening."

He turned away from her, stabbing the sweet potatoes with a fork and putting them into the oven.

"Good," she snapped. "Now, do you have any idea what I found in my slice of papaya this morning? No? Then I'll tell you. Seeds. Not one but *four* of them!"

"I am sorry, Madame."

"You must be careful about these things. You've got to learn to take pride in your work. I don't know what the problem is with you people!"

Mrs. Nordstrom crossed the cookhouse floor, her green cotton skirt crackling, and lifted the lid on the kettle of drinking water. "I hope you realize this water is not boiling, Bofio! And why aren't there two kettles? I know I told you to boil two kettles of drinking water!"

I slid quietly out the cookhouse door, a sickness roiling in my stomach. It was the same sickness I got whenever I saw that picture in the Frykmans' dining room, the one of Jesus wearing a crown of thorns and dragging a cross while a mob of people yelled and threw things. I decided not to visit Bofio again until the month was up, but the following Monday Patrice played hooky and upset my plans. My mother wanted to send a note to Mrs. Nordstrom, and as Patrice wasn't around, I had to deliver it. Afterwards I stopped by the cookhouse to see Bofio, who was inside ironing shirts and dresses.

It was one of those hot soggy rainy-season days when you wanted to wring the steaminess out of the air with your bare hands. The Nordstrom cookhouse was like the inside of a jumbo whitewashed oven, and I asked Bofio why he didn't iron outside. He said he'd rather work in the cookhouse because Madame of the Hard Words didn't like being in it, and he had a better chance of being left alone.

"Her voice scolds like a monkey at sundown, Grace, only it lasts all day," Bofio said. His peeled-back smile was gone, and he spoke as if he lifted a heavier burden than Mrs. Nordstrom's charcoal iron. He touched the bottom of the iron with his finger and frowned. "Too cold," he said. "The Madame will fire Hard Words like bullets."

He swung the iron in a swooping arc to heat up the coals, showering sparks and a few silvery ashes onto the concrete floor. Through the triangle-shaped holes on the side of the iron I could see the naked orange glow of burning charcoal. It was like peeping inside the heart of a fierce living thing, and I recoiled when the iron hissed and spat.

"I brought you an oatmeal cookie, Bofio," I said. "My mother made them yesterday. Our first cookies in many days, because your friend Patrice doesn't know how to bake." I handed the cookie to him, hoping I sounded pathetic and underfed.

"My heart pains me to hear it," Bofio replied, his voice dry as elephant grass before the rains. "You *mindele* always think you should have things exactly the way you want them. It's a habit for you. A bad habit. You should get over it before you get any older."

He sat down on the wooden bench across from the cook stove and ate my mother's oatmeal cookie. When it was gone, he tipped his head back against the wall, wiped his sweating face with a ragged handkerchief, and closed his eyes. "Have you noticed the moon lately, Grace?" he asked. "Strange things are happening up there. You Americans were unwise to upset the evil spirits, I think."

"Why should they be upset?" I wanted to know. "Both

Voice of America and the BBC said the astronauts just walked around for a while, planted a flag, and left."

"Maybe it was the flag," Bofio said. "I'm not sure. Anyway, the moon has been disturbed, and now the evil spirits are angry. They're coming down to earth, and they're driving people to madness. Only today Dawena told me about a *mwasi* in his wife's father's village who went completely *kili-kili*. This woman was fighting with her husband, and she picked up a basin of hot water and . . ."

"You should have finished the ironing long ago, Bofio! The patio has to be swept, and the pantry rearranged, and—Oh honestly, you people are hopeless. It would be quicker to do everything myself!" Mrs. Nordstrom stood in the cookhouse doorway clutching a blue enamel basin to her starchy front. The basin was filled with mangoes ripened to a lovely mottled rose. Mrs. Nordstrom's face was the same dusky mango pink, but on her it wasn't lovely. She shoved the basin at Bofio and said she needed the mangoes peeled and sliced for a pie.

"And this time I want thin, even slices," she told him. "My last pie looked like a five-year-old made it!"

I slipped past Mrs. Nordstrom and went home. The next day Patrice came back to work, and I gave him a full account of my visit to Bofio. Patrice made a sharp clicking noise with his big yellow teeth. "Bofio's told me about her," he replied. "Dawena too. Dawena says she gets angry about everything, and everything is always wrong. There are bugs in the flour and tangerine seeds in the fruit salad. The meat is tough, and the banana bread is heavy. The pineapple is too green, and the spinach leaves aren't clean. You could boil the whole river for drinking water, and it still wouldn't be enough to please her."

Sweet musky chunks of guava bubbled gently in a kettle on the back of the cookhouse range. I watched Patrice stir the fruit with a wooden spoon, my mouth watering as the soft seedy guava flesh disintegrated into a thick pink sauce. Patrice wasn't Bofio and couldn't bake, but he did have a way with guava sauce.

"Yes, it's a wearisome life, working for Madame of the Hard Words, but tomorrow is Wednesday. Tomorrow Bofio will have worked for her longer than anyone else ever has, and Alphonse is going to be a lot poorer than he expected!" Patrice laughed and waved the spoon, splashing a bit of guava onto the floor. "I have been invited to the celebration in Bofio's village tomorrow night. It's going to be a really tremendous *fête*, with fresh meat even! Bofio's rich uncle is butchering one of his goats."

I supposed Bofio deserved a party if anyone ever did, and it seemed he got one. By the time Patrice finally showed up for work on Thursday, it was well after noon and my mother had given up on him. A dense web of tiny red lines overlaid the whites of Patrice's eyes, and his skin had turned the bleached gray of a dead tree limb. He was touchy and sullen, spending what was left of the day slouched in a chair in the cookhouse. My mother wasn't in a good mood either. Her jaw had a stiff squared-off look. She collected every rug in the house and shook it hard. I decided to run over to the Nordstroms' and find out when Bofio planned to give notice. ("Hurry up and tell her, Bofio!" I would say. "Tell her you're going to work for *us* again, starting tomorrow—and tell her *right now!*") I was just rounding the corner of the cookhouse when I saw Mrs. Nordstrom, saw and heard her shrieking in Lingala.

I stopped, gripping my hands together. Missionary ladies never shrieked, not even Mrs. Nordstrom. I stood still, unblinking, flattening myself against the cookhouse wall.

"I have been gracious about your poor attitude. I have tolerated your laziness. I have even lowered my housekeeping standards, trying to give you a chance. But—but *this!*" Mrs. Nordstrom's voice soared up, then higher, and she began to stutter, throwing in French and English words when she couldn't find a Lingala one quickly enough.

"This *bet!* How *dare* you drag me into your filthy gambling schemes and make me the object of a bet! I'm just sick, absolutely sick. And you have the nerve to show your face here when you're hours and hours late for work and *reeking* of stale palm wine!"

Mrs. Nordstrom's eyes were furious blue slits, and her lips were white as sun-dried bone. She trembled with such condensed fury that I half expected her to explode like a tin of spoiled tomatoes in the sun. How, I wondered, had Mrs. Nordstrom learned about Bofio and Alphonse's bet?

"So this is our thanks for bringing you the Gospel! We sacrifice our entire lives—Fred's idea, *not* mine, *never* mine—and what do we get in return? Ugly nicknames!" *Pilipili* pepper-red spread across her face. "I don't *know* any words hard enough for you, Bofio, not after overhearing the gossip in the Frykman cookhouse this morning. You don't deserve all our efforts. You don't deserve this job either. Go back to Madame Berggren, if she'll have you. You're fired!"

She whirled around and stalked across the patio toward the house, her back straight as a papaya tree, her blue-checked skirt billowing behind her. The muscles in her calves clenched as her heels made an angry assault on the concrete. Her tight blond curls bounced on her rigid shoulders, and she swung her arms like an officer of the Congolese National Army on Independence Day.

As she thrust out her hand to yank open the kitchen door, Bofio emerged from the shadowy cookhouse and flung himself after her. His lips were drawn back from his teeth in a strange and terrible smile. His cheekbones gleamed in sharp points below his blazing eyes. Bumpy muscles bulged in his right arm, and I saw that he carried a steaming kettle. Bofio drew back his arm, raised the kettle high, and heaved four boiling gallons of drinking water after Mrs. Nordstrom. The simmering waterfall flashed like a prism in the orange late-afternoon sun, then caught her right between the shoulder blades. Hissing vapor swirled up, heated liquid splashed down, and Mrs. Nordstrom's outline blurred for a brief—and endless—moment.

She was still standing when the mist cleared, a stonelike shape with her hand outstretched, reaching for the kitchen door. Water streamed from all the sharp white edges of her body and flattened the bright yellow curls at the base of her neck. Her shoulders reared back in a parody of good posture, her water-soaked blouse clinging to her skin. Through the transparent fabric I could see narrow white bra straps and a large shining-wet mole. The mole sprawled across the straight ridge of her spine like a blackish brown ink blot. I stared at it, tracing the dark untidy borders while a deep jungle silence echoed in my head.

Mrs. Nordstrom's scream was high and shrill when it came, the frenzied cry of a pig being butchered. Her legs folded and she fell forward onto the kitchen step, her drenched back twisted, her stiff fingers spread wide open like two misshapen stars.

Bofio stared down at the empty kettle swinging from his fist. The kettle handle made a harmless squeaking sound, and Bofio looked puzzled. Then his eyes bulged and he stumbled backwards, half falling against the cookhouse wall. I felt the soft shudder of the bricks and heard Bofio's harsh breathing beside me. His teeth began to chatter as if he had malarial chills, and his white cook's apron fluttered on his chest. I saw his legs begin to tremble under his ragged shorts. The next moment the kettle slipped out of his hand, clanging on the ground. Bofio glanced wildly at

Mrs. Nordstrom's still body, at the other missionary houses, at me, and ran.

I ran too—but not away from the mission. I raced down the dirt path to the neighboring house instead, my nostrils filled with the crude smell of violence, my chest throbbing as if a whole village of drums pulsated inside me. I banged on the Carlsons' door with my fists, shouting in a hoarse voice that didn't sound like mine, "Hurry, Mrs. Carlson, please please hurry!"

"Of course she won't die," my mother told me.

But Mrs. Nordstrom was dangerously ill, and Dr. Birgie worried about infection. "You know how it is here," she said to my mother as she jabbed her ivory hairpins more deeply into her sagging bun. "Everything gets infected. Everything."

Visitors were not allowed. Since Mrs. Carlson was a registered nurse, she stayed with Mrs. Nordstrom nearly all the time, even at night.

"She talks in her sleep," Mrs. Carlson reported, snatching a five-minute lunch break with my mother and me. "And her dreams, June! All about picking blueberries by the shore of Lake Superior and finding the water too cold to wade in, the mosquitoes frightful, the blueberries black and shriveled. 'Why is everything always so disappointing, even in America?' she asks, and then she starts to cry."

I had dreams too, those weeks before they finally caught Bofio hiding out in the jungle near Esengo, the leper colony. My dreams felt like burns, and I longed for someone to stay with *me* all through the night.

The river is filled with steamboats and pirogues and water hyacinths, all glowing in the sun. I scramble into my swimsuit and grab my suntan lotion. I am halfway down the bluff when I see Bofio running toward me, his plastic sandals pounding the earth, his tattered shorts swinging from his brown hips. He carries a boiling kettle in one callused hand, a blistering pile of roasted peanuts in the other. Searing palm-wine madness burns in his charcoal eyes. White ashes spill like tears down his cheekbones. "I have failed my libeli," Bofio shouts. "And it's your fault. You Americans always get whatever you want. You should never have wanted the moon."

Purple Bougainvillea

ᴮACK IN THE TWENTIES a Swiss missionary and his wife, Monique, came to Boanda. They stayed for eighteen years, and in all that time Monique never ventured off the mission property once. She didn't learn any of the local languages either, according to old Mrs. Palmquist, her longtime neighbor. Each morning Monique's husband gave the cook his instructions in fluent Lingala while Monique herself slipped silently out to her garden. There she spent her days and years, working from early morning to sudden Congolese night, until she and her husband returned to Europe two weeks after V-E Day. Every Boandan knew the story of Monique's final morning at the mission, how she weeded the clover one last time, weeping all the while. How she cleaned her gardening tools with finicky care, wrapped them up in a watertight parcel, and buried them beneath the blooming jacaranda tree.

"A strange woman, that Monique," Alain remarked when Mrs. Palmquist first told him. "Yet what a grand passion for beauty. Truly grand."

Alain had lived in Monique's house for seven years now and had her garden all to himself. He had fulfilled his original teaching obligation long ago, but Alain said that Monique's garden was reason enough to stay on at the secondary school indefinitely. And he employed a full-time gardener to keep Monique's garden as beautiful as if she'd never left.

"A paradise within paradise," Alain called it, and my father agreed.

"Also an agricultural miracle," my father told him. "A lot of those plants need a drier climate and higher altitude. I want to study a soil sample one of these days."

The garden seemed larger than it really was, because Monique had done so much landscaping. With her own strong hands she had arranged logs, dripping with flowering vines and moss, under the cape chestnut tree. With her own muscle and cunning, she had pushed smooth granite boulders into perfect position between the traveler's palm and the crimson oleander. White jungle orchids with scarlet hearts bloomed good-naturedly beside mauve savanna orchids. Tea roses shared their bed with rosemary, thyme, and lavender. Scottish bluebells grew in the shelter of the moonflower and gardenia bushes, and filled in the cracks around the boulders and logs. The clover lay carpetlike, soft, dense, and green, tempting you to take off your shoes and curl your bare toes in it, careless of scorpions and tarantulas.

But Monique's purple flowers were best of all. If you stood in the middle of the garden and shut your eyes partway, any direction you looked was a gorgeous blurry splash of purple. Purple hyacinths and creeping phlox, purple pansies and heliotrope. Purplish blue lily of the Nile and bluish purple hydrangeas. The variegated purple of the camel's foot, the lilac purple of the blooming cape chestnut, the purple bell-like blossoms on the jacaranda tree.

"My favorite is that lavender rose by the veranda," my father said as we passed Alain's house on a Sunday-evening stroll. "I remember seeing one just like it in the Kenya White Highlands years ago. It's either a Belle de Crécy or a Reine des Violettes, but I'm not sure which." And then he added wryly, "I suppose Adela would know!"

My favorite was the bougainvillea, which draped the high hedge around the garden. It looked like an exotic flower-patterned shawl that some beautiful Spanish lady might toss over her bare shoulders. The bougainvillea was so deep and dark a purple that it appeared black on a dull rainy day. I'd never seen anything that color except for the grape Kool-Aid my aunt sometimes sent us from America.

Monique's garden made up for the crumbling interior of the house, at least in Alain's opinion. My mother often said she would hate to live in it, and not only because of Faith's mold and pollen allergies. "The army ants garrison all their Boanda troops there," she'd say, shuddering. "And if the termites ever quit holding hands, the entire building will collapse."

Alain would laugh and tell her that she worried too much, that she should deal with Africa *comme les français* and relax. "The army ants have chased me out only twice," he'd say in his most comforting voice. "And as long as I am not inside it at the time, it is nothing to me if the house falls down. It is only a place to sleep."

It was true that Alain was seldom indoors. Early mornings he spent behind the house in Monique's garden, eating French bread with tangerine marmalade, drinking coffee, and reading out-of-date Paris newspapers. During the day he was off teaching European history and philosophy at the secondary school. Late afternoons he usually sat on the front veranda, sipping his favorite drink that smelled of licorice while he watched the setting sun scald the river.

People were so familiar with Alain's routine that they ignored it. So when Alain suddenly reversed his habits in the summer of 1969, spending mornings out front and evenings in Monique's garden, no one but me seemed to notice. Even Mrs. Frykman didn't notice, for this was the summer of the leopard curfew, the summer of the American moon landing, the summer of the typhoid quarantine in lower Equateur province. (Not that we caught typhoid or knew anyone who did, but the adults spent a lot of time discussing precautions, symptoms, and ruined vacation plans.) Despite all these distractions, Mrs. Frykman had of course overheard Alain's latest reassurances to my mother, and she was still worked up.

"'It is only a place to sleep,' he says, innocent as you please!" Mrs. Frykman made a snorting sound way back in her nose, and gave my mother one of those mysterious adult looks a twelve-year-old wasn't supposed to notice. "Precious little sleeping goes on in there, if you ask me! First there was that miniskirted trollop with the red hair— What was her name? Ghislaine Pourcel, that's it! And who could forget the underdressed Portuguese female with the purple toenail polish, the giggly one who clerked at Soares on Avenue Bolenge! Or that dreadful chain-smoking atheist girl from Antwerp. And since then . . ."

"Since then, no one. You know that as well as I do, his cook being the awful gossip he is."

My mother glanced at me. I slumped deeper in my armchair, pretending total absorption in Miss Adela's latest *Woman and Home*, the one with Princess Anne on the cover wearing a royal blue dress out of the new polyester. (It was a formal, my mother said, but Miss Adela called it a dance frock.) "Why aren't you outside, Grace? It'll be dark soon, and it's been such a nice afternoon. You really should take advantage of it."

"I'd rather read," I said.

"You can read at school," she told me. "And you might be heading up there sooner than you think. Radio Kinshasa says there aren't any new typhoid cases, so the quarantine and travel ban could end this week."

I stood up and walked slowly toward the door, hoping to hear more Alain theories on the way. Mrs. Frykman often talked about him, and nothing she said was particularly nice. I never used to pay attention, but things were different this summer, this quarantine-extended summer now drifting lazily toward October. My arms and legs grew long and clumsy while my temper grew short, and at least once a day my mother embarrassed me by saying, "Well, well! I guess my late bloomer is finally getting around to it." Suddenly it seemed important that I know exactly what it was Alain did with all those European women.

"You honestly can't complain about his morals lately," my mother told Mrs. Frykman. "The girl from Antwerp married some Peace Corps engineer a few months back. Didn't they move to Addis? Or was it Khartoum? Anyway, since then I haven't seen any signs of—um—"

"Iniquitous moral failure," finished Mrs. Frykman. She folded her plump hands over her plumper stomach and looked fierce.

My mother gave her soft nervous laugh and passed Mrs. Frykman the plate of sugar cookies. "'Moral error' sounds a bit kinder, I think," said my mother. "And lately he seems different. Softer, somehow. A bit less cynical. I think he's under conviction by the Holy Spirit."

"Well, I grant you it would be a star in somebody's crown to win Alain Fougère for the Heavenly Kingdom," Mrs. Frykman said, "but I'm not holding my breath! I don't believe that man is interested in the Things of the Spirit at all. He's much too involved with Things of the Flesh."

She drained her coffee cup and set it on the end table. "Especially women!" she continued. "Did you see him chatting up Elsie Renquist at my Labor Day barbecue?"

"Oh, Hilda," my mother sighed.

It was a particularly good Labor Day barbecue, I remembered, featuring imported American hot dogs topped with American pickle relish, catsup, and mustard, all Heinz. I'd taken mine off to a quiet corner of the Frykman's back veranda, where I could watch and listen undisturbed. Alain *had* been charming to Miss Renquist. He had also been charming to Mrs. Palmquist, who'd gone on and on about the barbecues Boanda used to have years ago, before Mr. Palmquist died of sunstroke. And he was charming to Dr. Birgie as well, who got all flustered and young looking when Alain stole a few of her ivory hairpins. Alain had never attended a mission party without a date before, and no one seemed curious about it—except me.

"And then there's that garden, June! He's fonder of it than he should be, I think."

"It's amazingly beautiful," my mother pointed out. "Almost a work of art."

Mrs. Frykman frowned and began to fidget with my mother's favorite sofa pillow. It was an orange and black batik featuring a village dance complete with grass skirts and naked torsos, bead masks and calabashes.

"I suppose so. But if a missionary hadn't made it, I'd really believe it was a little too . . . too . . . something— lush, maybe."

I wondered if Mrs. Frykman had truly never noticed that her own sewing was lush, that the clothes she'd made for Carol, and now Régine, were almost works of art too. But probably that was different, since clothes were useful.

"Grace, what *are* you waiting for?"

There was an irritated edge to my mother's voice, and I

scurried out the door. It was time to leave anyway; I just hadn't wanted to seem too eager. I took the back path, hugging my private knowledge to myself, feeling a shame-faced superiority. They really didn't know, and I would never tell them.

The back path had no view of the river, so I didn't use it often. I worried I might miss something important: a croco-dile capture, a barge run aground on a sandbar, a European speedboat crippled by a hyacinth-clogged propeller. Be-sides, the river road was usually the most direct route to any place I wanted to go. But the river road ran right in front of the Carlson home—a drawback today, as I did not want to stop for Davina. If I couldn't pursue this latest adventure entirely alone, my pleasure in it would be destroyed.

Was it pleasure? I scarcely knew. But I had a deep intui-tion that neither Mrs. Frykman nor my mother would want me to think so. Maybe I needed to find a different word, a better and truer one.

The hedge was dense and high, with a narrow break behind the gardener's shed. As I had done several times in the past month, I squeezed through the gap and padded across the thick springy clover in Monique's garden. "*Mbote*, Wizamo," I said.

Wizamo didn't bother to turn around. He sat hunched over on a low wooden stool, his knees brushing his chin as he halfheartedly weeded the clover with his left hand. "*Ejali yo?*"

"Yes, it's me," I said, talking to his naked sweat-beaded back, since that was all I could see.

He said nothing more, dropping a fistful of weeds onto the wilting pile beside his stool. White-haired Wizamo had too much skin for his shrunken flesh, except where it was drawn too tight over his swollen knees and elbows. His face was the color of used-up charcoal, and his few teeth were chiseled to fine yellow points. I watched him for a moment, trying not to stare too obviously at the blunt stump where his right hand should have been. There was nothing beyond his wrist, absolutely nothing, and I knew why as well as anyone. Wizamo's hand had been chopped off more than sixty years ago, when he was about fifteen. The Belgian overseer at the plantation where Wizamo did forced labor had chopped it off because he didn't think Wizamo worked hard enough. His severed hand, all dried and withered so even Wizamo wouldn't recognize it, was packed into a basket with hundreds of others and shipped to the company headquarters in Antwerp.

My father told me those useless right hands were supposed to prove that strong measures were being taken to discipline the lazy people of King Leopold's Congo Free State. "Wizamo was lucky he didn't die of infection or blood loss," he said, adding, "He's just one of many this was done to, but you rarely see a one-handed Congolese anymore. They're either dead or very old, like Wizamo."

Wizamo never mentioned his absent hand, and I had never dared to. The circumstances of his loss, too horrible for discussion, completely absorbed and tongue-tied me whenever I saw him. But in my mind, the day it happened was always beautiful, atrociously beautiful, the sun filtering greenly through the semitransparent leaves. Turacos and parrots called overhead, and the sap dripped dazzling white from the scored rubber trees. The teenage Wizamo ran crazily this way and that, dodging vines and crashing through the underbrush as if he'd never heard of Gabon vipers and black mambas. Exhaustion finally overcame him, and he fell to the ground. He lay there gasping and weeping as a stout Belgian man with a sunburned neck and thick hairy forearms walked leisurely toward him. The man held a huge knife and spoke in bad Lingala, ordering two guards to hold Wizamo still. Then, in a hard quick motion too abrupt and ugly to see, he brought the knife down on Wizamo's trapped wrist. I imagined the warm rusty smell of blood as it splashed on European khaki shirtsleeves, on sandy topsoil, twigs, and greenery, on bare black skin. I imagined the shouting and screaming, the thrashing, sweating, and fainting.

"I'm leaving now, Mademoiselle. *Tikela malamu,* stay well." Wizamo's lined old face replaced the agonized young one, and the sudden perspiration dried on my forehead.

"*Kenda malamu,*" I said. "Go well."

I sprinted to the mango tree beside the veranda and climbed it, careful to avoid the rotting pegs some missionary father had pounded into the trunk ten years ago. In a few moments I was inside the tree house, settling myself cautiously on the termite-eaten floor. Several of the floorboards were missing, making it dangerous even though the tree house was only eight or nine feet above ground. Alain was always meaning to tear it down. ("If Monique knew about that repulsive object, she would have a crisis of the nerves.") But he never got it done.

Flat on my stomach, my neck craned for the best possible view, I watched Wizamo carry his trowel and wooden stool into the gardener's shed behind the jacaranda tree. He emerged a moment later, shrugging into a ragged brown plaid shirt that he buttoned with one hand. He passed right under the tree house but didn't look up, making for the veranda on clover-cushioned feet. As he climbed the steps, I could dimly see the network of deep dry cracks on his bare and callused soles. Those cracks reminded me of the patterns and lines on the brittle old Belgian Congo map taped to the wall of my father's office.

Wizamo walked around the open veranda to the front of the house, then out to the river road. This was the only proper way to exit Monique's garden, and since he was authorized to be there, Wizamo could afford to come and go properly—unlike me. Once I'd reached the tree house, the tree itself was my most discreet means of escape; I'd crawl carefully along one of the mango limbs overhanging the hedge until I could drop to safety on the grounds of the Catholic elementary school. It was lucky the mango tree was on this side of the garden, not the side bordering Mrs. Atwood's house.

The kitchen door scraped on the concrete veranda floor. Alain appeared carrying a dark green bottle and two long-stemmed glasses, which he placed gingerly on the top step. His hair had recently been subjected to a wet comb, I was surprised to see, and his shirt was tucked in. He even wore a belt! This last, as we all knew via his gossipy cook, Alain had not done for Ghislaine or the Portuguese clerk or the chain-smoking *agnostique* from Antwerp. And though I remembered hearing he'd tucked in his shirt the time he had dinner with Monsieur Adolphe of the Kisangani French Cultural Center, I didn't know if it was true. Something had happened since I last spied from my tree house observatory. Something remarkable.

"Double Gloucester cheese. It's amazing what Madame Vaske has in that shop of hers." As Mrs. Atwood came down the steps with a platter in her hands, I was bewildered all over again. Mrs. Atwood did not have Ghislaine's elegant slenderness or the Portuguese clerk's love of bright low-cut dresses. She was plain and skinny, her body dwarfed by a pair of oversized khaki pants and a blue shirt I'd seen her husband wear. Mrs. Atwood's light brown hair was straight as the trunk of a royal palm, yet she wouldn't bother with a permanent wave. She just tucked the fine shoulder-length strands behind her ears. Mrs. Atwood did have two claims to prettiness: a long neck that made me think of an Egyptian princess in our *Encyclopaedia Britannica,* and pearly skin as fine and white as my mother's Bavarian teacup. My mother did not permit us to touch that teacup, it was so delicate, but sometimes she held it up to the light so Faith and I could watch the sun glow through the thin porcelain.

John and Clare Atwood were from London. He was a linguist who believed the Bible had to be translated into every language on earth before the Lord could return and set up His earthly kingdom, the Millennium. ("A thousand years of peace and plenty, and Christian government *at last!*") Mr. Atwood spent most of his time visiting out-of-the-way fishing villages where they spoke dialects nobody had written down before. He said Mrs. Atwood could best help Further the Lord's Work by staying at Boanda and typing his translation notes and handling his correspondence. My mother didn't care for Mr. Atwood at all. Like Mr. Frykman, he thought soybean farming and Rhode Island Reds made my father a second-class missionary. What was worse, Mr. Atwood said my father was personally unspiritual, something Mr. Frykman would never have said, not even in that Millennium Mr. Atwood was trying to bring about for God. My mother did like Clare Atwood though, and worried about her to Mrs. Frykman. "She must be terribly lonely. It's a pity they have no children."

"There must be something wrong with her female plumbing," Mrs. Frykman would reply. "I've tried to find out, but you know how close-mouthed she is."

"They've only been here a year. Probably Clare feels she doesn't really know us."

"Well, she certainly could know us if she'd spend any time with us. But no! She's too busy running around the villages with her everlasting notebooks, writing down all those silly stories the old *tatas* tell her. She's the most undignified missionary wife I've ever seen, and she's headed for trouble."

Now I watched as Alain put a glass of wine in Mrs. Atwood's hand. All the times I'd seen her offered wine, she had refused, saying John wouldn't approve and she'd really better have a Coca-Cola. But this afternoon she smiled and accepted the wine glass, her cheeks glowing like one of Monique's moss roses.

Alain sat close beside her on the veranda steps. Usually he and Mrs. Atwood sat in well-spaced antelope-skin lazy chairs while they talked and laughed about curious things like whether or not the God of the Jungle could hear a tree fall when he was sleeping off several gourds of palm wine. Right now they weren't talking or laughing at all. They weren't even looking at each other. Alain twirled his wine glass between his thumb and forefinger while Mrs. Atwood stared off in the direction of the grape-Kool-Aid bougainvillea as if she had never seen it before. I lay still, so still that I could feel a strange pulsing somewhere under my skin. After a long moment, Mrs. Atwood made an odd throat-clearing sound that died away quickly, soaked up by all the trees and flowers in Monique's garden. When she spoke, her voice was so soft that I had to strain to hear.

"'When we were children words were colored. Harlot and murder were dark purple.'"

"Are you speaking of the bougainvillea or something else entirely?" Alain asked.

"That's Louis MacNeice," she replied. "A man with words for everything. Even this afternoon, here in your garden."

They were both silent, watching the harlot-colored bougainvillea blacken with the going of the light.

"What does he say about gardens?" Alain asked.

"'The sunlight on the garden hardens and grows cold. We cannot cage the minute within its net of gold.'" Mrs. Atwood turned to look at him, her eyes very dark. "'When all is told we cannot beg for pardon.'"

"My dear Clare, you are the best person I know. For what do you need to beg pardon?"

At the gentle sound of Alain's voice, a warm shiver ran all through my clumsy late-blooming limbs. I felt as floppy and loose as a stocking doll, the soft jointless kind that went limp without enough kapok stuffing. Where did this wild boneless feeling come from? There was nothing to see, just two people side by side on a concrete step.

Clare squared her narrow shoulders in the baggy blue shirt and looked directly into Alain's face. "I would beg pardon for what I should like to do, if only I could," she said.

Alain swallowed, a long lump running down his throat and disappearing into the opened collar of his shirt. I swallowed too, a strange lift and flutter in my chest.

"And you are so very sure you couldn't?"

"'You two should have met long since, he said, or else not now.'" Her voice sounded muffled.

Alain set his wine glass down. He did not move closer, just took both her hands between his palms and held them. After a moment she pulled her hands away, removed Alain's wire-rimmed spectacles in a slow dreamlike motion, and stroked his cheek with her thumb. He sat perfectly still, like I did when I coaxed Mr. Carlson's African gray parrot to light on my shoulder. At last Alain laughed, a shaky out-of-breath sound, and grabbed her face in his hands. They slid into each other's arms, whispering, laughing, rocking back and forth, her face burrowing against his throat while his hands pressed flat against her back. After a while his hands moved around to the front of her shirt. He murmured something as he unbuttoned it and slipped his hands inside, his fingers brown against her Bavarian porcelain skin.

They made unfamiliar urgent sounds, and I listened. They made unfamiliar urgent movements, and I watched. My nipples, with their developing tiny buds and sensitive pebbly cores, pressed hard against my T-shirt. I shut my eyes like Mrs. Atwood was, and deep purple bougainvillea shapes floated behind my eyelids. I knew now why I was here, what I had hoped and waited for, and it was pleasure after all. Iniquitous moral-failure pleasure. Pleasure as damp as the rainy-season air, the wet mango leaves, and the rotting mahogany boards I lay upon.

Alain stood up, drawing Clare with him, one hand curved around her Egyptian-princess neck. They moved slowly toward the kitchen door, their bodies touching and bumping as if blinded, and then they were inside. There was nothing to hear or see except my own quick breathing and the dimness of Monique's garden, where fresh daylight scents had given way to the sweet heaviness of evening.

I let out a hollow trembling sigh. After a moment I began to work my way cautiously along a sturdy limb of the mango tree. When I was out beyond the hedge, I swung down, my hands clinging to the thick-barked branch while my toes dangled several feet above the ground. As I let go, the branch quivered and the leaves trembled and rubbed against one another. I landed quietly, my knees braced for the red hard-packed earth of the Catholic-school playground.

"Mbote, mwana na mondele."

Shock surged in a cold wave from my stomach to my throat as I found Wizamo standing over me, dark against the hedge. A long bougainvillea branch reached across his shoulder, nodding deep purple blossoms at me. I usually saw Wizamo seated on his wooden stool, his back slumped as he weeded the clover with his single hand. I had forgotten he was so tall, so straight. His eyes, normally lowered or gazing off into the distance, bored into mine. They told me he understood better than I what Things of the Flesh were happening inside Alain's unlit house.

"I have watched you these weeks while you have watched them," he said, "and I believe I addressed you wrongly just now. You are still a *mondele,* a white, but you are no longer a *mwana,* a child."

So Wizamo knew. I had taken his silence for granted, but he knew about the strange hungering curiosity that sent me up the mango tree. He had watched me lying upon those decaying boards, visions of purple flowering behind my closed eyelids. He had seen the harlot-shaded self beneath my skin. I wanted to apologize, but for which of my sins I did not know. Because I wasn't a little child? Because I was a *mondele?* Because I'd been where I shouldn't be, feeling Things-of-the-Flesh feelings? Because I thought I might like to be one of Alain's European women in a miniskirt and purple toenail polish? I groped for a presentable reason, one that didn't reflect iniquitous moral failure.

"I am sorry about your hand," I said.

Wizamo took a step toward me. I took a step back. Everything was dark: the bougainvillea-draped hedge, the square shadowy outline of the Catholic school, the lanky shape of Wizamo's body, even the whitish grizzle on his head. Wizamo planted his blunt stump of a wrist against my shoulder, then ran it deliberately down the inside of my arm. The uneven ridge of bone, cartilage, and taut dry skin pressed hard against my own smooth flesh. I shivered, and this shiver had no pleasure in it.

"I see you are afraid," Wizamo said. There was satisfaction in his voice, and he withdrew his mutilated wrist. "I too was afraid. Greatly afraid. And my fear was justified because they did me a great evil, cutting off my hand with a saw. Back and forth, back and forth, across my bone." Wizamo tucked his wrist under his armpit. "But your fear has no reason, Mademoiselle. I am an old man, a very old man, good for nothing but sitting beside the fire and drinking tea. I cannot harm you, and even if I could, the price of harming a *mondele*'s girl child is too high to tempt me."

My unblinking eyes dried and stiffened in their sockets while my knees locked against the faintest trembling. Wizamo's face shone with the leftover heat of a long day in the Congolese sun.

"They paid no price for almost killing me, you understand, but I have paid for sixty years because I didn't work hard enough as slave labor on a *mondele*'s rubber plantation. I have pulled weeds from your *mindele* gardens and thought of murder. It is well for you, all of you, that you are too powerful to be touched."

Wizamo turned away, his shoulders high and square. He walked across the empty school yard toward the village. My rigid knees folded. I slumped down beneath the shadowy mango tree and stared up at the looming sprawl of night-blackened bougainvillea.

Burying Lumumba

I SLAMMED OUT the kitchen door and plopped down on the back veranda steps, my ears ringing with bad news. The raucous early-afternoon chirp of the cicadas made me lightheaded, and Matondi's loud singing didn't help. "The Blue Baboon Tune," Radio South Africa's latest jazz hit, was playing for the millionth time, but Matondi still had trouble pronouncing the English words. "It's sundown on the veldt, my love, sundown, sundown," he bellowed.

Matondi's machete sliced rhythmically through the grass, a bold metal blur against the backdrop of green jungle fringing our yard. His naked back and shoulders moved with the downward arc of his machete—bend and twist, bend and twist—regular as a metronome, until he struck a hidden rock. Iron clanged against stone, and vibrations shuddered up the length of the machete.

"Mafu!" Matondi threw the machete to the ground. He rubbed his hand, muttering Lingala words I didn't recognize, then snatched his blue T-shirt off the gardenia bush and wiped his face with it.

I was too fidgety to sit still, so I got up and wandered over to the fruit pail by the kitchen door. Several tangerines and a half dozen perfectly ripe mangoes covered the rusty bottom of the pail. As I poked one mango with my index finger, Matondi passed behind me on his way to the cistern pump.

"Those mangoes look good," he said over his shoulder. "Your tree has the juiciest ones in Boanda."

"I know," I said mournfully. "Do you want one?"

"Yes. But I need water first."

I chose the two biggest mangoes while Matondi filled the tin mug he kept by the pump, drained it, and filled it again. I sat down on the top step and turned the heart-shaped fruit over and over in my hands, staring at the tiny black speckles on thick, pink-orange skin. Matondi joined me, his Adam's apple bobbing as he gulped the second mug of water. Sweat rimmed the waistband of his baggy shorts, darkening the gray cotton fabric. The back of Matondi's neck glistened even after being towelled off, and sweat dripped like fat tears from his curly lashes.

"It's hot," I said as I handed him a mango.

"*Yango wana,*" he agreed.

Matondi took a knife from his pocket and began to peel the skin from his mango, his elbows resting on his wide-apart knees, his head and shoulders hunched forward. He looked relaxed, but the strips of mango skin flicked off his knife so fast that my eyes blurred with watching.

"Do you want to borrow my knife?"

"Yes, please."

Matondi's homemade knife had a blunt mahogany handle. I was used to my mother's sleeker American knives, and at first my fingers were fumbling and awkward. Matondi got that secretly amused look on his face, the look Congolese often had when *mindele* didn't do things right. Although the look was more tolerant if the white person was not an adult, it was also less secret and more frequent. My own clumsiness disgusted me, and I suddenly hated the juicy mango for slithering about in my hand like a bar of wet soap.

"Why are you so unhappy today?" Matondi asked.

"We're leaving for America in nine days time, right after New Year's," I said. I listened to myself with suspicion, a careful distance between my words and the real me, Grace Berggren, sitting on my veranda steps peeling a mango I wasn't hungry enough to eat.

"Going all the way to *mputu*, the homeland!" Matondi shook his head, then took a bite from his mango and let the bright yellow juice run down his chin. "Eee, that's bad."

Gratitude swelled thick and tight in my throat. "I know," I said. *"Merci."*

Matondi had cut our grass for two years, but I hadn't had anything to do with him until now. He started the same week that my sister Faith began at the Ecole Belgique and Mama Malia retired as her nanny. "That Matondi is a pushy, devious Luba," Mama Malia had warned Faith and me. "From the Kasai. And you have to watch out for those people from down there. They look very handsome and smile all the time, but you never know where you are with them."

Luba or not, at least Matondi understood how I felt. My parents didn't. I'd flown home only this morning—on a DC-4, even—piloted by a jolly Belgian captain who had tucked a sprig of holly in his cap and sung *"Il est né le divin enfant"* just before take-off. I was primed for a terrific Christmas vacation, and then after dinner my mother had fluffed her brand-new permanent with her fingers, smiled, and said, "Guess what, Grace, we're going home! Isn't it exciting?" I had assumed we were already home, and her disloyalty had shaken me so much I'd thought I might lose my mango pie. Then she'd said she planned to sew me a "going-home" dress to wear on the flight from Brussels to

New York City. "I've got three yards of blue dotted swiss, and we'll borrow a Junior Miss pattern from Mrs. Frykman. I think you're beginning to need clothes with a little shape. You know, dear—darts and such."

My father, all thrilled about an American winter, hadn't been much better. "There's nothing in the world like sledding, ice-skating, and cross-country skiing," he'd told me. "You'll love winter, Grace, I promise."

I wasn't so sure, but I did believe my father would love it, because he had a Currier and Ives winter scene hanging in his office above his desk. Whenever dry season got especially long, he would give the picture a hard narrow-eyed stare like he was willing himself inside it, holding the reins of the two prancing horses pulling a sleigh across a snowy landscape.

And then the real blow had fallen. I'd asked where the river was, and my father had said well, actually, as a matter of fact, New Goteborg, Iowa, didn't have a river. "New Goteborg is a good central location for raising money—lots of Evangelical Swedish-Americans—so that's where we'll live. Because fund-raising is going to be my job next year, Grace, not teaching and soybean farming. The mission has a serious financial crisis. Very serious."

"The Frykmans and Miss Renquist will be going home to raise money as well," my mother had added brightly. "And Dr. Birgie plans to make a quick trip to address her alumni association this spring."

"No river at all?" I'd struggled to squeeze out the words. "Not even a small one like the Ubangi?"

"I'm afraid not, although the Mississippi is just a two-hour drive east," my father had replied. "About a hundred and fifty miles, I think. Come to the office and we'll look at my map of North America."

I'd glared mutely at my father. Did he really think his

maps would do me any good? Losing the Congo River to the Ubangi nine months out of the year was bad enough, but *this?* I couldn't talk to these people, didn't even want to be in the same house with them. And if the mission was so dreadfully poor, why did I have to have a new dotted swiss Junior Miss dress with darts in it? Why wasn't my girls'-size-fourteen green plaid with the white Peter Pan collar good enough? I'd stalked out the back door in search of someone who would understand how I felt, who would agree that going to America was a terrible thing. I had found that someone in Matondi.

"Here is your knife back," I said.

"I suppose it's possible your *mputu* won't be so bad," Matondi remarked. He wiped the knife against his shorts before tucking it in his pocket. "You might really like it. Other people do."

"Other stupid people," I muttered.

"Maybe. But I have heard many people say they'll come back, and then they don't. They have too much fun being rich Americans. I can understand why. I've seen pictures of their houses."

"You have?" I asked, momentarily distracted. "Whose houses?"

"Don't you remember that movie the American Embassy people showed at the Boanda primary school last year? It was all about big houses in America. The houses of *Mondele* Washington and *Mondele* Jefferson and *Mondele* Lee."

"Oh," I said. "Well, we're not rich Americans. We're in financial crisis, my father says. But we'll be back. It's only for a year."

Matondi laughed, short and sharp, then spit his mango pit into his palm. The bone-colored pit was completely stripped of mango fibers. I had never figured out that special trick of using my teeth to scrape a mango pit clean.

Now I'd have to put off learning it for another year. New Goteborg, Iowa, probably didn't have mangoes.

"*Wapi, mwana!* You are plenty rich," Matondi said.

The afternoon sun shone on his sloping cheekbones and square, dimpled chin. I understood why Mama Malia said that people from the Kasai were handsome, but I didn't like his expression. He wore the secretly-amused look, and the tolerance was missing.

"But we won't have a *likambo* over it," Matondi said. "I can see you're much too sad to argue today. Besides, here comes the child of *Mondele* Carlson."

I turned to see Davina hurrying across the backyard. She cradled something in her arms, and as she drew closer I realized it was her cat, Lumumba. The cat's sleek black head flopped over Davina's forearm, strangely docile for an animal that disliked being held.

"Lumumba's dead," Davina said flatly, holding out her arms so we could take a look. "He ate some of the DDT my father bought for his tomato plants."

Matondi pressed thin, hard fingers into Lumumba's soft belly.

"This *pusu* was a beautiful animal," he observed. "Lots of nice fat. What do you plan to do with him? A little *pilipili* pepper, maybe a few spinach greens, and he would make a fine meal."

Davina reddened, her cowlick bobbing with outrage. I jumped in before she could say anything rude. "*Ekoki te,*" I said. "You could get terribly sick. Davina says Lumumba was poisoned."

"Ah. That's too bad. So wasteful." Matondi withdrew his hand, and suddenly his heavy-lidded eyes opened very wide. "*Nakamwi!* You named your cat Lumumba? After a Congolese revolutionary hero?"

Davina nodded. "I liked the name," she said.

Matondi started to laugh, shaking his head and slapping his sweaty knees with mango-stained palms. "You Americans! He was assassinated by your own CIA! Your CIA thought he was too *charismatique*, and they didn't like his Russian friends."

"What's the CIA?" I wanted to know, for I hadn't run across this term before—not in *Good Housekeeping*, not in Miss Adela's *Woman and Home*.

Matondi folded his arms across his chest and rolled his eyes. "*Centre pour l'Interference des Affaires Africaines*," he said.

"Then it's not my CIA," I told him, and he grinned.

Davina and I laid Lumumba gently on the cool concrete step and caressed his rich black fur. We cautiously stroked the slender paws which he had never permitted us to touch.

"I don't mind he's dead," Davina said, gazing pensively at Lumumba. "Not really. We haven't liked each other much since I first went downcountry to the American school. You know."

I did.

The numbing buzz of the cicadas drowned our will to talk, and we sank into a hot unhappy lethargy. Now and then we roused enough to give Lumumba's fur an absent pat, our hands accidentally meeting over his sleek cat's body, then retreating to our separate laps. I was vaguely aware of Matondi slouching against a pillar, out of the sun. He was watching us even as he tossed his mango pit high into the air and caught it again.

"Maybe you girls ought to have a funeral for your *pusu*, Lumumba," he suggested. "A big village one, with a feast and mourners. The real Lumumba, Patrice Lumumba, he didn't have the right kind of burial, you know. Murdered people never do."

I looked first at Davina, then at Matondi. Devious smiling Matondi, who came from the Kasai, that place filled with handsome pushy people. I knew perfectly well most adults had their own entertainment in mind when they suggested pet funerals. They wanted us to give them a reason to laugh, especially if they had other worries. Could Matondi be worried about finding a new grass-cutting job after we left for New Goteborg, Iowa? Was he having a financial crisis? On the other hand, a village-style funeral sounded satisfying, and that come-and-go tolerance was back in his eyes.

"It could even be a Protestant missionary village funeral, I suppose," Matondi said. "No palm wine."

"Of *course* no palm wine!"

If my mother ever found out Matondi stashed a Kraft Miracle Whip jar filled with palm wine behind the cookhouse woodpile, she'd fire him.

"Palm wine is good for funerals though. It gets you started mourning real well." Matondi jiggled the mango pit in his cupped palm. "Do you remember when Madame Brorsen died from the yellowing disease a few years ago?"

"The Norwegian Baptist lady in Mbandaka?" I asked. "Sure I do."

"Well, I was at the Madame's funeral, because one of my friends worked for her. And her husband, that cold *Mondele* Brorsen, he should have drunk *lots* of palm wine. I watched him and watched him, but he never cried, never mourned at all. His heart was a stone."

Matondi shook his head, clicking his beautiful white teeth together like castanets. "Yet when she was alive, he had seemed to think much of her, bringing her gifts and treating her kindly even though she had no children. If I hadn't already known, I would never have guessed that the funeral was for his wife—and certainly not his first and only wife. He hid his grief as though Madame Brorsen had been his *deuxième bureau.* Maybe even his *troisième bureau!*" Matondi paused, frowning. "It was not well done of him, I thought. Very disrespectful."

A second and third office? My father had only one, and while it was too small for all his maps, animal husbandry books, and butterfly charts, I couldn't see why anyone needed two or three. I glanced inquiringly at Davina, but she was busy picking burrs out of Lumumba's stiffening tail.

"What is a *deuxième* and *troisième bureau?*"

"Oh, a second or third—ah—wife," Matondi said, and then grinned. "But not arranged by the families, you know. More informal. Secret."

And wicked, I supposed. Like polygamy. I knew I shouldn't ask—Davina would think I was childish—but I couldn't resist.

"Do you have one?"

Matondi burst out laughing.

"Eeee, no, I can't afford one!" he said. "I'm not a *patron,* a big shot! Anyway that was not the point. We were talking about *Mondele* Brorsen not mourning his wife properly."

"But Christians aren't supposed to mourn other Christians very much," I told him. "Death is bad if you're an Unbeliever, because Unbelievers go to Hell forever, but dead Christians go to Heaven. So death is really something to look forward to—isn't it?"

I wasn't sure what prompted me to convert a truth I'd always known into a question. Was it the quirky slant of Matondi's smile as he listened? Was it my own fear of being classed with the stony-hearted Mr. Brorsen? I was already alarmed by my changing body; now I worried my mind was taking on an unfamiliar shape as well. And I doubted Mrs. Frykman's Junior Miss patterns would help me.

Matondi balanced the clean mango pit on his curled forefinger, then flicked it with his thumb into the gardenia bush. "Death comes soon enough in the Congo," he remarked dryly. "We don't waste time looking forward to it."

The gardenia leaves rustled back into place. Matondi got up and rinsed his hands under the pump.

"Anyway, you girls ought to have a real village funeral," he continued. "Not a cold white one. Down by the riverbank, I think, where the soil is soft and easy to dig. I worked hard this morning, so it's all right for me to *kobuma tick-tock* for a while. If you bring food for the feast, Grace, I'll dig a hole for Lumumba."

Kobuma tick-tock, to kill time, was the very latest slang from the capitol. I could tell Matondi expected me to ask him what it meant, and I was pleased I already knew.

"*Soko bongo,*" I said. "But only if Davina wants to."

"*Soko bongo,*" Davina said.

It was the hottest hour of the day, and my parents were napping in their bedroom with the curtains drawn against the sun. I went to the kitchen and filled a plastic bag with food: oatmeal cookies, a chunk of Spam, bread slices spread with peanut butter and pineapple-mango jam and folded in half. I hurried back outside where Davina and Matondi were waiting. Matondi eyed my bag and said, "Oh, Spam! *Malamu mingi,* very good." We went around to the front yard, crossed the gravel road, and followed the steep path down the bluff to the river. We took short mincing steps to keep from pitching forward into the green and yellow shadows of palm and bamboo, Matondi leading the way.

"It's sundown on the veldt, my love," Matondi sang, energetically whacking his machete from side to side, clearing out all the overgrown razor grass and kudzu. I followed, with shovel and bagged feast in hand, watching a thin glistening trail of sweat snake down Matondi's back. Davina brought up the rear with beautiful dead Lumumba clutched to her shirt front and her aqua cat's-eye glasses falling off the end of her nose.

When we arrived at the bottom of the bluff, Matondi looked around and said, "This is a good spot, I think. Flat ground, and no tree roots. Do you like it?"

Spears of sunlight pierced the green ceiling of flamboyant trees and fell in bright crazy patterns all around us. Vines hung from the umbrella trees like giant green arms, heavy and muscular. There was little undergrowth but lots of pale savanna grass almost as tall as Matondi, and several feet beyond flowed the river. Lumumba would be lucky to be buried here, I thought.

"I like it fine," I said, and Davina agreed.

Matondi leveled some of the savanna grass with a few hard slashes of his machete, and the long blades folded gracefully to the ground.

"Did you girls bring any of Lumumba's favorite food to scatter on top of his grave?" he asked.

I glanced at Davina, and she shook her head. "Sardines?" I asked. She nodded. I told Matondi I could go get some if he thought we really needed to, but Matondi said never mind, a few bits of bread would do just as well since Lumumba was only a cat, not a person. Davina asked why Lumumba needed food sprinkled on him, and Matondi said it was just the way some Congolese funerals were done.

"What is necessary to a man's life should accompany him to the afterlife," he explained. "Only last year the richest man in my friend Petelo's village died. This man had a big house with white-people glass windows, lots of manioc and corn fields, lots of children. He even had a *quatrième bureau!*

But he loved his phonograph player and his Frank Sinatra and Jacques Brel records best. At his funeral they were broken up in pieces and scattered on his grave."

"What a terrible waste," Davina said reprovingly.

"No, no!" Matondi replied. "You children would understand if you weren't *mindele*, but it can't be helped. Now give me that shovel."

While Matondi dug a hole deep enough to keep the wild animals from digging up Lumumba, Davina and I collected several extra-large leaves from a banana tree and wrapped Lumumba in them. He made a sloppy green parcel which we tidied up using several yards of kudzu vine for string. We placed him in the hole, squashing him a little so he would fit. Matondi stood by, leaning on the shovel and remarking that he hadn't realized the *pusu* was such a long creature or he would have made the hole bigger. Then Matondi replaced all the red clay soil, tamping it down with a few good blows of the shovel, and I winced.

"Which of you is doing the funeral service?" Matondi asked.

I glanced around to make sure no white adults had shown up to watch or laugh. At twelve, with a Junior Miss dress in the making, I was *much* too old for cat funerals.

"I wouldn't mind preaching the sermon," I told Davina. "Unless you'd like to."

"He's my cat," she said, pushing her glasses back on the bridge of her nose. "I'll preach. In Tshiluba."

I sighed. Tshiluba was a downcountry language I didn't know.

"Don't be snooty or I'll sing in Ngbaka," I said, and Davina backed down.

"All right, all right, English then."

Davina stood behind the flattened dirt mound that was

Lumumba and cleared her throat while Matondi and I found two large stones to sit on. Matondi plucked a thin tough blade of grass and used it like dental floss, sawing up and down between his white teeth. I sat completely still on my stone, feeling the sun-soaked heat of it through my cotton shorts. Then Davina began to preach, and I was caught in a dreamy deafening undertow of familiar words. Every so often I would surface, catch a flowing phrase or two, and sink back down in my own thoughts again.

"Lumumba drank from the well of salvation . . . left this sinful world to be glorified in Heaven . . . his trust in the Lord an inspiration to us all."

The clouds were dense and fluffy, their flat bottoms subtly veined with blue and gray. Dry season had begun, but these were rainy-season clouds. If Davina didn't hurry, there wouldn't be time to mourn, feast, and go for a swim before the rain came.

"God will wipe away our tears . . . Behold, the old is passed away, and all things are become new."

How could I possibly get in all the swimming I wanted— needed—before we flew to America? And what would I do in New Goteborg, Iowa, once I got there? A hundred and fifty miles to the nearest river, my father said. And even then it wasn't the Congo.

"O Death, where is thy victory, o Grave, where is thy sting . . . safe in the arms of Jesus . . . Let us bow before the Throne of Grace, rejoicing in the eternal life of our friend Lumumba."

The strip of soil between Lumumba's little red grave and the water's gold-brown edge was very narrow, I noticed. Two yards at most.

Davina said, "Please join me in our closing hymn, 'Shall We Gather at the River.'"

Matondi spat and tossed away his makeshift floss. I stood
up to sing, wondering what to do with my hands since I had
no skirt to smooth down, no hymnal to hold.

> "Shall we gather at the river,
>   Where bright angel feet have trod;
>   With its crystal tide forever
>   Flowing by the throne of God."

A light breeze ruffled the long grass and set the traveler's
palms swishing gently like enormous green fans. The river
lay broad and blue beneath the early-afternoon sun, so
smooth that the billowing clouds cast perfect reflections.
There was no traffic on the water, save one lone pirogue
gliding west with the current. A tall thin man stood in the
back of the pirogue holding a steering pole, and his laughter drifted across the wet spaces. I watched the water hyacinths float downstream, tangled clusters of green tipped
with lavender, their river-loving roots sunk deep in water
instead of soil. I knew those hyacinths lived the river as I
never would, resting in unnamed lagoons and roaming trib-
utaries that didn't exist on my father's maps. They could
wander fifteen hundred kilometers, from the Kisangani
white water to glassy Malebo Pool, and never leave home.

> "Yes, we'll gather at the river,
>   The beautiful, beautiful river,
>   Gather with the saints at the river,
>   That flows by the throne of God."

"You can toss those bread crumbs on the grave now,"
Matondi said.

Davina and I stopped singing and looked at each other,
thrown off balance. I took one of the sandwiches out of
the plastic bag and handed it to her. She broke it into
sticky peanut-buttery pieces, which she scattered on the

hardpacked mound of precious, dead Lumumba. Matondi said he really ought to get back to work, and as long as we had the bag of food open, he'd like to have his feast now. We gave him his share of the Spam, sandwiches, and cookies, and he sat back down on his rock, already eating. Davina stared down at Lumumba's grave. She looked so confused that I knew she had lost her place.

"Verse three," I said, planning to try out my tentative alto.

> "On the bosom of the river,
> Where the Saviour-King we own,
> We shall meet, and sorrow never—"

My vision blurred. A terrible pressure built up behind my face, throbbing and pushing against my skin. I twisted my head from side to side, my throat so thick I couldn't sing any longer.

"Come on, girls, mourn!" Matondi finished his Spam and started in on the cookies. "I don't know why you people can't do it properly."

"Mourn? I am mourning," I choked.

Matondi finished his share of the cookies and reached for the feast bag.

"Can I have another of these?" he asked. I nodded. He said *merci*, pulled out one with lots of raisins, and took a big bite.

"If you're really mourning, show me," he said, his heavy-lidded eyes bright above his handsome Luba cheekbones.

All my banked-up tears gushed forth, running down my cheeks in twin rivers of hot salty water. The pulsing pressure moved from my face down to my chest and pounded against my rib cage.

"Mourn!"

A host of village funerals crowded my mind, all peopled

with grieving Congolese who didn't waste time looking forward to death because it came soon enough. I saw a young mother beating her own head and shoulders at her baby's funeral, an old man groaning in the dust beside his wife's fresh grave. Wailing men with clay-daubed skin, and the shining tear-scored faces of weeping girls. I heard the shrieks of shriveled old women flinging their bone-china-brittle bodies to the ground.

"Mourn, now. Or I'll give you palm wine to get you started!"

I pictured New Goteborg, Iowa, filled with snow-covered American houses and blue dotted swiss Junior Miss dresses instead of mangoes and the dry-season sun. A place without Lumumba graves of any kind, mourned or unmourned, buried properly or not. A place without a river.

River pleasures clumped together in my thoughts like a jumble of water hyacinths. Could any American winter replace the long afternoons floating in the sun-dappled water or building river forts, making catfish traps or playing in abandoned pirogues? Where in New Goteborg could I skip through the slow dragging sands of a white-gold sandbar, or race to shore with the first thunderclap of a rainy-season electrical storm? I loved to swim out as far as the strong Congo current allowed, shouting *"Bonjour! Mbote!* Hello!" at the strangers on the Kisangani-bound steamboats. I always waved madly, treading water as the boats passed by, remembering only at the last minute that Kisangani people spoke Swahili. "Oops! *Jambo!"* I would call, choking on laughter and churning brown water. *"Jambo! Habari gani!"* Could I do these things anywhere but here, on the Congo?

Mama Malia's cousin Alphonse had promised to take me fishing for Nile perch next summer. And I'd hoped by next summer I would finally be strong enough to swim to the Otraco shipping docks and explore the underwater caves where the Congo dragon once lived. Now my summer river plans would have to wait. My whole life would have to wait. I would do nothing for a whole year but *kobuma tick-tock* until I was finally home again.

I threw myself on the machete-felled grass and dug my fingers into the soil, ignoring the stab of rocks and twigs. I smeared handfuls of red clay on my teary face until I was covered from neck to hairline in muddy paste. My jaws were clenched, but my mouth opened wide and square as I began to wail. I slipped into a rhythmic keening as if I'd always known how, my low moans rising to a harsh scream, falling, then rising again. My howls crested like river waves in a high wind, surging ever higher, flooding my head until it spun with thick anguished blood. I pounded the ground with my fists, pounded and pummeled it as if it were the Currier and Ives winter scene complete with sleighbells and frozen pond.

"You're doing well now. Mourn!"

When my fists were too sore to pound any longer, I snatched an armload of bobbing water hyacinths from the river and threw them onto Lumumba's bread-crumb-strewn grave.

Margaret Meyers was born in Brussels, Belgium, and grew up in Zaire, formerly Congo. Daughter of missionary parents, she lived at nine different mission stations in the Equateur province. Her four happiest years were spent at Bolenge Mission, a venerable place even in Conrad's day and mentioned in his *Up-river Book*. She attended boarding school in the Ubangi district, graduated in 1976, and moved to the United States to further her education.

Meyers received a Master of Arts in Philosophy from DePaul University in 1988 and a Master of Fine Arts in Creative Writing from the University of Virginia in 1995. Her awards include the Phalin Fellowship at DePaul University and a Henry Hoyns Grant at the University of Virginia.

In her varied work life, Meyers has been a creative writing teacher, a nurse's aide, a library assistant, a hotel maid, a nanny, a textbook buyer, a shipping clerk, a security guard, a house cleaner, and—for two memorable weeks—a church secretary. She is currently at work on a novel.

Designed by Will Powers.
Typeset in Charlotte, Centaur, and Cochin italic types
by Stanton Publication Services, Inc.
Printed on acid-free 55-pound Glatfelter paper
by Edwards Bros.

Somebody Else's Mama
David Haynes

The Importance of High Places
Joanna Higgins

Circe's Mountain
Marie Luise Kaschnitz

Persistent Rumours
Lee Langley

Ganado Red
Susan Lowell

Tokens of Grace
Sheila O'Connor

The Boy Without a Flag
Abraham Rodriguez, Jr.

Confidence of the Heart
David Schweidel

An American Brat
Bapsi Sidhwa

Cracking India
Bapsi Sidhwa

The Crow Eaters
Bapsi Sidhwa